NATIONAL SERVICE,
CITIZENSHIP,
AND POLITICAL EDUCATION

SUNY Series in Political Theory: Contemporary Issues
Philip Green, editor

NATIONAL SERVICE, CITIZENSHIP, AND POLITICAL EDUCATION

Eric B. Gorham

State University of New York Press

Published by
State University of New York Press, Albany

For information, address State University of New York
Press, State University Plaza, Albany, NY 12246

Production by Christine M. Lynch
Marketing by Fran Keneston

Library of Congress Cataloging-in-Publication Data
Gorham, Eric B., 1960–
      National service, citizenship, and political education / Eric B.
Gorham.
          p.   cm. — (SUNY series in political theory. Contemporary
issues)
      Includes bibliographical references and index.
      ISBN 0–7914–1075–7 (acid-free). — ISBN 0–7914–1076–5 (pbk. : acid
-free)
      1. National service—United States. I. Title. II. Series.
HD4870.U6G67   1992
355.2'236'0973—dc20
                                                              91–23388
                                                              CIP

10 9 8 7 6 5 4 3 2 1

To my family

CONTENTS

ACKNOWLEDGMENTS

I must thank all those who have helped me throughout the past few years. Professor Charles Anderson taught me the most important lesson I learned as a graduate student—to think openly about political philosophy. Professor Booth Fowler taught me the second most important one—that doing political analysis and criticism means reading and writing carefully. I feel privileged to have worked with both of these men. Professors Diane Rubenstein and Alan Ware have supported me throughout the years and have demonstrated in their extraordinary work why politics, policy, philosophy, and language are worthwhile and inseparable objects of study. Professors John Armstrong, James Farr, and Marion Smiley helped me more than they know at the beginning, middle, and end of my graduate studies respectively. The Departments of Political Science at the University of Wisconsin-Madison and Loyola University, New Orleans have allowed me to pursue my studies in an atmosphere of open inquiry and collegiality. Professors Stephen Esquith, Philip Green, Richard Green, Fred Newmann, and David Vogler have given me the opportunity to discuss these ideas with a wider audience—their advice has made this a better book. Special thanks go to Clay Morgan, Christine Lynch, and Jim McKenna of SUNY Press for their outstanding editing. My colleagues Phil Dynia and Stan Makielski helped me think more clearly about the final chapters. My friend Brit Smith did wonderful editorial work on chapter 6. My uncle, Alan Gorham, helped with a bit of last minute detective work. I have some friends to thank for their support—Dan Levin, Hans Mathews, Ray Webb, Margaret Schabas, Steve Nadler, Jane Bernstein, Ed Cohen, Peter O'Brien, Adolf Gundersen, Mary Geske, Nancy Garber, Dave Hejna, Cathy Rogers, Susan Heidenreich, Jon Roth, Mary Troy Johnston, Connie Mui, Mark Bjerknes, Nora Schaeffer, Kris Falstad, Eugenia Paulicelli, Jeff Mayer, Mike Stein, Chip Myers, and Jim Ascher are only some of the people who have helped make this book a labor of love. My other friends in Madison, Chicago, New York, New Orleans, and elsewhere inside and outside of the United States, have also been a constant source of strength; and some have probably been wondering what I've been doing in front of a word processor all these years. Finally, my family—my parents

Sue and Howard, my brothers and sister, Jim, Roger, and Bev (Gorhams all), and my grandmother Minna Unger—taught me to think openly, be careful, play with language, discuss politics, and make friends. All of the above are in some measure responsible for what and who I am, and for that I am glad. They are not necessarily responsible for what you are about to read. I am.

E. G.
New Orleans, Louisiana
December 6, 1991

INTRODUCTION

This book is not really about national service. It is about ideology, discourse, and political organization, but it does not detail a particular policy or set of policies, because, as supporters are quick to point out, national service is no "one thing." It is, as of now, an almost purely speculative program. In November 1990, President Bush signed into law the National and Community Service Act of 1990, but it contains only the rudimentary structures and funding of various programs that could affect the lives of thousands of people. The idea of national service holds great appeal for many, yet no study has challenged the premises upon which the discussion has been taking place.

Many criticize the program, but much of this criticism is well worn: national service violates freedom or rights, it is a costly government program, it presages a draft, it threatens union jobs, etc., etc. While these are powerful critiques of the program, all fail to grasp what I take to be its fundamental nature: an institutional means by which the state uses political discourse and ideology to reproduce a postindustrial, capitalist economy in the name of good citizenship.

And this is what the book is really about: how language is deployed to promote a public policy that may not benefit the public; how political philosophy can be used in the interest of bureaucrats, technocrats, and beneficiaries of late, postindustrial capitalism; and how its use helps justify public services. National service does not simply mean "serving the public," it means serving the public under particular political and economic institutions, it means serving the nation in an age of nationalism, it means constructing the nationalism which it serves.

I do not discuss all of the issues surrounding national service—in fact, I limit my analysis to very specific topics. I do not examine the "social needs" of the United States, nor do I necessarily doubt that there are many worthy of attention. I do not scrutinize the relationship between national service and the military, and I do not focus on the argument that national service presages a draft. I speculate on how to make national service a practical reality, but I do so only contingently and in the most abstract terms. While these considerations preoccupy the minds of most writers on

1

national service, I cannot offer any particularly new insights here, and emphasizing them would most surely bore the reader. Rather, I investigate issues that have hitherto remained unexamined by writers on national service (and by many professors of political philosophy).

This book is comprised of two parts, chapters 1–7 and chapters 8–10. In the first chapter, I critieize the planned institution of national service as an exercise in "good citizenship" on the ground that it will socialize young people toward certain norms, not educate them for citizenship. I support this claim in chapters two through four by examining various institutional arrangements currently being discussed for national service. I discuss the educational aspect to service in chapters five through seven, and I suggest that the notion of "service-learning" is more complex, and less helpful or benign, than proponents of the plan suppose.

In the second part of the book I begin to set out an alternative argument for a democratic, participatory national service, one that focuses on citizenship instead of service. I present these chapters as an example of how one *could* argue this case. However, I remain skeptical throughout that any plan of national service is a good one. My argument is strictly a contingent one: *if* one believes national service to be a good thing, and *if* one believes that it ought to have something to do with inculcating citizenship, then this is one way in which policy makers might think about arguing for, and developing, such a program.

This book is not meant to support or oppose national service for all time, it is meant merely to reveal the hidden political and economic assumptions guiding policymakers on this issue, and to suggest that our current thinking on the program needs to be reoriented. It is also meant to demonstrate how difficult it is to inculcate democratic citizenship in a program of national service. Consequently, I address those political philosophers who seek communitarian or republican policy alternatives. At least one of these alternatives—national service—may have to overcome insurmountable obstacles to achieve civic or communitarian goals in a postindustrial, technological society. And that alternative may perpetuate, however unintentionally, the very society that is being criticized.

Part I

A Critique of National Service

CHAPTER ONE

National Service, Political Socialization, and Citizenship

Many politicians, academics, and planners define national service as a nation-wide program of community work that citizens, mostly young people, enter for one or two years. It is either voluntary or coercive, and employs participants in public sector or "voluntary" sector jobs at subminimum wages. In the process, participants serve the needs of the nation, acquire job and life skills, and learn the essentials of American citizenship.

This definition has evolved from William James's conception of national service in the early part of this century. James argued that the "gilded youth" of America ought to be required to serve the nation in order to "toughen" their spirit, and help them recognize the poverty which afflicts their country. James proposed a "moral equivalent of war" in order that Americans may become more concerned with their communities, and in order that a "peaceful" alternative to the military be offered to the public.[1] Individuals could then view their country from different perspectives and not merely conform their behavior to certain nonmilitary standards.

After James, a number of other prominent Americans accepted his idea on principle, but offered competing proposals for a service program. Franklin Delano Roosevelt proposed that programs were needed to put young people to work during the depression. On March 21, 1933, he announced his intention to create the Civilian Conservation Corps (CCC):

> We can take a vast army of these unemployed into healthful surroundings. We can eliminate, to some extent, at least, the threat that enforced idleness brings to spiritual and moral stability.[2]

For Roosevelt, the CCC was necessary to employ underprivileged youth, not James's "gilded youth," and to provide them with certain physical and moral standards by which they could improve their lot.

After World War II, James's theme of educating youth returned in the form of John F. Kennedy's Peace Corps proposal. An international "moral equivalent of war," the Peace Corps offered thousands of privileged youth the opportunity to work selflessly for their country and for others. A domestic program, Volunteers in Service to America (VISTA), was established to provide similar opportunities for work in the poorer regions of America. More recently, there have also been a number of university programs that promote service—like Campus Compact and the Campus Outreach Opportunity League (COOL).

At the same time, various administrations have experimented with employment programs for youth. The Johnson Administration instituted a National Job Corps program, and that program has had various incarnations throughout the past twenty-five years. Regional conservation programs were created; among the most prominent have been the California and Wisconsin conservation corps. Finally, cities have developed service programs for their young citizens—for example, the New York City Service Corps or Seattle's Program for Local Service. These programs are aimed at giving young people job skills while teaching them the values they will need to prosper as adults.

The apparent success of such programs has recently sparked interest in a national program of voluntary service. These programs would create a new institution—generally in the form of a national service foundation—to oversee a comprehensive program of citizen service for young people. The arguments for this program are generally threefold: (1) the nation has needs that remain unfulfilled, like environmental conservation, day care, health care, etc.; (2) young people need to develop themselves morally, and national service can help (here supporters commonly cite such problems as drug dependency, crime, idleness, and teenage pregnancy); and (3) Americans, especially young people, need to develop a stronger sense of citizenship. Proponents of national service believe that the program can enhance the well-being of the nation and restore a sense of community to American public life.

Since the late 1970s, national service has become a very important issue. Numerous bills have been introduced in Congress promoting versions of this proposal, new books have emerged on the subject almost every year, national politicians have endorsed the idea, and public and private conferences and commissions have been held every few years on the matter. The most publicized proposal has been the Sam Nunn–Dave McCurdy national service bill

(SR3-1989), which ties federal education aid to service programs. On a smaller, less systematic scale, the Bush administration has introduced the Youth Entering Service (YES) program, which earmarks twenty-five million dollars for voluntary service work for young people.

On November 16, 1990, President Bush signed into law the National and Community Service Act of 1990 (PL 101–610). This national service law differs from previous efforts in one very important way—it attempts to merge service programs for both "gilded" and underprivileged youth, in order to provide the youth of America with a common set of norms and opportunities. It is a comprehensive law which includes a variety of youth service schemes, and it is designed to test the feasibility of national service for a number of different socioeconomic groups.

All service programs, whether for rich or poor, have had one component in common. Proponents maintain that young people must learn citizenship, and either they argue that such programs inculcate this generally, or they have attached particular programs designed to increase the civic competence of young adults.[3] Indeed, the rhetoric of citizenship justifies the program ideologically; that is, it defends national service on moral and political grounds, rather than instrumental ones.

NATIONAL SERVICE AND THE PUBLIC PHILOSOPHY

The idea of national service is thus significant today not only for its political import, but also for its philosophical implications. It speaks to an important philosophical debate about the civic competence of the individual. It suggests particular kinds of discourse about citizenship and its attendant rights and duties. In the remainder of this chapter, I want to examine this discourse in order to de-mystify the relationship between the concept of citizenship and the program of national service.

Historically, American political philosophy has been dominated by the Hartzian argument that the public philosophy of America is a Lockean one. According to this approach, Americans are liberal individualists who hold the tenets of Lockean contractarianism so closely that they do not even recognize it as a conscious ideology. In the past twenty years, though, some have challenged these theoretical assumptions. Such historians as Bernard Bailyn, Gordon Wood, and J. G. A. Pocock contend that the ideals that were to nourish American civilization took root in the renaissance, and grew out of the practice of civic humanism. These historical arguments have coincided with sociological and philosophical ones that maintain that America needs a civic philosophy—one that abandons the principles of atomistic individualism found in liberal philosophy.[4] Instead, the argument goes, American public philosophy ought to be grounded upon an ethic of community and republican virtue—one that recaptures the lost or submerged language of shared citizenship.

National service is identified as a policy that can contribute to this public ethic. The leading proponent of the idea of citizenship through national service, Charles Moskos, cites the works of the most important philosophers of this school (Michael Sandel, William Sullivan, Benjamin Barber, and Michael Walzer) as evidence that American public philosophy is recovering the civic. He suggests that "in the emerging political philosophy, national service is regarded as a form of civic education," and that a "civic-oriented national service must ultimately rest on some kind of enlightened patriotism." Moskos recommends that such service could provide a "renaissance" for American political culture, and that it would "entail a search for a new balance after an indiscriminate weakening of the sense of citizenship duty."[5] National service, then, can be a concrete policy that introduces the notion of civic obligation to a population of individualists largely ignorant of the notion.

Furthermore, some of the philosophers Moskos cites also call for a program of national service. Benjamin Barber argues that "universal citizen service" is one of many significant institutions in the quest for "strong democracy." He maintains that it possesses many virtues: (1) it is realistic and workable, (2) it complements representative institutions today, (3) it offers safeguards and opportunities for minorities, and (4) it gives expression to participation and citizenship.[6] National service, then, can be one institution among many that inculcates "citizenship"—a necessary condition for "strong democracy." Barber's vision is a participatory one, which affords individuals opportunities for deliberating over public issues and learning the virtues of "citizenship."

Barber also argues that national service can improve citizens psychologically and morally. For instance, service fulfills a "growing desire to do service" and nurtures "membership in communal associations." Moreover, he deploys common metaphors used repeatedly by proponents to describe the program. The need to serve must be met by healthy democratic forms of community in a democracy or it will breed unhealthy and anti-democratic forms: gangs, secret societies, conspiratorial political groups, hierarchical clubs, and exclusive communities.[7]

Service, then, not only satisfies the individual citizen's need for community, but it can help cure the pathologies of a society. This medical metaphor emerges in the discourse of all strong supporters of national service, as we shall see in the last section of this chapter. Finally, Barber contends that "compulsory" national service should be a duty, not an altruistic act. "It assumes that our rights and liberties do not come for free."[8] The exchange metaphor also reappears in the discourse on national service, especially in those texts where there is an emphasis on the service "contract."

Similarly, Michael Walzer contends that national service may be a policy which can help create the civic society. He maintains that national service can be part of a domestic work force which does the "dirty work" of society. He justifies this on grounds of equality, that such work may "break the link between dirty work and disrespect," and maintains that it (perhaps) ought to be done by the young because "it isn't without educational value." In this way every young citizen, at least, will have a "working knowledge of the working days of his hardest working fellows." But Walzer cautions that national service is only a temporary solution: "over a longer period, the work can be covered only by an enhanced sense of institutional or professional place."[9]

Walzer also suggests that national service might be a way to socialize distribution within the welfare state.[10] Through national service, both deliverers and recipients of social service empower themselves, and learn the value of participation.

> [I]t seems to me at least possible that participation in the delivery of services might constitute a kind of training for participation in the management and direction of services.[11]

National service, then, requires an ethic of egalitarianism and participation, and instills a civic sense into its participants. At the same time it alters the political economy of the state very subtly. For Walzer, national service inculcates civic education, but it also reorganizes society and institutes democracy and participation in the everyday lives of the participants.

In short, contemporary public philosophers support the idea of national service on the grounds of civic education, participation, equality, and democracy. They contend that this new institution might be part of a general program grounding American political culture in an ethic of community and obligation. Moreover, such an ethic helps overcome the atomism afflicting the culture today. Thus, national service expresses institutionally the ideas of authors who argue for a new civic philosophy in America.

But these arguments give rise to a number of questions. For instance, how well can the practice of national service fulfill its theoretical goals? What does "inculcating civic education" mean in concrete terms? In what sense will national service offer opportunities for democracy, equality, and participation to those who serve? Is the goal of citizenship appropriate to all people, regardless of their race or gender? Does national service contribute to citizenship in any material way? Furthermore, how should citizenship be nurtured? Do the ideas of the planners of national service coincide with those of the philosophers who might view it as appropriate to their ends? This study hopes to answer these questions, and especially the last one. For the question remains as to whether the practice of national service, as it has been and is being devised, fulfills the promise of the ideal. If not, one would need to argue for such an institution on grounds that do fulfill those ideals. Furthermore, as these questions indicate, what constitutes the "civic" is debatable, and one needs to *incorporate* this ambiguity into the program.

I contend that the concrete practices of national service, as planned by theorists who address the subject directly, may not fulfill the civic hopes of the philosophers who support it. Planners of national service see it as a vehicle for the socialization of a variety of groups in a pluralist America. They do not focus on the issue of civic education as a means for the intellectual and civic training of the citizen. Rather, they focus on national service as a partial solution to many of the nation's social problems. As will become apparent later in the study, by focusing on the socializing possibilities of national service, planners have neglected or derogated its educational possibilities. And, as I argue in the next section, political education, not just political socialization, ought to ground a civic philosophy. The following study helps clarify the institutional context within which a civically oriented republic can be realized. Consequently, I hope it can contribute to the debate over the public philosophy of America.

THE CONTESTABILITY OF CITIZENSHIP

I begin my argument with two premises—first, that national service is a good idea and that it ought to be involved in the activity of citizenship.[12] Most, if not all, contemporary proponents of the program assume these premises as well, and for good reason. One could construct some sort of community service without recourse to arguments about citizenship, but the citizenship argument gives youth service its particularly national character. Without the rhetoric of citizenship one cannot easily find ideological and ethical reasons for youth service (though one might have practical and economic ones). The citizenship argument emphasizes that youth service has a political purpose. Otherwise the program becomes the mere administration of manpower programs to fulfill the economic and social needs that go unfulfilled in a market economy. Finally, the citizenship aspect to national service sheds light on the nature of citizenship and citizenship education, and helps us understand better those political theorists who put the concept at the center of their ideological agenda. Thus, the study focuses on the rhetoric and ideology of national service, on its ability to instill good citizenship, not on its economic and social utility.

My second premise is that citizenship is a contestable concept. One cannot simply posit a single definition of citizenship and then construct some sort of service program that seeks to fulfill a concrete goal.[13] Or if one does posit a single definition it ought to include contestability as the overriding characteristic. National service can encourage citizenship by accepting its conceptual contestability, and by exposing adults to what the grounds of the argument might be. Contestability is one characteristic necessary for a democratic polity governed by the consent and participation of the governed. Each citizen should be able to reason toward his or her own understanding of what citizenship means because this will strengthen his or her cognitive ties to the community.[14] Where national service helps individuals think about why they consent to, and participate in, their government, it strengthens their commitment to democratic processes.

In the first part of the study I argue that national service planners do not accept the contestability of the concept—they base national service, and its philosophy of citizenship, on a particular definition of citizenship, and they assume that young adults can somehow be socialized toward its ends. On this understanding, citizenship becomes a defined end that can be measured with relative precision.[15]

But as Michael Walzer reminds us, to define American citizenship invites controversy, because the American people are too diverse: "America has no singular national destiny—and to be an 'American' is, finally, to know that and to be more or less content with it."[16] Where national service nurtures this diversity it promotes American interests. Yet some of its proponents see its strength in its ability to unify and homogenize a variegated people. I argue this point in the next section.

Furthermore, the very concept *citizenship* describes activities of deliberation, discussion, and participation that involve contestation and conflict. To be a good citizen—in definitions ranging from Aristotle to Locke, Rousseau, Marx, and Dewey—means to be independent, politically active, politically aware, and engaged in the issues of the community. From this general definition, though, it becomes difficult to specify its terms. Should "good citizens" participate actively in all the central political decisions of the country? Should they merely serve as a democratic check on their elected representatives? Is citizenship a political status, or does it also help constitute the individual self and identity? Are there ethical norms to which citizens ought to conform, or does citizenship imply a measure of independence from the dominant cultural ethic? And if we are citizens, to whom do we owe allegiance: the local community, the city, the state, the national government, the global order? Clearly theorists and concerned citizens offer many different answers to these many different questions.

One clear example of contestation over the meaning of citizenship emerges from feminist scholarship. Here the practice of modern democratic citizenship belies its essentially patriarchal and fraternal roots. Carole Pateman maintains that the original Lockean contract (upon which American ideas of citizenship are premised) is a fraternal one. The civic contract between political subjects and the labor contract between workers and employers hide a marriage—or sexual—contract between men and women.[17]

> During the genesis of civil society, the sphere of natural subjection is separated out as a non-political sphere. The non-political status of familial and private life is confirmed by Locke's label "paternal power" for its constituent relationship. Sex-right or conjugal right, the original political right, then becomes completely hidden. The concealment was so beautifully executed that contemporary political theorists and activists can "forget" that the private sphere

also contains—and has its genesis in—a contractual relationship between two adults.[18]

In other words, political obligation (a constituent element of modern citizenship) is historically and culturally constituted and rests
upon a particular imbalance of power between men and women.

On what grounds can women's political obligation be justified? Women have not been incorporated as citizens in the
same way as men; women's 'contribution' is deemed to be
private, nothing to do with citizenship; and the benefits of
the welfare state have usually been distributed to women
not in their own right as citizens, but as dependents of
men, as private beings.[19]

Pateman calls this "Wollestonecraft's dilemma." Women, who have
historically been the care and welfare providers in western societies, are excluded from participating in the rights and entitlements of the modern welfare state, because their work has not
been publicly and officially branded as "welfare" or "service." This
marriage contract emerges in certain other spheres as well—the
social and legal acceptance of date rape and rape in marriage, minimal economic assistance for day care, and systematic discrimination in the labor market.

Where national service recognizes the existence of this contract it helps remedy the imbalance of political power between
men and women. For instance, if national service educates men on
the issue of date rape it makes them more aware of the sexual contract. And where national service participants lobby and educate
lawmakers to change laws regarding marriage rape they advance
the juridical status of women. But most national service proposals
expressly forbid such political activity, and in doing so they relegate women's issues to secondary status. Coercive national service
proposals can potentially separate families, as mothers (and
fathers) are called to duty. Voluntary programs do the same for
families where the parents use it to escape poverty.

Finally, the contractarian, quid pro quo nature of the service
program reinscribes an autonomous, instrumental manner of
thinking at odds with the ethic of care that many feminists argue
is relevant to women's experience.[20] The actual tasks of service cor-
respond to care-giving, but the incentives and punishments offered
in entering service, whether voluntary or coercive, sustain the gen-

dered act of contracting one's citizenship with the state. Where national service "contracts" empower women and men to begin thinking and acting in noncontractarian ways, and where they make the sexual contract and its implications clear to all participants, they contribute to equal citizenship among Americans. Where they do not, they help perpetuate a fraternal order.

In the first part of this book, I conclude that national service *in its most prevalent forms* does not inculcate citizenship, because these rest on the idea that citizenship can be defined or that a definition can be assumed or agreed upon. This has led its main proponents to contend that the program should socialize young adults toward preestablished norms of morality and citizenship.[21] However, if national service can be reconceptualized so that it accounts for the contestability of citizenship, then, maybe, national service can be justified ideologically and rhetorically. If it cannot be reconceptualized in this way, its justification rests strictly on economistic and utilitarian arguments—arguments which do not have strong moral or civic force.[22]

In the second part of the book, I account for the contestability of the concept of citizenship, and I devise an alternative argument for national service accordingly—one grounded on principles of political education. By appreciating the contestability of citizenship, the national service participant can glimpse more clearly into the workings of political democracy, and understand better the ideals of participation and collective deliberation. In this way, the individual citizen understands his or her role in a democracy and reproduces that democracy more faithfully.

The ideas in this book are open to debate, thus my conclusion is provisional. *If* national service is a desirable institution to create, then it ought to be constructed with education, not socialization, as its goal. I have not resolved the problem of *whether* it is desirable to create such an institution in the first place. Rather, I hope to redirect the grounds of the debate, understanding that the debate will progress anyway, and that many policy-makers remain convinced that the idea of national service is a good one.

POLITICAL SOCIALIZATION, POLITICAL EDUCATION, AND CITIZENSHIP

Political socialization is the means by which society transmits basic political and social orientations, and the processes through which individuals learn to behave appropriately in political and social contexts. This definition focuses less on developmental processes, or psychological mechanisms of political learning, for I consider these to be aspects of political education. Rather, institutions of socialization transmit norms which help guide people's behavior, and often establish an attitude of civility between individuals. We will see that some proponents of national service seek to inculcate this idea of civility in all young people. While this goal is an important one, service planners have often made it the central, or the only, purpose of youth service, and the cornerstone of good citizenship.

Political education consists of those processes that help individuals to think about politics and society, and to reason about the purposes of the political community. This model of political and social learning emphasizes the critical assessment of a polity, on the behavioral norms of that polity. Democratic education engages individuals in a critical dialogue with their society, and encourages people to learn about their society by participating in it. Democratic political education, then, is not a process of transmission, it is a two-way exchange between the individual and his or her society— one in which the individual learns from others but in which others also learn from him or her.[23] Political education treats political concepts as material for discussion and learning, and thus citizenship becomes an ideal about which students can reason.

Amy Gutmann argues that political socialization is the process of unconscious social reproduction, while political education is the process of conscious social reproduction.[24] Her distinction is generally apt, though it avoids the question of how educational institutions socialize individuals. Nevertheless, Gutmann suggests rightly that democratic education instills character in individuals. Character is necessary because moral freedom in society demands it—individuals must know how to make correct moral choices (that is, choices which reproduce a democratic society). And they must also be afforded the choice to identify with their communities. In this sense, they are not being socialized to their communities, but are learning how to reason about their communities and how to come to a thoughtful decision about joining them.[25] Consequently, democratic education teaches democratic social virtue—"the ability to deliberate, and hence to participate in conscious social reproduction."[26] In sum, political education strengthens the citizen's commitments to democracy, political socialization merely transmits those commitments.

Citizenship, I would argue, is a matter of political education, not only political socialization. The civically competent individual ought to understand his or her society and polity critically, and ought to engage that society in a discourse in order to learn *how* to think about it (not necessarily *what* to think about it). By participating in a critical discourse with society, the citizen can also reason about the problems that afflict society. Thus the citizen can hold values such as independence, self-reliance, and tolerance more deeply because they are values which the educational process forces that citizen to defend rationally.

Political education involves self-government, and citizens are charged with the responsibility of maintaining and transforming political institutions as their ideas of justice dictate. In this way, learning to be a citizen is learning the diverse means by which rational people govern themselves in a democracy.[27] Citizenship means being conscious that one is responsible to a polity, and this idea of responsibility is one that an individual must recognize through both loyalty and reason. For a citizen should understand what it means to act responsibly if he or she is to do so. Citizen self-government, therefore, is a part of an intellectual learning process that is ongoing for however long the individual resides in a particular community.[28]

By this definition, citizenship also means participation, and participation leads to political learning.[29] Participation is possibly the most important means by which individuals come to learn useful public and moral knowledge and political judgment. Political judgment is an exercise in practical reason, and can be learned by deliberating with others about the ends of a particular community and by acting with others to advance certain common ends. It rests, then, on political conduct—a way of acting appropriately with others on political and social matters. Within a democracy, political judgment means knowing how to comport oneself with other, equal citizens.

On this understanding, conduct signifies more than behavior, rather it is the means by which individuals understand the politics of their community rationally in order to act in the best interests of the community.[30] In a democratic community one ought to understand how to treat others with respect, how to tolerate difference, how to contest issues, how to deliberate collectively about problems, and how to resolve those problems without repression or discrimination. A system of political education that involves participation offers individuals numerous ways of learning the rules of rational political conduct, and gives them the opportunity to learn through experience. This method of learning seems most appropriate to individuals who have finished formal schooling, who have received a rudimentary education in democratic conduct, and are prepared to educate others to do the same.

Citizenship education should inculcate civic virtue, the cultural disposition apposite to citizenship. Such virtue involves a number of elements: (1) a willingness to assume the burdens of public office, (2) a willingness to subordinate private interest to the public concern, (3) the capacity for rational choice in order to understand the requirements of (1) and (2), and (4) a willingness to learn those things necessary to make rational choices.[31]

The fact that the individual ought to be prepared to assume the responsibilities of public office signifies a number of things. First, the citizen ought to be a self-governing person who recognizes that one must participate in order to perpetuate the democratic traditions of a society. In this way, the individual exemplifies democratic conduct to others, and can teach others to act democratically. Second, as a public officer, the citizen comes to understand how he or she transcends his or her own private interest, and works for the good of the community. In this way, that citizen holds the common good in trust for the rest of the community. The citizen becomes a public representative of the community, and is thus responsible to that community for the actions he or she takes. Thus, the citizen will be inclined to act prudently, and not for his or her own narrow interest.

Moreover, the person will not only be a public representative, he or she will be a public person. In this way, that person's identity is partially constituted by the public acts in which he or she engages. Thus, political participation and the responsibilities of public office have a psychological role to play in the development of the good person. In fact, one contemporary proponent of civic education claims that such education ought to foster the good person more than simply the good citizen; and he argues that citizenship education is a moral education, not merely a political one.[32] Active citizenship may also help individuals come to a greater understanding of themselves and of the practices of the community that help define them as citizens and as persons.[33] Consequently, occupying public office is not merely a lesson in moral reasoning, but can also be an exercise in self-consciousness. It helps the individual citizen come to his or her own conclusion about what it *means* to be a citizen.

Inculcating civic virtue also means overcoming political apathy. Political apathy, and even alienation, in America is well known—we have very low turnout rates at the polls for elections at all levels, social scientists have recorded increasing evidence of political distrust and alienation in all age groups, races, and classes in society, fewer Americans are identifying with a particular political party, and fewer social movements are developing (with some notable exceptions—the abortion issue is one). Political apathy often precludes the search for solutions to political and social problems. Apathetic residents of the national community either assume that there are no problems with that community, or that such problems cannot be resolved through public effort. In response to these problems, individuals return to their private concerns, thus aggravating the seriousness of the problems by ignoring them. An apathetic public also abdicates responsibility for solving political problems to representatives and administrators (who, in a democracy, are checked by an active public).

Individuals can overcome political apathy by becoming engaged in political debate or activity, thereby learning to conduct themselves in the public sphere. At the same time, they can generate interest in politics by being educated to think critically about politics—by analyzing political and social problems, and how those problems are resolved most profitably. Hence, political interest may not be generated by the process of socialization as I have defined it. For socialization trains people to behave toward certain norms, and if one of those norms is apathy, then the problem I have just described perpetuates itself. Rather, in a polity that reproduces an apathetic citizenry, some form of counter-socialization may be necessary, one where individuals are educated and activated in order to transform the social conditions which breed political apathy. I would argue, then, that political interest can be taught, and not merely transmitted between generations.[34]

Finally, civic or political education can also be ennobling in ways that political socialization cannot. Education and political activism can teach citizens the nobility of that office. Through learning about politics, either by discussion or activity, individuals experience the political ideas that have significance for the national community. Political socialization merely provides the behavioral context in which individuals are taught to act in particular ways, without necessarily engaging them in political issues. Thus, by being socialized to particular norms, the individual is not compelled to understand why those norms are worthy ones, or why the community in which he or she lives is worth defending.

NATIONAL SERVICE AND POLITICAL SOCIALIZATION

A number of authors contend that national service ought to be one means which teaches individuals citizenship. Morris Janowitz, Donald Eberly and Michael Sherraden, Charles Moskos, and Amitai Etzioni argue most systematically for the plan. They believe that national service must first socialize individuals toward certain norms, and that this socialization constitutes citizenship. Even their occasional comments about "civic education" concern socialization rather than education.

Morris Janowitz maintains that national service helps individuals achieve "civic consciousness"—"the process by which national attachments and obligations are molded into the search for supranational citizenship."[35] Janowitz argues that we must move beyond narrow self-interest, and promote voluntarism as a way of solving collective problems effectively. Yet he seems to hedge on this point a bit when he declares that "no matter how one defines citizenship, to be a citizen implies that one is an effective consumer, anchored in the economic system."[36]

Janowitz declares that states persist because of the "powerful ideas of mutual obligation," rather than self-interest.[37] And he wishes to harness this sense of obligation in order to promote a more stable polity and a deeper sense of civic pride. He contends that citizens of liberal democracies must be obligated in ways that express their loyalty to the state: taxes, education of the family, military service, electoral participation, jury duty, membership in voluntary associations, and "promoting the welfare of the community." The idea of national service comes under this last category, and Janowitz suggests that it supplement the more traditional institutions of civic education—the schools and the military—in order to create a loyal citizenry.

What is civic education, though? It is an education that involves

a) exposing students to central and enduring political traditions of the nation, b) teaching essential knowledge about the organization and operation of contemporary governmental institutions, and c) fashioning essential identification and moral sentiments required for performance as effective citizens.[38]

Yet this definition conforms more to what I have been calling socialization. Students are "exposed" to certain traditions—that is, these traditions are transmitted to them, they do not play a part in the learning process. An important goal is "identification" with the state and teaching "moral sentiments" to individuals—not pressing them to think critically about their country. Finally, "teaching essential knowledge" of American government does not advance the students beyond elementary civics; it confirms what they have learned in school without challenging them to think critically about the national political community. In short, "civic education" here signifies little more than socializing Americans toward particular norms.

Janowitz bases this argument on the failures of the post-War era. He discovers two causes of the decline of "civic consciousness" in America since 1945, and especially since the 1960s: "new communalism" and the influence of social science on mass education. Combined, both have engineered a decline in the civic pride of the citizens of the United States. From the time of the first wave of Eastern European immigrants in the late nineteenth century until World War II, civic education was concerned with assimilating immigrants. This was important for a growing nation because it ensured a stable and loyal citizenry, and created the political conditions necessary for a successful economy and foreign policy. However, at the same time ominous forces were at work: the school was becoming more professionalized, "civics" were being transformed into "social problems," Deweyite teaching methods were coming into vogue, and citizenship was being taught as a set of rights, not obligations or duties. According to Janowitz, these forces would explode into what he calls the crisis of the post-War years.

The responsibility for this crisis rests first on the shoulders of the "new communalists"—minority communities who focus concern on their problems to the detriment of the larger whole. Blacks, hispanics, and women's groups thus contribute to the decline of citizenship in America. Janowitz blames the busing and black power movements of past years for fomenting black communalism, claiming that "frequently black nationalists turned into another youth gang." He also charges Afro-American studies programs at universities with encouraging black separatism, and complains that university unrest had implications outside the academic setting. For some it "regularized middle-class college attendance" for blacks, but for others, "at the level of the underclass, the new communalism often became a rationalization for purposeless violence without a facade of educational aspiration." Further spending for education has not assuaged this, thus Janowitz suggests a civilian and military service program to aid in the assimilation process. Janowitz traces the history of blacks in the modern military in order to show that they can be socialized through service institutions.[39]

Janowitz also analyzes the "communalism" of Mexican-Americans, and argues that Spanish-speakers, and Mexicans in particular, have not become assimilated into the American social fabric, rather they still keep to themselves. He contends that Chicanos are colonizing vast segments of the southwest, that they are "transplanting a segment of [their] society to a new and expanded locale," and even that they may be recolonizing land lost in the nineteenth century.[40]

This is a problem because Mexican-American values are different from the traditional values of Americans. For one, Mexican-Americans "are more concerned with their rights than their obligations." Also, Mexican "familism" resists acculturation, a phenomenon of which Janowitz approves because it provides them with "self-esteem," and a belief that they are "special." However, there is a subversive element simmering under all of this, for "the strong sense of group identity has not prevented considerable criminality and deviance among the young." Thus Mexican familism leads to social pathology, or at least does nothing to prevent it. A further peril is the fact that Mexican-Americans are "easily the most fertile" ethnic group. These "social pathologies" imply that Mexican mothers have failed to assimilate their children to "American values."[41] In Pateman's terms, Mexican women have not fulfilled their part of the sexual contract in America.

Finally, Mexican civic and educational standards are poor: "Mexican-Americans have not been preoccupied with educational achievement," and their rates of political participation are very low (except of course over the issue of bilingualism). Janowitz concludes that all this bespeaks a Mexican "cultural and social irredenta" in the American southwest; the "irredenta" is inherently unstable not only for the reasons given above, but also because Mexico itself is an unstable country whose "agitations and demonstrations...will no doubt influence the pattern of immigration to the United States in the years ahead." In sum, the communalism arising out of black separatism and Mexican immigration has upset the "delicate balance of toleration." For these "new immigrants" are "deeply involved in a communal lifestyle which blocks the development of a sense of citizenship."[42]

These arguments imply that service ought to be a mechanism of cultural assimilation, not merely acculturation or pluralism. Civic "education" ought first to provide all residents of the United

States with a common set of values and norms, and the program should try to assimilate those residents who might not normally adapt well to those norms. It also suggests that national service ought to help eliminate "new communalism." Yet this implication could justify using national service participants to restrict the practices of these groups. Thus some proponents suggest that national service participants could become part of a border patrol corps, designed to supplement the professional border patrols.

Janowitz's argument also implies that national service is to be developed in a national, not an international, context. For example, he does not ask why Mexicans are coming to the United States, or whether this migration may be tied to an international political-economic order on top of which rests the United States. The very way Janowitz establishes the problematic of new communalism, especially in relation to the "Chicano problem," suggests that the United States lives in a geopolitical vacuum. This reflects the perspective with which he presents the notion of "civic consciousness": it is a turn inward in order to reestablish some mythical normative ideal that Americans may have once had. It is, in short, a turn toward civic socialization. Yet this could reinforce the ignorance Americans have about the outside world, and it would make it easier for them to accept the potentially racist argument that, for instance, Mexican values violate the basic principles of the nation.

Janowitz argues that it is not only the "new communalism" which has created the sociological conditions for the decline of civic education, but also the "widespread demoralization of teachers." This demoralization has a number of sources: the horrible conditions in inner city schools, the decline in the "mental caliber, prestige, and authority" of the American high school teacher, the practice of tenure and the power of the unions to prevent the removal of bad teachers, the "hidden curriculum" of dissatisfied teachers on the Left, and the dominance of images from the mass media.[43] I would argue, though, that these are social, even sociological issues, not educational ones. Janowitz offers a plan for a new order in society, and does not suggest ways in which individuals can learn. Moreover, given the prominence of women in teaching positions, Janowitz indirectly blames the "ills" of modern American society on the failure of women to transmit the appropriate values to children.

Janowitz maintains that to achieve this reordering, individuals ought to engage in national community work, to "affiliate the individual into the larger social structure."[44] He presents the Civilian Conservation Corps as an example of such work, and suggests that contemporary programs ought to model themselves after the CCC. This sort of program would, like the CCC, reinforce "the social and moral meaning of work." Indeed Janowitz argues that similar programs of the 1960s, like the Job Corps, were inadequate to the task, because they were not residential outdoor programs. Such programs are necessary in order to control the antisocial behavior of "frustrated youth" who are "largely black, but include other dispossessed minorities."[45]

Yet Janowitz suggests that "affiliation" is necessary not only for desocialized youth, but for all youth. He argues, for example, that college students could be relieved of their "bored, restless, and unclear" goals through a program of civic service. However, Janowitz realizes that many of these young people will be against the program, and marshals some very questionable arguments against those young people who oppose national service on principle. Some young people fear national youth service because, on the surface, they wish to retain their personal freedom and power of economic self-determination. But, he assures the reader, "if we probe more deeply," we find that this is merely a cover for the real reason underlying the fear: national service would "interfere with the personal search for pleasure" and the spread of sexual freedom.[46] Resocialization, then, is also necessary to restrain the hedonistic and individualistic desires of American youth.

Despite the number of young people who might favor national service, or who are indifferent to it, Janowitz fears that there are some who will still refuse to join. For this reason, he supports a voluntary service at least in the immediate future.

> Obligatory national service would mobilize a very small minority who are in blind opposition based on personal deviance or criminal-like personality. I would estimate that at least five percent of youth would fall into this category. Neither the armed forces nor the civilian component would want to act as a reformatory for delinquents. It does not take many deviants to wreck or severely strain a program. Administrative leaders would have to maintain a system of rules which would allow for easy withdrawal of those who had an oppositionist mentality.[47]

This argument implies that national service will not, for some, be the way they can realize the American dream or learn citizenship values, because their "oppositionist mentality" will preclude them from even being enrolled. It also suggests that national service might be an instrument by which officials can locate those with "personal deviance or a criminal-like personality"; thus national service serves as a means of making visible to the public eye those who refuse to accept the principle of national service (through "easy withdrawal"). It may also intimate that opposition to national service on principle is difficult, if not impossible, without being labeled deviant or criminal. All these criticisms suggest, most importantly, that Janowitz's plan is designed primarily to socialize youth.

Michael Sherraden and Donald Eberly take a slightly different approach in defending national service, though they share many of the same goals for the program. In one article they examine the rights and responsibilities of citizens in America. The authors suggest that, contrary to the dominant trends in Western culture, one ought not to think of rights and responsibilities as opposites, but rather as complementary to each other.[48] After centering themselves between "libertarians of the Right and Left," Milton Friedman and Erwin Knoll, the authors offer a panoply of new "rights" which imply responsibility, and which national service can offer: the right to employment, the right to "seek out a new and enriching experience," and the right/rite to a "promising future."

They maintain that a philosophy of rights and responsibilities should undergird a "new social institution [that] can in fact restore and augment individual opportunities."[49] Sherraden and Eberly situate individual opportunity within a socioeconomic vacuum and address the issue of "rights and responsibilities" to an audience of libertarians: "In short, there has been a diminution of the role of the individual in meeting the needs of the society, and an accompanying alienation of individuals from government and from each other."[50] Yet by focusing the problem on the "role of the individual" Sherraden and Eberly also imply that socialization can cure the problems afflicting America. Moreover, they ignore the intermediary institutions and organizations that prevent alienation from that society, and pose the problem as one of the individual versus society at large. We would expect their solution to be one that actually creates state institutions to enable individuals to meet "the needs of the society." And their proposal in the article confirms this, for they recommend a national service program that "would be a *de facto* civilian service created by the expansion of the conscientious objector provision in the draft law."[51] Thus they suggest that national service become a "new social institution" (and not, for example, a new *educational* institution).

But their arguments for socialization go beyond abstract notions of the alienation of the individual in society; they offer concrete social problems which must be solved. For instance, they argue that service is necessary because of the social problems afflicting urban youth.

> Urban cities are burning constantly from within, like the underground coal fires which burn for decades. Only rarely is an explosion heard at the surface. Unemployment is like oxygen for these subterranean fires. Unemployment eats away at whatever sense of community once existed. Businesses decline. Crime increases. Anyone who can possibly afford to leave does so. Buildings are abandoned.... Everything declines.... This is the vortex of poverty, and it is very much connected with unemployment.[52]

In addition there is a great threat in recidivism, which needs to be controlled. Add to this the rise in alcohol and drug use among young people, and the increase in vagrancy—the "deinstitutionalized," transient, and those who "live by handout, petty crime, or prostitution"—and the "vortex" becomes more threatening. National service can be a means by which these "problem cases" are resocialized into normal members of society, not dysfunctional or dangerous.[53] It is a way to prevent the cities from erupting into "flames," and to ease the "economic costs of crime." "Why national service" then? To eradicate the "signs of a youth problem."[54] Why national service? To correct for the failures of the ghetto family and single-parent (read "female-headed") households.

Charles Moskos begins his argument for national service with an appeal to youth and to an "emerging public philosophy."[55] He contends that national service must involve the young people of the nation because they are more "flexible" than adults, with fewer familial obligations, and are not as involved in the nation's economy. Moreover, they have the physical capabilities of performing certain tasks, "notably military and conservation work. But there is also an intangible: focusing national service on youth makes it a rite of passage toward adult citizenship, dramatizing its importance."[56] Citizenship, then, involves not only rights and obligations, but rites of obligation. National service becomes a *state-sanctioned* rite of adult citizenship in a way that, say, giving birth and caring for a child does not. Furthermore, service rites can only be civic in specific ways—they do not involve picking cotton for the Sandinistas or cutting sugar cane for the Castro regime, nor do they involve working as an evangelical in missions across the world.[57] Moskos thus implies that civic involvement by the young should not be tied in with strong moral beliefs about a particular political regime or religious purpose.

Moskos also suggests that American political culture is "in crisis," that there is widespread alienation, "democratic overload," a declining influence in the world, an egocentric identity—in short, a "crisis of legitimacy." Ultimately this reflects back on our historic failure to maintain community:

> The need for national service as a vehicle of civic education is especially strong now because of the relative weakness of other forms of community. In the United States, national community can only be grounded in citizenship because Americans really do not have a *patrie,* or fatherland. America does not claim solidarity and unity by virtue of a claimed common ancestry or some divine foundation myth. America is the immigrant society par excellence. Our cohesion depends upon a civic ideal rather than primordial loyalties. At stake is the preservation of the United States of a shared citizenship that serves to knit this increasingly ethnically diverse society together as a nation.[58]

In his use of the concept *patrie,* Moskos recalls the patriarchal and fraternal origins of the American contract, and reissues a gendered account of the civic. In the last sentence of the quote, one also sees a possible similarity between Moskos's communitarian justification and Janowitz's argument for assimilation, at least in its emphasis on "knitting together" an "*increasingly* ethnically diverse society." It also indicates that for Moskos the central problem is one of "cohesion," and that this cohesion depends upon a "shared citizenship." Yet, as I tried to argue earlier, citizenship rests on a nobility of thought, and active, critical participation in society. Such practices may not always ensure cohesion, but rather an informed citizenry.

Throughout his book, Moskos makes arguments which support his claim that cohesion is the most important aspect of a shared citizenship. Yet the practices which ensure cohesion may succeed at the expense of individual rights and diversity. For instance, he suggests that national service ought to be a requirement in order to "avoid stigma." He also recommends that national service be used as an alternative sentencing program directed at teens "who are likely to get into or already have been in serious trouble." How will "counselors" discover teens "who are likely to get into serious trouble" and how will they be made visible to service planners? Moskos further warns that if national service is not implemented "the richest country in the world will enter the twenty-first century crippled by an unemployed, unassimilated, and embittered underclass." Thus, the "crippling" of American society is a function of an unassimilated, not uneducated or unenlightened, citizenry.[59]

Moreover, Moskos wishes to tie this program explicitly into the military, implying that the program will be operated by centralized state institutions.[60] He calls the national connection between civilian and military service the "double helix." This signifies that civilian service will generally have the same socializing functions as military service—that is, both will establish national norms of behavior for young citizens to follow.

Moskos also hopes that national service allows the government to put deinstitutionalized mental patients back into institutions, and provide day care for welfare clients so that they can go back to work.[61] At a recent conference Moskos made this rather extraordinary claim:

> In recent years U.S. cities have been inundated with the deinstitutionalized mentally ill. Many of these would be better off back in institutions, but staff costs make this financially infeasible. National service, which would provide low-level personnel for work in mental hospitals, offers a way out. The alternative is to allow cities to become increasingly crowded with people incapable of taking care of themselves and to make Americans increasingly callous toward the plight of the mentally ill on their doorstep.[62]

Note the rhetorical strategies Moskos deploys. He treats the "plight of the mentally ill" as if it existed in a sociopolitical vacuum, as if it is merely a problem to be solved by returning the ill to mental institutions. He also treats these institutions as if *they* existed independently of politics. Thus, the "financial infeasibility" of labor costs appear as a given, instead of as something that might be negotiated in collective bargaining. Moreover, it hides the argument that the profit margin at private hospitals is simply too important to afford the "charitable" care of some of the mentally ill. Moskos ignores the political and economic context in which the business of caring for the mentally ill thrives, and this allows him to make ideological statements under the guise of fact.

Finally, and most revealingly, he argues that without national service "the alternative" will be cities crowded with insane and cold-hearted people. *The* alternative? I suspect there might be other equally feasible solutions.[63] In applying this sort of cure-all, or sure-fire cure, discursive strategy, national service becomes more than just another policy, it becomes *the* alternative.

In claiming that national service can solve these problems—the deinstitutionalized mentally ill and unemployed welfare recipients—national service emerges as part of an extensive system of socializing strategies involving not only the servers, but the recipients as well. National service demonstrates that "the obligations of citizenship will act as a solvent for most of the differences among the various kinds of national servers."[64]

Amitai Etzioni also lobbies for national service, and includes the plan in his analysis of American society. Unlike the others, he focuses his attention on the psychological development of young people in an individualist and ego-centered society, and argues that national service is a remedy for the pathologies that society inflicts on its young.

Etzioni begins with the clinical question, "what must be done to rehabilitate America's individuals as government is cut?"[65] The goal of his therapy, of his rehabilitative techniques, is "civility." He contends that civility, and rehabilitation, are necessary because America has been "hollowed"—with big government has come the egoistic attitude of extracting benefits from it and the decline of supporting intermediary communities. In response, Etzioni suggests renewed "mutuality": the ego and the other must "attend to each other and their shared world."[66]

> The underlying reason for our need for bonds with others is that human attributes grafted upon our biological base are difficult to sustain. Even without full isolation, they require continuous reinforcement or they will erode.... In short, we *are* all each other's keepers. Children "validate" their parents; workers, each other and their supervisors; and so it goes.[67]

The bonds of mutuality have been eroded by the secular mentality of individualism, increased social and geographical mobility, isolated living, and a pop psychology that promotes a "consuming preoccupation with the self." He suggests that government may have stepped in as a community of "last resort" to replace these weakening ties. Yet big government does not solve the problem adequately, and "rehabilitation" demands that individuals become more involved and dutiful.[68]

One achieves "civility" (i.e., one is socialized) by three means: (1) playing by the rules, (2) committing oneself to the public realm, and (3) involving oneself in commonweal matters (e.g., public safety and national security). The first technique demands that one abide by rules from faith, not from instrumental calculation, that one police oneself and others when this fails, and that one modify these rules when one's perceptions of them change.[69] Yet "playing by the rules" involves understanding, and reasoning about, those rules; thus, Etzioni diminishes the importance of education in the inculcation of civility. He also suggests that we strengthen parties and restrict interest groups in order to ease public participation in government. Finally, he argues that institutions must be altered or created in order to address "commonweal issues." This is the realm of national service. Etzioni suggests that national service contribute to the care of the elderly and of mental patients, to public safety, and to citizen education on consumer product information. All these practices, he argues, will create civility by involving individuals in the affairs of the community.

Etzioni also recommends that the basic institutions of society—family, school, church, unions, etc.—be "restructured." Along these lines, national service supplements the school "experience" and help develop "character" within the young. Again, in attacking the family, the school, and the church, Etzioni indirectly attacks the ability of women (who constitute most of these "realms") to care for their children and teach them appropriate norms, and thus seeks "alternatives." At the same time, these alternatives contribute to a growing need for *national* bonds, which have faded since World War II. Finally, America needs to be "reindustrialized" and he devotes the latter half of his book to this end. This means "being sensitive to human, social, and environmental costs, *but* economic, technological, administrative, and security considerations will have to take on, for a decade or so, the status of high values, priority, and core project."[70] Despite Etzioni's claims, one can still defend the seriousness of "human, social, and environmental costs." In any event, reindustrialization may lead to the sort of strength that is at best ambiguous.

His message is also about restructuring and rehabilitating the very processes of human thought. It is

> a return to a higher legitimation of rationality and its corollaries of self-discipline and deferred gratification... reducing the violations of rationality by impulse or by conflicting values, without returning to the narrow rationality of the nineteenth century.[71]

Thus, Etzioni's observations (e.g., "reducing the violations of rationality by impulse") inform an argument similar to Janowitz' comments about the private hedonism of individuals and their sexual excesses, or at least in the operational categories it presents as relevant to the individualist American.

Moreover, it "returns" to a particular way of thinking: "rationality." Here *rationality* means a number of things: (1) a greater reliance on "logical-empirical explanations," (2) more respect for science and technology, (3) more respect for bureaucratic regulations, and (4) the closer connection between reward and effort. Yet, following Weber, one could argue that respect for bureaucratic regulations augments government. Moreover, as rewards and efforts become more closely connected, individuals might be led to think more instrumentally, and thus egocentrically. Finally, the claim that Americans need more respect for science and technology seems intuitively wrong. Americans appear to be very respectful of science and technology, as evidenced by our support for research and development, the growth of home computers, the proliferation of science magazines, the high status we attribute to doctors, etc.

Etzioni wishes to completely resocialize individuals, and his ideas for national service reflect this. He envisions national service in the most efficient of ways: as a set of "total institutions" that radically reform the "character" of young people in the country.[72] Moreover, it permits the young person "to grow beyond his animal origins and become a mature member of human society."[73] Yet it is not only "animals" who need such "growth"; the "overeducated"— the modern day "gilded youth"—do also in order to provide a "strong antidote to any ego-centric mentality" that is imparted by education.[74] Like Janowitz, he sees conservation work as the most useful, *because* it must be done in residential camps where young people can be most easily assimilated to "basic values."[75] In sum, "work camps" are an efficient vehicle of socialization.

CHAPTER TWO

National Service: The Debate over Current Proposals

In this chapter I examine the fundamental issue of whether national service ought to be compulsory or not. The terms of this debate can be rethought, and service programs that are considered at odds with each other will be seen to be two sides of the same coin.

COMPULSORY VERSUS VOLUNTARY: EXPANDING THE DEBATE

The architects of national service contend that the fundamental philosophical dilemma surrounding the program is whether or not individuals ought to join the service voluntarily. They maintain that any practical proposal must address the issue of compulsory service versus voluntary service. Compulsory service generates problems that voluntary service bypasses—for example, how to accommodate large numbers of enrollees, and what to do with those who refuse to comply. Thus, the argument goes, the institutional structure of the programs must differ in order to account for the nature and extent of the program. The actual tasks in which the participants will engage will be the same, however, regardless of the voluntariness of the program.

A compulsory program requires a year or two of national service, which must be fulfilled before the participant reaches a particular age, or else he or she will be subject to civil or criminal penalties. In the eyes of most supporters of national service, regardless of their personal preferences on the issue, compulsion involves the use of state power to force individuals to enroll in a national service program. A voluntary program is one which allows the individual to decide whether he or she wishes to join national service, without the threat of civil or criminal penalties. In this sense the individual wills him- or herself into the service freely and purposively.

The debate over the voluntariness of the program is the most fundamental issue facing the supporters of the plan, because it is the basic organizing principle of the program. Voluntary and Compulsory systems have different consequences for the labor market

31

as well as military enlistment; their costs and constitutional status differ as well. The philosophical tenor of a voluntary program also differs from that of a compulsory one. A voluntary program emphasizes free choice, the autonomy of the citizen's will, and suggests that planners adopt a liberal attitude toward its implementation. Furthermore, voluntariness implies that the program is a stepping-stone for its participants. A compulsory system indicates a concern for equality of condition and socialization, the notion that there is a general good toward which all can be socialized, and it de-emphasizes individual freedom in the program (possibly for a conception of collective freedom). A compulsory program might also suggest that the planners of national service consider the problems facing the nation to be very serious indeed. Finally, the question of voluntary versus compulsory would affect the distribution of educational benefits associated with the program.

But the distinction between compulsory and voluntary national service is not always a useful one, because in certain instances one may feel compelled to enroll in the service despite a structure that appears voluntary. Put in other terms, volunteerism cannot occur in a vacuum, but manifests itself in a particular socioeconomic context. For instance, a desperately poor individual may feel that national service is his or her only hope for a steady income. Or an individual who wishes to go to college, but can only afford it if he or she has completed a term of national service, can be said to have his or her choices constrained, and thus has not willed his or her participation in complete freedom. Finally, one may experience enormous social pressure from family or school authorities to enroll in a national service program. In all of these instances, one could not say that these individuals volunteered for service, without stretching the notion of volunteerism beyond an acceptable limit.

Alan Wertheimer reconceptualizes the notion of coercion based not on empirical evidence of force but on the moral condition of the person being coerced. Wertheimer maintains that one can be in a coercive context despite the fact that the empirical evidence does not indicate the use of what might commonly be called "force." Rather, the moral choices presented to the coerced person are such that he or she is effectively coerced. Wertheimer suggests that people perceive such coercion by establishing a "moral baseline," which judges the morality of the allegedly coercive proposal. This is grounded upon two principles: (1) that A's proposal creates a choice situation for B such that B has no reasonable alternative but to do X; and (2) that it is wrong for A to make such a proposal to B.[1] The second principle involves the moral condition that might reveal a coercive context despite the presence of alternatives.

Wertheimer describes a variety of choice contexts where coercion might be present, and suggests that an account of voluntariness begins from a "moralized account" of B's situation.[2] One context he suggests is that of describing inducements—"particularly when they are thought to be inappropriate or so great as to make refusal completely irrational."[3] I will argue below that such inducements characterize what I call compulsory systems of national service, and that in a very real sense they constrain the choice of potential participants.

In addition, the very definition of *volunteer* as used by the proponents of national service is suspect. The Coalition for National Service suggests that a volunteer is "a person who serves of his own free will," but this describes very little about the motives for serving in the program.[4] Donald Eberly, the leading advocate for national service over the past twenty years, defines voluntary work as that in which "the monetary value of that person's service exceeds the actual income that he or she receives for that service."[5] This definition presumes that in a capitalist economy each worker receives a just income for the work that he or she does, a position refuted by Marxists and non-Marxists alike. Ironically, Eberly's definition of volunteer corresponds closely to a crude version of Marx's analysis of surplus value; and one could argue that many workers do not receive the proper, even the market, wages for their labors. Rather than volunteering their time, these workers are exploited. The definition thus fails to distinguish between exploited workers and true volunteers. It becomes more problematical where one tries to make the distinction between a subsistence, a minimum, and a decent wage, a consideration that the designers of all national service programs must confront. People do not always receive such low wages because they volunteered to accept them. Nor does Eberly's definition distinguish between the service task and the job of homemaker. Does a mother serve her children when she is not compensated for it monetarily, or is there something more complex at work here?

Finally, one advocate of the program argues that the purpose of the program would be to maximize the numbers of "true volunteers" who would sign up. He implies that a compulsory service may be necessary to instill a sense of voluntariness in young people.[6] This same argument is made by a journalist who contends that compulsory national service could help make young people voluntarily accept the service ethic.[7] Unfortunately, this puts the cart before the horse, and implies that volunteerism is a quality unconnected with the exercise of free will. Moreover, the idea of voluntariness often contradicts the designs of most of these programs, for they present a carrot and/or a stick in front of all potential enlistees.[8] To be a true volunteer would mean to think outside of the carrot/stick mentality, and to act primarily for reasons other than self-interest. Currently no proposals ensure this.

I propose a different scheme for organizing this debate. Instead of a bipartite discussion of compulsory versus voluntary, I suggest a tripartite arrangement: coercive, compulsory, and voluntary. This threefold distinction makes the choices involved more analytically clear. It keeps the moral distinction between voluntarism, compulsion, and coercion. This then highlights policy choice as a moral choice. It also helps clarify the institutional practices that conform to these categories. Finally, it allows for a psychological distinction to be made, especially in the notion of compulsion. By adding the psychological component, one can help clarify the coercive context in which the choice to join national service is taken, yet still retain a moralized notion of what it means to be compelled into joining.

A coercive system of national service has traditionally been called "compulsory." That is, it is one in which the state threatens individuals with legal and political sanctions for not enrolling in a national service program. These sanctions could be criminal penalties, imprisonment, fines, suspension of privileges (like voting, driving, or drinking), or the imposition of a special tax above normal tax obligations. The state could even rest the juridical qualifications for citizenship on such a program, and require all naturalized citizens to engage in such work. Only a few individuals would have the moral compunction or political and economic resources to refuse national service when faced with restrictions like these. In this way the state guarantees the participation of virtually all those required to serve, or at least it guarantees that all national service positions be filled. If the state wished all individuals (or all individuals in a particular age group) to serve, then coercion might be the only means to accomplish this end.

One could justify a coercive system if, beyond such necessities as decent wages and working conditions, it provided two things: the opportunity to participate in and the opportunity to learn how to judge the political system that created the program. By "opportunity to participate" I mean that individuals ought to be able to participate in the polity that creates the program and to determine the means and ends of the national service program itself. As I argue in Chapter 1, participation helps develop active citizenship, and this is the end of national service programs described in this chapter.[9]

Besides the test of participation in making and acting within such an organization, the service program ought to help people come to an understanding of their government—enough to know if that government is legitimate. The government ought to be a "true authority, one whose subjects are obligated to obey it...one to which they ought to consent."[10] For coercion could be justified if it brought individuals to a greater understanding of the moral and political choices open to them. This is so, to follow Wertheimer's lead, because it helps us understand each other's "moral baseline"—that is, at what point we concede there to be a coercive context. In short, coercion might be justified if the system resulting from it allowed us to understand the nature of that coercion, and helped us to decide if we wished to consent to a government that had imposed the coercive context upon us.

We come to this understanding through education. Moreover, we come to this understanding by participating in our own education. We determine whether a government and its policies deserve our consent by participating in its institutions in order to educate ourselves about the politics of our communities. In this sense, our opportunity to participate has a purpose: to help us judge whether our government deserves consent, and whether its policies are just. Pitkin suggests that we need "to know much more specifically when resistance is justified and what might count as justification" and that we learn this "by assessing the nature and quality of the government."[11] Where national service satisfies the conditions of political education (to give people the opportunity for more active citizenship), it could be justified on coercive grounds. Then, at least in theory, the coercion could enhance the political freedom of individuals by making their political choices more comprehensible to themselves and to others. In this way they could better understand the very nature of the coercion, and come to a more reasoned understanding of when the government is justified in acting the way it does.

Where national service is justified on grounds of socialization, it should not necessarily be coercive. First, participants do not necessarily advance their understanding of government and how to judge it, because such education is not the purpose of the program. Second, there is little incentive to participate, because a program emphasizing economic needs or civic socialization derogates the idea that individuals are enrolled in the program to learn, and instead focuses either on the services the program can provide, or on the norms toward which the enrollees will be socialized. Finally, if the program is constructed around a principle of socialization, it could reinscribe central American norms that service is supposed to reform: individualism and the calculation of self-interest. To coerce individuals into an institution that may ultimately foster individualism is contrary to the spirit and ethic of citizen service. In sum, coercive service, I argue, is justified only if it meets certain very specific conditions—conditions allowing for participation and requiring political education.

But universal service does not necessarily depend on a coercive system, for it could exist theoretically under what I shall call a compulsory system of national service. Here the state urges, constrains, or obliges individuals morally or economically to join a national service program. The state does not use legal or political sanctions to fulfill its quotas, rather it encourages social sanctions or economic obligations that compel certain individuals (even, under certain circumstances, a majority) to enroll. Thus a compulsory system might involve tying all educational aid to the completion of a prescribed term of national service. Or the state could make future welfare or social security dollars dependent upon the completion of service. Moreover, the state could engage in widespread advertising campaigns to represent national service as a normal part of growing up, or otherwise abet local communities into exerting moral pressure on young people to enlist. In each of these instances, some individuals will face present and future economic and social sanctions for not enrolling in national service. They would not necessarily be coerced by law into enlisting, but they would be compelled to do so, given their economic or social status.

I would categorize those who join a national service organization purely out of self-interest as acting from compulsion. These individuals do not enroll because they wish to be part of a service organization, or because they have an altruistic sense toward others. Rather they believe that national service is the only or best way by which they can achieve their own personal, and material, goals.[12] In some instances it may be the only way of achieving those goals, as in the examples I gave in the preceding paragraphs. In other instances, those concerned may believe that it is the most efficient way, in which case they act instrumentally. By acting instrumentally, they constrain themselves in terms of what they want from the organization, and the state abets them insofar as it encourages this sort of instrumental thinking. In any event, they are not serving the public freely for they are not serving it selflessly. And where they do not serve the public selflessly, they cannot be said to be engaged in "service," and especially "national" service. They are not thus serving the nation, or the public, with integrity. Where individuals do not serve with integrity they cannot be said to be serving autonomously and freely, and a state that encourages the loss of an individual's integrity makes that individual's quest for material goods more compelling.

Lastly, national service could be in the form of a voluntary service. Here individuals enroll in national service freely and fully responsible for their actions. In this form of service individuals enroll because they want to engage in service for its own sake, or for the sake of others. The state encourages this altruism without the use of coercion, legal penalties, or social and economic sanctions. The state provides national service in an atmosphere where individuals decide to join and act with full integrity, and does not reward them materially for such a decision. This does not mean that they would not get paid, for participants deserve a decent wage like everyone else; rather it means that they do not get *rewarded*— they do not get special privileges for being in national service. Nor should the state encourage groups in civil society to reward individuals for service. National service, under this proposal, is one where the integrity of the individual and his commitment as a citizen, are at stake. True voluntary national service, then, does not mean simply the absence of legal penalties for nonenrollment.

Most contemporary proposals for national service fall under the category I have called "compulsory." Either they provide economic or social sanctions for nonenrollment, or they encourage the individual to join national service involuntarily—that is, without integrity, for instrumental purposes, or without the necessary desire for service. Some proposals reflect a coercive approach in the hopes that this will ensure universal service, or a service which fulfills its quotas. But very few proposals for national service can be considered voluntary in that they remain loyal to the idea of public service.

COERCIVE SERVICE

Currently, there are no proposals in Congress that would coerce individuals into enlisting in a national service program. In recent history, there have not been many proposals for such a program, largely because most congressmen have hesitated to consider them seriously. Many complain that such a scheme violates particular freedoms and rights of individuals, as guaranteed by the fifth and thirteenth amendments. They are also wary of the cost; few congressman advocate great increases in governmental spending in the contemporary political climate. Thirdly, there has been no need so far for conscription, and so the desire for a civilian service option to that system has lost some immediacy. Finally, they are skeptical of its practicability; congressmen do not want to support a project that has little chance of being implemented, and thus little chance of doing something for their constituents.

Nonetheless, coercive programs have been proposed by academics, consultants, and even the odd House member. For instance, in 1979 representatives Paul McCloskey (R-Calif.) and John Cavanaugh (D-Nebr.) each presented bills which would require all young people to give some form of service to the state. McCloskey, a long time supporter of national service, proposed that all young people register at age seventeen, and a year later be required to do one of the following: (1) two years of military service, (2) six months of active duty and five and one-half years of reserve duty, (3) one year of civilian service, or (4) enter a lottery pool for six years of draft liability. While it was theoretically possible to avoid serving in any capacity, the odds against this were strong because of the labor demands of military and civilian positions. Such a program was coercive in that a teenager would engage in a gamble, where the odds were stacked in the state's favor—so much so that any rational person would choose one of the first three options. As McCloskey reasoned: "I don't believe that reasonable young men and women are going to volunteer for the military service unless the draft, the possibility of the draft is in the background."[13]

Representative Cavanaugh's plan was similar in most of the details to McCloskey's plan, except that individuals could be forced into entering civilian service in a service lottery. Those who failed to register would be subject to a fine and/or jail term, and those who failed to complete their service obligations would be denied future federal money of any sort (except, apparently, social security and medicaid).[14] Neither of these bills survived the legislative process, and to date no other bills have been proposed that rival these in assuring universal civilian service.[15]

But a number of academics and consultants have sought to universalize service. Perhaps the most original proposal is the one suggested by Richard Danzig and Peter Szanton in *National Service: What Would It Mean?*[16] Though they endorse coercive service only hesitantly, because they worry about the costs accompanying such a project, they claim that it "would be the most likely to fulfill the visions of proponents of national service."[17] As a manner of enforcement, they would impose a civil, rather than a criminal, penalty for noncompliance: a five percent surcharge on an individual's taxes every year, which would be forgiven after that individual had completed one year of service. This is a unique plan because it is one of the very few which encourages all individuals to serve, and not just those in a particular age group. They argue that it also prevents the rich from escaping their obligations because the surcharge affects a large portion of their income, but the very rich would probably not miss even five percent.[18]

The arguments for coercive national service, are quite compelling, especially where they can be enforced. For one, they guarantee that the obligation to serve would be equal on the part of all individuals. This is an important moral ideal in a democracy. At the same time it would be the most practicable way for individuals to meet and work with each other on equal footing. The power relationships based on class, gender, or ethnicity could be minimized, in that all participants would be constrained comparably by the requirements of service. This constraint could nourish the new relationships people would develop with others from different backgrounds or of different ages, because people would develop true friendships, not relationships based on inequalities of power.

In a service program constructed appropriately, coercion almost guarantees that all individuals share common experiences. This is important where national service offers significant educational opportunities for individuals, and where service informs those individuals of their political and social rights. In this way the state promotes the positive freedoms of all equally, by offering each the opportunity to learn more about his or her society. This helps those who did not know their rights or capacities beforehand, and in this way, coercive service extends the freedoms of individuals. Thus, while service may be coerced in one sense, such service may actually enhance freedom in another—the freedom to understand oneself, one's rights, and the capacities of others. Coercive service offers the state the means of educating all individuals equally toward responsible citizenship.

Finally, coercive service might actually be more cost-efficient than voluntary service. For one, it would be more predictable, in terms of the positions filled and resources needed, and so would be less likely to cause fluctuations in government outlays. The program would not have to worry about accomodating changing numbers of volunteers from year to year, even if those numbers are relatively small. Secondly, the government could phase out those programs which might overlap with national service, though there is the danger of eliminating worthwhile programs. Thus, the coercive service organization would absorb such programs as the Peace Corps and VISTA. A voluntary service organization might set up additional agencies because it is too small or focused to encompass these sorts of programs.

Of course, the objections to coercive service are, under most circumstances, quite significant. Some contend that America cannot afford one more governmental program, even if the program is not a useless one, and that coercive service would cost a great deal of money. This need not be true, though. Many service proponents argue that such a program could be decentralized, and that most of it could be administered by voluntary or private agencies.[19] Moreover, the argument that the United States simply cannot afford more government in an age of billion-dollar deficits is only partly true. Though our deficit precludes the addition of new programs in the minds of many, it also represents a set of priorities that one might question. For instance, does it make sense to say that the government cannot afford national service when it spends much more on defense? The research money desired for SDI alone would be more than enough to establish a national service program with minimal organization, and allow peaceful scientific research to continue apace. In short, to say that the federal government cannot afford national service implies a set of budget priorities that ignores the process as political, wrought with social and economic choices.

Another, more intractable, problem is that coercive national service violates freedoms and constitutional protections. While very strong legal cases can be made against such a plan,[20] the moral case against coercive service is even stronger. Coercive service violates the fundamental rights of freedom of expression and freedom from involuntary servitude that are a basic part of what it means to be human. They violate these basic characteristics which define human nature, and as such infringe upon the capacities of individuals to live a full life with corporeal autonomy and intellectual integrity. Moreover, coercive service violates the individual's right to property, and does so without the due process of law.

This objection can be addressed in a number of ways. First, individuals would be coerced into national service not because they are human, but because they are citizens of the United States. As such, they have responsibilities to the state as well as rights, and they must fulfill those responsibilities in order for their rights to be protected. Thus, it is not necessarily their natural rights that are being violated—for freedom of expression and property can be defined in a number of ways—rather their civil or societal rights are being earned. Individuals are not only entitled to particular rights and privileges from government, they are also obliged, through a moral duty, to preserve the social structure and culture which ensures those rights and privileges.[21]

Second, the argument that we must move away from an individualist conception of the citizen comes into clear relief here. For national service can be a vehicle by which people come to understand that they owe duties to the national community, and that they are not merely the recipients of federal benefits and privileges. That is, national service can be a way for individuals to increase their understandings of their political communities, and by doing so become more clear about their rights and privileges. Through political education individuals can come to a more immediate understanding of their capabilities as human beings, and so augment their freedoms rather than have them restricted.

This last point also implies that national service need not be national servitude. Where people object to coercive service they do so because they assume the program is in some sense servitude; but a program could be designed which minimizes its servile characteristics. As I discuss below, none of the contemporary proposals for national service do so, because they emphasize the work and socializing aspects of national service. These proposals thus presume that most enrollees would serve a particular project or industry that they would not normally. But were national service to be founded on political education, critics could not easily argue that coercing people into such a program violates their rights. The purpose of the program would be to apprise participants of their rights. This could be a program where individuals are taught the workings of government as well as new political ideas; in such a way they could come to a greater understanding of their capacities as citizens. Indirectly, this may help them assess their abilities as human beings.

The argument becomes stronger where a national service organization teaches individuals to criticize their government, and to think independently about political and social issues. For here the state does not coerce individuals into being its servants (or the servants of private industry), but rather forces them to retain an intellectual stance independent of the government or its operatives. In the same way as Gutmann argues for democratic education, national service could teach adults to think critically and creatively about politics and their government. Thus, national service could actually free people from the constraints of government, and teach them to participate in that government.

VOLUNTARY SERVICE

Truly voluntary service, as I describe it above, has never been seriously proposed in Congress for a few reasons. Firstly, most proponents of national service believe that a service program requires incentives to attract individuals to fill the openings. They believe that altruism is not powerful enough a motive for individuals to serve their country. Moreover, it is difficult to estimate how many people would join such a service were it made available, and so allocating funds for it becomes problematic. In addition predicting what sorts of tasks the participants would prefer makes appropriating and administering the program's budget a bit of a guessing game.

Occasionally, though, voluntary service plans are presented to the Congress for approval, though all to date have failed to pass. The most recent plan coming closest to the voluntary ethic is Senator Barbara Mikulski's bill, S. 408, introduced on February 9, 1989.[22] Entitled the National Community Service Act of 1989, the bill seeks to establish a corporation to administer a national volunteer service program. It does not force individuals to join, nor entice them with large amounts of federal money, and it only requires them to complete a minimum of nine hours of service per week in any way they want (but preferably on weekends). Thus the form and content of service is left largely up to the individual. Moreover, the corporation supervising such a service would not be "considered an agency or establishment of the United States Government" (section 201[a]). Finally, a significant part of the program would be educational: individuals will engage in "general training in citizenship and civic and community service" (section 106[a][2][i]).

Nonetheless, while Mikulski's bill is the closest to the ideal of a purely voluntary service, it shares some characteristics with the compulsory bills I discuss below. First, it offers vouchers for the purposes of education or homeownership, so its incentives abet the individual to think instrumentally about service. Second, it conceives of service purely in terms of work, viewing service as jobs that do not involve challenging individuals intellectually to any great degree.[23] Despite these drawbacks, though, it remains the closest congressional proposal to date of an ideal of strictly voluntary service.

The most important merit to voluntary service, as the Mikulski bill demonstrates, is that it does not violate the integrity of the individual, while it trains that individual to think more deeply about politics and political ideas. It does not appeal to the instrumental passions of the citizen, and in fact provides the citizen with a means of expressing his or her public spirit. And where the program engages in conscious political education, it may validate and develop the citizen's notions of freedom and justice. Moreover, it does not advertise national service as a way to cure the country's ills, but simply offers it up as an option for the activity of concerned citizens. In this way, the expectations for national service are not too high, and its advantages and accomplishments can be viewed in a more realistic light. Voluntary service cannot be indicted for failing to cure society's problems because it does not offer itself as a cure, but merely as an outlet for the free and public expression of individual citizens.

Thus, voluntary service may be the purest expression of citizenship. It is at least the means by which public-spirited individuals can demonstrate to the rest of society that altruism and community spirit still remain in America. It then further enhances the development of responsible citizens, and recommends itself to those who may be looking for a means of developing their capacities as citizens. It neither coerces individuals into becoming citizens, nor moralizes to them to do so. Finally, it does not entice them into serving with the promise of material gain. In short, it is the ideal form of service that represents a civic concern.

Yet many national service proponents call this form of service a pipe dream. They contend that a completely voluntary service based on the altruistic and civic senses of citizens is a lie, and that some incentive or force is necessary to coax anyone to enlist. They claim that pressuring some minimum number of enlistees are necessary in order to accomplish the public goals set out by the program, an approach which implies that the program intends to remedy particular social problems or improve the conditions in some particular geographical locations.

A more difficult problem is that such service undoubtedly excludes the many individuals who choose not to enlist presumably because of the opportunity costs in doing so. Thus, one could not argue for voluntary service as a prospective means of enhancing the civic qualities of the community or the individuals who make it up, because most of these citizens would not benefit from such enlightenment. Therefore, to call such a program "national" is a bit misleading, because it serves only a very few individuals, and thus may not serve the public at large. One may question whether such a program even deserves to be considered in an analysis of national service. For this reason, I hesitate to include it in my review of national service programs, despite its good intentions.

COMPULSORY SERVICE

Compulsory service is, by far and away, the most popular form of service for proponents of the idea, because it is practicable. It contains elements of voluntary and coercive service and offers material incentives so that people will enlist in it, thus filling quotas. Moreover, it pretends to solve some of the problems America faces, so congressmen can credit themselves with doing something to improve both the nation and their districts and states. Lastly, such proposals are often compromises, so they appeal to their proponents as the most pragmatic method of implementing national service.[24]

Proponents of compulsory service also contend that incentives are necessary because they ensure an adequate supply of labor, and thus help achieve the particular goals set out in individual programs. Advocates justify national service not on grounds beyond mere service, but on what such service can accomplish, in material terms, for the nation.[25] Thus it becomes a public means of producing services.[26] Its productivity then justifies offering material incentives to individuals to enlist. Incentives imply that where a worker is not productive, or where the program is not successful in some material way, the incentives will be withdrawn.

There are two problems with this. First, productivity is not the same thing as public service, and one could argue that a society productive for its own sake derogates the public character of the services. It undermines the ethic behind public service, because one does not merely serve "selflessly"; one does so to produce services. Where productivity motivates service, other motives, like good citizenship or the cultivation of friendships, often become secondary considerations. There is also no reason why productivity *per se* is a good thing; one cannot abstract productivity from the culture in which it thrives. One must be productive *for a reason*, and the simple fact that an organization or a nation is highly productive does not give it any special *moral* status (though it may give it political and economic power). Therefore, productivity cannot be used as a moral argument for national service.

Because it cannot be a moral argument for national service, productivity may be a goal that does not contribute to the moral purposes of the individuals who work in the service. For those who benefit are the enrollees and the individuals whom they serve (the elderly, drug addicts, the mentally ill, etc.). Where service concerns productivity, the people involved may become incidental to the program's purposes. The incentive system, then, represents a moral and economic outlook that puts services first and people second. This is precisely the sort of ethic national service proponents wish to alter in the United States. This ethic does little to teach individuals the meaning of political obligation, and it reinforces the policy that the abstract functioning of service industries supersedes the actual needs of the people who receive them.

Second, there is ample evidence that the "products" of such service do not always serve the public, but rather particular groups within the society. For instance, an earlier service program—the CCC—created thousands of parks and forests for the public to use. But is also helped develop forestry techniques that the forestry industry began to employ for their own private purposes. Moreover, conservationists complained that some of these techniques ultimately destroyed parts of the landscape that the CCC was meant to preserve.[27] The CCC also built many roads that eased interstate commerce, thus helping private businesses move their products more efficiently, without forcing them to pay a direct tax for the privilege. Finally, the corporations that supplied the corps's uniforms, buildings, food, and recreational items, made quite a bit of money from its nine year term. This occurred in the depression when F.D.R. decided that the government had to spend in order to trigger a recovery.

In times when there is no depression, a similar response could be a gift to some corporations. And given the size of a national service program, only the largest corporations could supply the program with goods and service most efficiently. Thus, if a program required work camps, or uniforms, or school equipment, or leisure equipment, those who could provide these for the cheapest cost would be called to do so. All versions of the program either state explicitly or imply the need for this support. In the end, someone invariably profits from such an arrangement, and that profit will most likely not be distributed evenly among a large number of people. In short, the products used by the service participants and the "products" generated by them are not strictly in the public interest. Private industry reaps the rewards of a national service program. Where private industry is rewarded, the program cannot be said to be only in the public interest, and where it is not in the public interest alone, it does not function with the integrity its proponents wish to give it.[28]

The most well-known example of compulsory service, as I use the term, was the bill proffered by the Democratic Leadership Council (DLC). This bill was introduced in the Senate by Senator Nunn (D-Ga.) on January 25, 1989, and in the House of Representatives by Representative McCurdy (D-Okla.) a few weeks later. The Senate bill, S.3, was entitled the Citizenship and National Service Act of 1989, which indicates that its sponsors considered citizenship to be a priority. And in fact, its first purpose was stated thus: "to renew the ethic of civic obligation in the United States and spread the responsibilities of citizenship more equitably" (section 3[1]). In fact all of its stated purposes considered only the welfare and development of persons, with no mention of any public purpose except "to deal with pressing social problems" (section 3[3]). It did not indicate that producing goods or services is important to the fulfillment of the program.

The DLC's plan establishes a "citizens corps," which involves three types of service: civilian service, military service, and service by senior citizens. The plan indicates appropriate (section 206[a][2]) means of service and sketches an organizational structure for the program. I examine these issues more closely in the next chapter, when I describe the types of jobs a national service program provides.

Despite its stated purposes, the bill gives the service administration enough leeway to put its objectives before those of the individual server. For instance, section 105(a)(4) states that if "the council determines (after consultation with the applicant) that the applicant is better qualified for a position outside of the area, the council may refer the applicant for placement to another national service council," or to another agency accepting members in the citizens corps. There are a number of potential problems with this. First, and most obviously, what is the nature of "consultation"? Does it mean that an individual can refuse to be transferred even if the council thinks he or she may be better qualified elsewhere? Second, what is the nature of "qualified"? Does it mean that the individuals would be unhappy in their home districts because there are no jobs which would suit their tastes? Or does it mean that if the national service organization needs a particular individual to do a particular job, that individual must go for the sake of the program? If the latter, it may fall into the same sort of productivity ethic I describe above, and may actually cheat an individual out of his or her original choices, or out of an education in community that can only come from being near home.[29]

I call the DLC bill "compulsory" largely because of the regulations concerning benefits for participants in the citizens corps. These consist of one hundred dollars a week stipend, health insurance, and educational or housing benefits (amounting to about ten thousand dollars for each year of service).[30] The one hundred dollars a week is a subsistence wage, though there are very few places in America, especially in the cities, where one could subsist on that wage. This is even more true for those individuals who have to provide for themselves and possibly a family, without another source of income. The time responsibility that comes with national service precludes a second job.

Section 402(a) states that,

after the end of the 5-year period beginning on the effective date of this Act, no individual shall be eligible for post-secondary educational assistance from the United States under any programs providing loans or loan guarantees unless such individual is a member of the Citizen Corps or has successfully completed a term of service in the Citizens Corps under section 103.

The parents of a dependent undergraduate student "shall not be eligible for loans...unless such a student is a member of the Citizens Corps or has successfully completed a term of service...under section 103" (section 402[6][c]). In short, the authors of the bill hope that citizens corps benefits will replace current federal higher education loan and grant programs, and they suggest that Pell and SEOG educational grant programs (section 403[a]) be phased out for most individuals.[31]

The obvious objection is that this unfairly places the burden of service on poorer students who must rely on educational loans for their future. But this merely points up some deeper implications of the proposal. First, it not only burdens poor young people with service, it compels them to join the service for reasons of private interest.[32] It does not merely provide an option for getting money to go to college, it may effectively be the *only* way to pay for college. Consequently, national service becomes a requirement for enrolling in an institution of higher education for many individuals. It also validates the belief that national service is a way to get ahead in society, thus derogating the civic aspects of the program. Service may then be seen as a way that individuals receive benefits from the federal government, indeed the only way they can receive those benefits. This does nothing to alter the perception that government is some institution foreign to their immediate experience and which serves as an instrument for their private success. By reinscribing their inclination to think instrumentally, this sort of national service program encourages an individualist, self-serving ethic.[33]

This sort of instrumental thinking stretches into the plan for funding the program. In its booklet, *Citizenship and National Service*, the Democratic Leadership Council justifies the Nunn-McCurdy proposals on grounds of "citizenship" and "civic obligation." But the council's "public spiritedness" is questionable because it insists that such a program can be paid for without new taxes.[34] Whether or not this is true is debatable, but the council certainly appeals to the self-interest of the taxpayer. Thus, civic obligation does not involve the taxpayer in this case. This paints the Democrats as being very opportunistic, without a serious commitment to the ideas behind the proposal.[35]

Since the bill was first introduced, Senator Nunn and his co-sponsors and Representative McCurdy and his co-sponsors have backed down from their commitment to tying educational aid firmly with national service. But this has only been for pragmatic political reasons: they want to get some form of the bill passed in order to win votes and appease a national constituency. And in fact, they were successful in the passage of the "National and Community Service Act of 1990." This does not mean, however, that they will not try to make the tie again, because the link is part of the policy platform of the DLC.[36]

As I have tried to point out in this section, the debate surrounding the compulsoriness and voluntariness of national service is spurious. The terms of the debate must become clearer. But as I have also tried to show, the most practical solution, what I have called "compulsory," is in some ways the most unfair. Moreover, it reinscribes the instrumental and atomistic traits that characterize American society.

A GUIDE TO THE ADMINISTRATIVE STRUCTURE
OF NATIONAL SERVICE

Regardless of how voluntary or coercive national service is meant to be, all plans for it involve programs and training sessions that are remarkably similar. A number of individuals and organizations have begun to propose potential structures for such programs and training. These structures involve fairly detailed descriptions of the particular institutions and agencies who are to be involved in the program. They also suggest that a national service program must address three basic issues: (1) improving the moral character of the individual, (2) helping remedy social ills, and (3) contributing service where the nation needs it. In this way national service programs improve the quality of citizenship in the United States as they improve the quality of life.

These organizational principles have generally been formulated with minimal regard to how many individuals enroll in a national service program.[37] Coercive, compulsory, and voluntary national service plans all have the same basic goals and constituent units, regardless of which formula is used. The only difference tends to be in accomodating different numbers of enrollees, and in the enforcement of the program in the cases of coercive and compulsory service. With the exception of Danzig and Szanton's proposal, these enforcement policies all involve criminal charges for noncompliance. Nonetheless, the types of services offered and the character of the agencies involved remain very similar whether the program is voluntary or not.

Thus all its proponents agree on some fundamental things about the nature of national service. They all assume that it is primarily an institution that encourages individuals, usually young people, to work. More precisely, individuals work at service jobs— they do not create consumable goods, but are employed to fill human needs above and beyond the basic necessities of life. National service participants (NSPs) generally do not produce food, clothing, or shelter, though they may assist in the distribution of these goods.[38] Rather NSPs serve the country by providing the human labor necessary to improve its social conditions. So the jobs that all its proponents foresee are tasks like day care, meals on wheels, conservation, teaching, criminal justice, library and museum work, and national defense. National service means serving people, not producing goods for them.

The structural organization of these service programs has obviously not been elaborated, but some designers have gone into surprising detail about what sorts of agencies and special programs would be necessary for a successful venture. These involve two basic categories: the administrative apparatus of the national service organization, and any special programs necessary to train the participants in the desired manner. In the following chapters I examine both these aspects to national service in order to see to what extent they fulfill the hopes tied to it. In the next chapter I look at some aspects of the proposed administrative organizations of the program. In this way I question how national service, as a form of administration, instills "in our citizens a more robust ethic of civic duty and mutual obligation."[39]

In chapters 4 through 7 I examine specific proposals designed to educate the NSP, or otherwise improve him or her morally or spiritually. I contend that such proposals, if implemented, would not cultivate a sense of civic obligation, and in many instances would abrade the integrity of the citizen. Rather than strengthen the citizen, some of these programs could further individuate and atomize its participants.

In these chapters I cite evidence from proposals offered by some of the most eminent politicians, public interest groups, and academics working on the problem. But their arguments are still speculative, because national service is not yet fully a reality. Therefore, in order to supplement their claims, I also present evidence from past attempts at instilling the same sort of ideals that national service is supposed to do. Because there have not been many of these in recent American history, I rely occasionally on evidence from the Civilian Conservation Corps (CCC)—especially in chapters 4 and 7. The CCC remains the only large-scale experiment which sought to serve the needs of the country as it trained its participants morally and civically.[40] All other attempts at this dual goal were (and are) either too small, too focused, or too regional to engage in what might be called "national" service. For example, the Peace Corps only enrolls a very small percentage of Americans from only a few socioeconomic groups to do work that occurs outside of the boundaries of the nation. Similarly, VISTA involves only a very few people, and neither it nor the Peace Corps make pretensions to training people for citizenship. Smaller scale employment programs for young people, like the Job Corps,

ACTION's PLS (Program for Local Service), or regional employment offerings like those of Seattle and New York, are simply too limited to be considered national programs. Finally, present-day conservation programs, like the Youth Conservation Corps or the California Conservation Corps, have been restricted in scope and funded too inadequately to be considered serious models for national service. Where national service appropriates specific ideas or policies from these organizations I will refer to them (for instance, in Chapter 6).

CHAPTER THREE

The Creation and Structure of National Service

Here I present and evaluate proposals for the institution and development of a national service program. In the development and justification for the actual structure of national service, one sees programs which emphasize the socialization of citizens. The chapter highlights those issues involved in creating and instituting a program of national service that most service proponents have chosen to ignore. In this way, the chapter does not so much criticize the idea of national service, but warns that the advantages of service are not as self-evident as many individuals believe.

THE DEVELOPMENT OF NATIONAL SERVICE

Most supporters of the idea agree that national service can not be invented overnight. Rather, it must develop from a series of well-planned experiments, and must expand from a pilot program into one encompassing most, if not all, communities in America. In fact there is evidence that this is already being done to some extent, with the help of private foundations.[1] Its designers make no secret of the fact that, despite its initial charter, national service ought to ultimately incorporate all young people (and possibly senior citizens). Thus, a study done for Senator Nunn and the armed services committee of the Senate over a decade ago concludes that even a "minimally coercive" initial program is only a "first stage" effort and that it should be expanded into a more universal and coercive system.[2] Former U.S. Senator Gary Hart agrees and argues that "at least in its initial stages, a national service system would need to be voluntary."[3] The Committee for the Study of National Service declares that the country should "move *toward* universal service by steps and by incentives but without compulsion."[4] The Carter Administration argued that a compulsory-based lottery system was the "most promising alternative."[5]

Moreover, many of its proponents envision it as part of a general youth strategy, and as the leading edge of an educational and socialization system that needs to be completely revamped. Amitai Etzioni sees it as a "remedy for overeducation" leading to a "down-

53

ward shift" of educational resources that reorients the educational priorities of America.[6] He suggests that it could reform the "ego-centered mentality" of American youth. Samuel Halperin adds that "youth service must become an integral part of formal education."[7] Donald J. Eberly and Michael W. Sherraden claim that national service should "join education, employment, and military service as a fourth cornerstone of our unwritten national youth policy."[8]

The development and expansion of national service could only be done through "rational planning," according to the participants of a conference held twenty years ago in Washington, D.C. To one participant, "it requires a combination of statistical, demographic, sociological and psychological data" that no single government agency could compile.[9] A contemporary advocate contends that "the important thing in planning for national service is to base decisions on real data, not hypotheses."[10] The "real data" requires painstaking research by a number of governmental agencies, and a thoroughgoing investigation of many individuals.

> What is required is the creation of a series of typologies (with typical profiles or case histories) which could function as significant categories for planners in creating new volunteer services. Such typologies would have to include information regarding educational histories, social and economic class, race, occupation, motivation, regional differences, age, and values and future plans of a large segment of the American population in the group from 18 to 25. It could most appropriately be undertaken by the Department of Health, Education, and Welfare, if that agency has not already done so.[11]

The information gathered by the appropriate agencies, according to strict scientific method and careful experimentation will lead to "pilot projects."[12] Morris Janowitz states that "voluntary national service will come as the result of pragmatic and piecemeal innovation."[13] Yet the researchers may not fulfill the requirement that science be objective and impartial. For example, the most vociferous supporter of national service, Donald Eberly, maintains that such a pilot project could only be tested in a "receptive area," for testing the project in a "hostile" area brings in a built-in negative bias.[14] Eberly argues in addition that the results of the test would be measured by a special agency within the national service program itself, which would "conduct its research in accordance with the project objectives."[15] Finally, an advisory board would ultimately approve or disapprove research requests by private agencies. Such a board "could rule on the legitimacy of such requests and minimize the effects of the Heisenberg Uncertainty Principle by keeping research studies from seriously affecting the project itself."[16] Many national service supporters argue that the National and Community Service Act of 1990 allows for greater testing of a national service program.

These policy recommendations indicate a number of unsettling things. First, a small-scale national service program is only a temporary and experimental plan in the minds of its proponents. Thus *any* plan for national service, no matter how voluntary or tentative, must be seen as a first step toward a more comprehensive and universal program.[17] Even voluntary or compulsory plans have coercive intent. One can therefore discuss national service as if it is going to be a universal, and possibly coercive, system.[18]

Second, if it is tested in the way prescribed above, the success of *national* service may be a foregone conclusion. For it will most likely be tested in a location that supports its creation, by the agency governing national service itself. That agency will have an interest in ensuring that the experiment works. The agency can support its findings by regulating the nature and extent of independent tests carried out by private organizations. In the name of the Heisenberg uncertainty principle it can actually prevent negative results from ever being discovered. In short, even before national service begins, plans for it can restrict the free exchange of ideas, and a fledgling agency can serve as an agency of disinformation.

FEDERAL OVERSIGHT

Once established, national service requires a new bureaucracy, though not necessarily a large one. Because national service is such a large and unique project its administrative apparatus would be correspondingly unique. Its structure blends the imperatives of a nationwide and possibly (or at least potentially) universal program, with the contemporary desire to decentralize authority. Indeed, all its proponents argue that any practical national service program must be implemented at the state or municipal level. Regional implementation prevents an enlarged federal government and makes the individual programs more manageable and accountable. Thus a workable national service requires both federal supervision and regulation, and local control.

The apex of the structure consists only in an independent, non-profit corporation overseeing the program.[19] This corporation would be separate from other governmental agencies and "shall not be considered an agency or establishment of the United States Government."[20] How this can be is a bit sketchy, for it requires the government to deny the very act which created it. Questions of logic aside, though, the corporation consists of eleven members appointed by the president with the advice and consent of the Senate, with the majority presumably coming from the president's party. These members would be "eminent citizens," and their term of office would be seven years. They would receive minimal pay for their efforts.[21] Moreover, such members head a corporation that is "nonpolitical." Nonpolitical here means not contributing to or supporting "any political party or candidate for elective office"; though it obviously does not restrict the members from being members of a political party, or the president from appointing them for that reason. In this sense, even the enabling legislation creating the corporation manifests the political nature of the oversight agency.

Such politics may be vitally important given one of the tasks of the corporation—to "specify the types of national service activities appropriate for members of the Civilian and Senior Services."[22] The sorts of private agencies or groups in line for federal funding or approval may thus be narrowed to those which support one political party or the other. Even where one party does not dominate the approval process, the corporation may be empowered to restrict greatly the sorts of tasks appropriate to national service. Thus, individuals would not be able to serve freely in any sort of service organization they choose, but only in those approved by the corporation. This is significant, because if participants want to receive a political education, they may want to serve in political or advocacy organizations, and the corporation has the legal power to prevent this.[23] In this way, despite claims of decentralization, the national corporation practices a great deal of discretion over how a national service system would be constituted. Its power to allocate grant money to states in support of appropriate forms of service accentuates this argument.[24] The corporation also serves "as a clearinghouse for information on national service opportunities" and issues "rules for administering and monitoring the performance of national service."[25] And at least one advocate maintains that it would be the storehouse for record-keeping of all sorts.[26] Thus information about participants and employees would be centralized in Washington, D.C.

This is in fact what happened under the CCC, and we can see some parallels between its agency and the national corporation projected for national service. The CCC was governed by an agency independent of other departments or agencies within the administration, though it was never considered to be independent of government. Other agencies had influence on the CCC and this often led to internecine warfare among the departments of war, interior, and agriculture over policies; these disputes crippled the agency.[27]

The one clear power the agency had was the setting of rules and regulations. Ironically, many former CCC members recall fondly the diversity of the men found in the camps, yet the agency struggled against this diversity. The administrative imperative was to make each boy conform to a particular behavioral pattern. This was more than just ridding society of a latent criminal element in each boy, it was an attempt to instill particular values and mores in him. The agency believed that through its regulations it could provide individuals with a uniform legal and ethical code by which to live their lives. And these regulations filled volumes.[28]

A present-day national service corporation can learn from the experience of the CCC. It can learn to avoid the institutional paralysis that occurred in the CCC when it became the site of interagency battles. Indeed, one wonders if such an organization can have any influence without allies in the various departments. Thus it would not be surprising to see its directors negotiate with, and around, other agencies. This means that its status as a nongovernmental agency would be severely compromised.

It can also learn that its power to make rules and regulations can go a long way in restricting or standardizing the behavior of service participants. The corporation, like the CCC, could have the authority to make extensive health, safety, educational, and other regulations—regulations which limit the free association of individuals and the free exchange of ideas. For, like the CCC, once participants enroll in a government-sponsored organization, it is quite possible for them to be subject to a whole series of rules to which they would not normally be subject as private citizens.

In fact, the Selective Service Agency already has rules governing alternative service. For instance, its regulations define alternative service as "civilian work which contributes to the maintenance of national health, safety, or interest, as the Director may deem appropriate."[29] Moreover, the director can authorize specific activities and can even act to ensure certain "standards of performance" and standards of "conduct, attitude, and appearance."[30] Thus both the example of the CCC and current rules suggest that the corporation's regulatory powers will be fairly extensive. Consequently, any argument that emphasizes the decentralized nature of national service may be a pretense for relatively widespread federal regulation of behavior.[31]

Even where federal regulations do not apply, state and local regulations might. For the rest of the program is to be governed by state and local bureaucracies, and any private agency participating in the program must comply with guidelines established at these levels. Samuel Halperin of the William T. Grant Foundation, and a member of Youth Service America, contends that "we must insist on standards for service that are every bit as rigorous as the standards that govern our best schools, business, and factories."[32] And these standards can be ensured only through some sort of regulation. At some level the individual participant, and the agency involved, will be subject to more state power than he, she, or it would be otherwise. The claims that these individuals volunteer or that the constituent agencies are voluntary conceal a compulsory structure to the system.

THE SERVICE ACTIVITIES:
SOCIAL AND POLITICAL ASPECTS

The civilian tasks established for the participants, will be largely in the service sector, regardless of how voluntary the program presents itself to be. These tasks include day care, help for the mentally and physically disabled, primary and secondary school instruction, library and museum work, conservation work, and criminal justice apprenticeships. All proposed programs have a military component, and incentives to join the military would be raised sufficiently to ensure that the forces meet their quotas.

All service tasks will be, in some sense, *state sanctioned;* thus, service will be juridically defined. Those individuals who serve, who provide care, who contribute to the welfare of the society, without official designation will not be considered to be providing service. The most significant group excluded, then, would be parents, especially mothers. Certain tasks (e.g., day care) will be sanctioned precisely to free parents from their familial responsibilities—and will serve to correct the failures of the family in serving the moral and psychological needs of the young.

All the civilian work types are tasks in the area of human relationships, with the exception of conservation work.[33] Thus, participants serve both civil society and the state. In society, they serve the needy, those people requiring special services to live a decent life. Participants help teach inner city children, repair houses in poor rural areas, and provide care for senior citizens, the mentally retarded, runaways, pregnant teens, and drug abusers. As all proponents of the plan admit, there is no shortage of needs to be addressed. "For national service programs of even the largest foreseeable kind, the work is there to do."[34]

Yet NSPs also serve the state, for they fulfill tasks that many individuals, and many state officials, believe the state should provide. This service will probably be official—that is members of a national service will be registered as state, or quasi-state, functionaries of some sort, and will be subject to the rules and regulations governing federal or state employment in some way. At the very least, the private agencies who administer particular services must abide by state regulations, and will thus impose certain restrictions on their workers.[35]

In any event, individuals provide service on behalf of, and for, the state, and so could be considered state workers. This would have immediate political consequences for the party in power: its members could take credit for the work accomplished in the program. Because the needy would receive valuable services, they would be less inclined to oppose the policies of incumbents. There may also be ways for congressmen and state legislators to use plum service positions for patronage, both legally and illegally.[36] In this way, more people will become obligated to the elites of the state, thus further tying their fortunes in with those of the state.

A certain paradox arises here, because proponents of national service insist that the tasks of the participants will not be political, or at least ought not to be political.[37] One conference on national service concluded that the purpose of national service

is not to invade communities and cities, upsetting the power structure. While in some situations political action is needed, the impact of National Service experience would emerge after the person returned home, having completed his period of service, and engaged in local affairs as a private citizen.... Certainly there will be interaction between persons in National Service and people in towns and cities, but, insofar as participants are carrying on approved projects under National Service, it is assumed that the activities will be primarily technical.[38]

Eberly also implies that the sorts of jobs specified by the various bills presented in the 1980s must be the only ones allowable, because "there has been enough research and experimentation to narrow down the viable alternatives."[39] So these "nonpolitical" jobs are the legitimate ones because they have been validated "scientifically." Moreover, Moskos argues that national service will actually "work against ideological polarization" between the political parties.[40] Thus the tasks themselves are not only "nonpolitical," they depoliticize partisans.

Moskos also argues that service will provide a sort of moral Keynesianism, that is, it will even out the cycles of political and social involvement that have afflicted young people in the history of America.[41] Building on Albert Hirschmann's work, Moskos suggests that the service nature of the tasks helps even out the "shifting involvements" young people seem to have between intense interest in public issues and "an almost total concentration on private happiness."[42] In place of these ups and downs, national service helps focus the attention of young people on both areas in a balanced way, so that their moral life can grow at a steady rate.

> This is not to say that national service will do away with predicted cycles of private hedonism versus political activism, but it does promise to flatten the curves, thus helping to avoid the exaggerations of the recent past and contemporary period.[43]

Thus, national service is not only nonpolitical, it both depoliticizes and sometimes politicizes, to maintain a set of consistent morals for youth.

These arguments are curious because, where they are not incoherent, they represent particular ideological positions on the nature of politics and political involvement. First, the statement that national service will "not invade cities or communities" is both wrong and cynical. It is wrong because the very purpose of national service is to provide services that cities and communities cannot provide. It is cynical because it conceptualizes cities and communities as independent of the program. The very ethic of national service ought to embody cities and communities as sources of pride, and must accept them as part of the public domain. One might argue that good citizenship, regardless of the definition, is not taught by machine politicians or defenders of an antiquated system of patronage. Moreover, where certain cities and communities are invaded, and where the power structure is disrupted, young men and women can redefine their ideas of citizenship.

Second, the idea that someone can be a private citizen, as the conferees believed, only demonstrates one aspect of the concept of citizenship. By distinguishing public citizens in national service and private citizens in local politics, the conferees tacitly state that politics is a private affair, or at least an affair that is relevant to only certain public activities. I have already argued that citizenship is a public and participatory activity as well. Thus the authors focus on an ethic that imagines politics to be a means of private gain. The conferees fall victim to the instrumental reasoning that helps lead to "private hedonism" on the part of youth. By defining the political sphere in the way they do, they help perpetuate an individualist and hedonistic culture.[44]

Moskos's comments reveal a cynicism toward youth, a hostility toward politics, and a misunderstanding of the nature of politics. Moskos's argument that service will even out the cycles of youth is pretentious, and belies a dangerous technocratic urge. He assumes that national service will alter a postulated character trait of young Americans in the late twentieth century, without giving any evidence for this. Indeed, one could argue that such a trait may be inherent in young people. But even if it is only a recent phenomenon, how can he explain the cycles experienced in countries with universal military service and a civilian option, like West Germany. Moskos can only hope that such service would even out fickle youth, though their capricious nature (if it exists) may fade with age. And where it does not fade with age, maybe one cannot blame such attitudes on youth, but on the particular socio-political context of the time (a context created by adults). In short, Moskos needs to support these assertions with evidence.

Furthermore, while "Hirschman's theory provides a good framework for analyzing the long-term political dynamics of national service," it actually requires the analyst to come to the *opposite* conclusion.[45] Hirschman argues that an expansion of services leads to greater disenchantment with those services.

The argument about the high disappointment potential of these services becomes a great deal stronger in times when a substantial effort is made to expand rapidly the supply of these services with the intention of making them more widely available. Under these conditions, the average quality is likely to drop substantially.[46]

Under these conditions, the cycle of public and private action becomes exaggerated, and rather than smooth out such cycles, national service might actually perpetuate them. National service might create such great expectations on the part of all involved that its failure to fulfill them may cause an even greater privatization of lifestyles than we are currently experiencing. If Hirschman is also correct that disappointment is an important structural consideration in modern Western economies, then national service cannot assuage its effects, because those will necessarily remain with us.

If Hirschman is correct in his analysis, and if we are not at the nadir of our private cycle, then national service is an inappropriate corrective, historically, for our way of life. National service is a way that *government* induces the citizenry to become more active. Consequently, the cycle becomes ahistorical, for it implies that we can correct for history. This may not be what Hirschman intends.

Moskos also narrowly defines politics as mere partisan debate. He assumes that jobs like day care, teaching, or historical preservation are somehow nonpolitical. But they represent the central political and, even ideological, concerns of a community. Indeed, the very process of educating children is as central a political task as exists in any community. Furthermore, organizations like a police corps, or border patrol corps, or criminal justice programs are fundamentally political because they represent the ways in which the state organizes its own security.

Finally, and in many ways most importantly, jobs like day care, meals on wheels, border patrol, police corps, clerical work in libraries or other public institutions, and conservation work have one very important element in common: they are tasks that do not require individuals to use their intellects to the highest capacity. Virtually all the proposed jobs in almost all national service schemes are purely service jobs. But service more often than not means clerical, or manual tasks, and tasks that do not challenge the individual. Rather, they are tasks requiring that citizen to memorize and repeat a few key procedures.[47] Even where there may be more complex procedures to understand—as in a police corps—these are, ultimately, procedures. Innovative and creative thinking may not serve NSPs well in most of their tasks.[48]

〝 The situation implies that simply doing community service work cannot guarantee that one learns civic responsibility. In a study of community service programs in eight high schools, Rutter and Newmann found that "the performance of a socially derived service in a technically proficient way will not necessarily result in greater social responsibility, commitment, or political order."[49] Moreover, there is no guarantee that such work is significant to individuals' understanding of themselves or others. Service participants, in carrying out their appointed rounds, may not be given the opportunity to think independently of the particular procedures they must follow. They are not necessarily encouraged to develop their own ideas about those procedures or about the particular agencies within which they work. For they are charged with administering the tasks of a particular agency, not helping to formulate its policy, or discussing ways in which to improve the administration of tasks. This sort of education teaches all people, but especially young people, to follow orders, not to question those orders or rethink them. Many educators today argue that such programs must have a reflective component to them—like a seminar or writing program. This is only now being developed by national service planners, however inchoately.[50]

In sum, most service participants will be required to engage in the sort of work one critic has labeled "new work." Yet this is no advance on the sort of drudgery experienced by, say CCC workers, because though

the New Worker may not be climbing up freight cars to crank down hand breaks or sweating double turns in a steel mill or putting up roof bolts in a coal mine...most [will] continue to do what the old workers have always done: a lot of scut work, often at relatively low pay, in many cases for the most demanding of bosses.[51]

Moreover, one report found that youth service programs offer little hope that individuals will acquire the sorts of skills necessary to engage in meaningful or dignifying work.[52] What they do provide, however, is training for a future postindustrial economy—an economy that demands an extensive service proletariat.

Service proponents also maintain that service work benefits the moral and intellectual development of the young citizen. But there is a growing body of research that suggests quite the opposite. Social psychologists now argue that, while young people learn some skills on the job and make friendships, they also learn behavior that is at the very least questionable. The research evidence contradicts service proponents in a few areas: the development of responsibility, success in school, deterrence of crime and delinquency, and the improvement of employment prospects in adulthood.

Some social psychologists claim that service work generates gender differences in levels of personal responsibility.[53] In experiments done at the universities of California and Wisconsin, teenage girls were found to develop a slight sense of self-reliance, while teenage boys were not, and neither gender developed a sense of social responsibility. Moreover, these researchers speculate that work may be the setting where young people practice already aquired work habits, rather than develop new ones.

These same researchers suggest that work may inhibit academic performance for those teenagers who work while going to high school. They also suggest that employing high school youths is a distinctly American practice, partly due to our "less demanding" educational system.[54] Their findings suggest that national service, as work, may not be able to make up deficiencies that a poor educational system creates. Furthermore, they indicate that, given finite resources, the country may want to focus its energies on improving that educational system before it resorts to national service. Or, the results imply that if the policy of national service is pursued, maybe it should reinforce the *educational* role of the schools.

A series of different studies demonstrate that work does not reduce delinquency and may, in fact, "promote some forms of deviant behavior."[55] This deviance is promoted in middle class youth because their increased disposable income helps them lapse into drug use and the criminality that that use generates. Job stress can also be a cause of deviance, and this, along with an ethic of greater materialism, becomes an unanticipated consequence of youth employment. In all the studies cited, Greenberger and Steinberg found that young people had greater cynicism toward work in general after being on the job for a while. Finally, they argue that service work for teenagers does not really increase the employment prospects for these persons in adulthood.[56] All of the above hold true both for students in private employment and for those holding positions in school- or government-sponsored programs.[57]

In short,

> jobs that provide only limited opportunity for decision-making or cooperation are not likely to foster healthy independence or social responsibility.... Jobs that involve youngsters in repetitive, unstimulating tasks are not likely

to facilitate the growth of higher-order intellectual skills; prepare youngsters for adult employment; inspire feelings of self-esteem, mastery, competence; or foster a clearer sense of identity.[58]

Let us now see what kinds of jobs national service participants will enjoy.

SERVING THE STATE:
CIVILIAN JOBS IN A SERVICE PROGRAM

Before turning to the actual tasks done by participants in a national service program, I must make two prefatory remarks. First, I only consider civilian jobs, because the purpose of this essay is to critique the concept of national service beyond its military component. Second, the tasks I list are not arbitrary, but have been agreed upon widely by academics, politicians, and bureaucrats alike.[59] Moreover such tasks are the very ones the government has designated essential to the future of the American economy.[60] I argue that, while such tasks are no doubt noble, they may harbor within them possibilities for injustice—injustice for the participants and toward the recipients of those services.

More precisely, a successful program of service may leave some recipients of that service worse off than they were before. At the very least, it leaves open the door for substantial changes in federal policy toward the poor, the homeless, illegal aliens, drug addicts, and other marginalized people in society. In this way, national service is on the cutting edge of a change in wide areas of federal social policy. In this section I discuss some of the possible injustices involved in these changes. I also argue that, despite the rhetoric, most tasks performed by the participants in such a program may neither enhance them morally, nor give most of them any real skills upon which to build a future. In fact, most of the needed tasks involve clerical work or unskilled manual labor.

The categories of what are popularly called "unmet social needs" number five: (1) public school and general education (including work at libraries and museums), (2) child care, (3) health care, (4) criminal justice and public safety, and (5) conservation. In each of these areas there are real social needs, but the programs that would be administered would not necessarily be as benign as one would think. For example, "health care" may involve the use of NSPs as objects of medical and psychiatric experimentation. "Criminal justice and public safety" may include programs to close up the borders of the country. At the same time, participants in this task may impose the state's definition of citizenship on themselves and those who "receive" the services of such agencies as a police corps, prison guard corps, or border patrol corps.[61]

Education

I begin here because educational tasks are probably the most intellectually satisfying tasks of any proposed. Both the public school system and public cultural institutions have many openings that need to be filled, and national service participants can be an economical and efficient way to fill them. One author suggests that this might trigger major school reform in the United States, by offering "new choices for ways to improve the quality of what schools offer."[62] Beyond this, participants themselves might learn quite a bit about the world of ideas by engaging in this sort of work, and so improve themselves intellectually. They would also come into contact with other adults and school children in an atmosphere of learning, and so friendships based on their mutual learning are established. These contacts theoretically cut across social and economic boundaries, and so go further toward the equal provision of quality schooling. Finally, the use of national service participants frees up teachers to do what they want to do—namely teach. And it allows them to do so with more dignity and shorter hours.[63]

Senator Edward Kennedy has proposed a bill which establishes a "teacher corps" throughout the country. The bill offers scholarships of up to eight thousand dollars a year, in exchange for five years of teaching. Former Mayor Edward Koch of New York also proposes a similar idea to increase the number of teachers in New York City, so the idea is gaining some support. The *New York Times* endorsed these plans.[64]

Yet the most well-developed plan for utilizing NSPs in the educational field suggests that only a very small percentage would actually teach. Danzig and Szanton, following Theodore Sizer's work, suggest that responsibilities in the educational service be graded. They recommend three different categories of teacher's assistant, based on a sociopsychological study of each applicant: mentors, teaching auxiliaries, and management auxiliaries. Only the highest qualifiers could be mentors, and would actually teach; and these are "only a small fraction of NSPs." Teaching auxiliaries supervise tests and drills, while management auxiliaries are responsible for school maintenance and clerical work in the schools.[65]

There are a number of problems with this. First, only a very small percentage—Sizer calculates it as the top ten percent[66]— qualify as Mentors. Thus, only a very few receive the intellectual benefits from being in the educational service. This ten percent might reflect the sociological makeup of the program, as students from the best high schools would be allowed to participate as mentors. Such a policy reinscribes class differences, which contradicts the argument that national service is a great equalizer. At the very least, mentors are a privileged group in a program that is theoretically egalitarian.

The teaching auxiliaries and management auxiliaries do not really benefit from being part of the educational system because their tasks are largely noneducational. That is, they do not develop the skills necessary for teaching, though the teaching auxiliaries may learn by observing. The management auxiliaries would be no different from apprentice clerical or janitorial workers, and so could accomplish their tasks under any institution. Therefore even the name "educational service" is misleading, for most of its participants would not actually teach, but would merely contribute to the bureaucratic routine of the schools.

For the ninety percent who do not teach, the advantages that come with being an NSP are very few. How do cleaning blackboards or mopping up the cafeteria inculcate a sense of citizenship? How do these tasks improve the long-term job prospects of the participants? How do clerical tasks in the principal's office help an individual decide upon a career? How will following bureaucratic routines in the principal's office, or at the office of the school board, inculcate good morals or a sense of Aristotelian friendship? Where is the incentive for a clerical assistant to get off drugs? The answers to these questions remain mysterious, and the futures of the NSPs are shrouded in this mystery.

These same problems afflict participants who work in cultural institutions, like museums or libraries. Though here the problems might not be as severe, and the presence of NSPs could trigger more federal money toward these institutions. Exposure to these institutions could also enlighten the participating citizen. Nonetheless there is no logical reason to presume that simply engaging in essentially bureaucratic tasks has a moralizing or politicizing effect on individuals. If they are challenged intellectually, then maybe these same individuals can go far in developing their capacities, and work in libraries and museums must challenge them to have this effect.

Child Care

There are few things as important as the care and nurturing of the very young, and there are fewer needs more pressing than safe and capable child care for millions of young women and couples. With the rise of the two-income family and the feminization of poverty, child care has become one of the most urgent demands to which this country must now respond. At the same time, experts warn of the psychological and sociological dangers to latch-key children, and the need for more assistance at orphanages, child shelters, and adoption shelters. Moreover, all these problems may increase with an increase in the birth rate, and with more mothers working. Under these conditions, it could be useful to have an army of day care workers ready to staff the needed positions in this field?

What sorts of tasks would NSPs do in the day care centers?

> NSPs might assist with cooking and serving food, perform clerical services, serve as drivers, or help with maintenance and upkeep. Others, especially the more responsible or imaginative, could work directly with the children, tutoring, supervising play, and reading stories.[67]

In this way NSPs could lower the "quite high child to staff ratios" found in most day care centers. And the federal government could guarantee their quality by offering reimbursements to day care centers if they agree to be administered by a nonprofit agency which provides training and technical assistance.

Unfortunately, these arguments and plans ignore some very important aspects to the day care problem, and do not indicate how participants will benefit from day care experience. First, day care has become big business. There are profits to be made, and the large day care centers do not welcome competition from the government. Where participants work for these large centers, they are not be serving the public, but serving private industry. If the program places them in smaller, more community-oriented centers, those businesses might become more dependent on federal money and more subject to federal regulation. This may not make it profitable for these businesses to remain open. Furthermore, a study by the Child Care Employee Project has discovered that child care staff turnover in for-profit centers almost tripled between 1977 and 1988, and that turnover was highest at large, for-profit day care centers that paid very low wages (about $4.10 an hour).[68] The study also found that children at centers with a high turnover of staff members "were less engaged in social activities with their peers and scored worse on vocabulary tests" than children at other centers.

This augurs certain problems for national service involvement in the field. It suggests that poorly paid day care workers do not perform well at day care centers, and that this affects the level of education the children receive. It also points up the poor care children receive at corporate centers—centers which could benefit from national service labor.[69] Lastly, it demonstrates that high turnover in day care centers is not in the best interests of the children. National service participants will of necessity be short term and paid at a subsistence level. Therefore, the problems cited in the study remain.

Another problem is that the sorts of tasks required in these day care centers parallel those I have just described for the schools. They are mostly clerical or maintenance jobs, and so are of uncertain value in the inculcation of citizenship. Moreover, where participants learn their "craft" in privately owned, corporate centers, they adapt themselves to corporate time, corporate space, and corporate aesthetics. Deborah Fallows notes the uniformity of corporate day care in her descriptions of the interior of a center, and of the daily timetable used.[70] She further notes that "life in day care centers is also more homogenous than life elsewhere. The day's format is always the same...surprises and variety...are kept to a minimum."[71] This sort of atmosphere is not necessarily conducive to the intellectual development of participants. Nor are they learning any lessons about communal liberty because the center itself is not the source of the worker's identity. It suggests that variegated and interesting jobs in a day care center are few and far between, but that bureaucratic routine is everywhere. Such routine can *only* become more pronounced with the inclusion of thousands of national service participants, because they will be expected to follow instructions, and because the centers themselves (even the smallest ones) can only get larger. Even where centers remain small, routine might be refined.[72]

Finally, there is the danger, not only of such jobs being routine or clerical, but gender biased too. It may turn out that, upon analysis of the profiles of national service candidates, women are found to fit such work better.[73] Even where this is not so, many mothers or couples may feel more comfortable placing their children into centers where most of the caretakers are women. This underscores the need for responsible participants, and points up the need for careful federal regulation and the close scrutiny of potential service workers. Thus the surveillance of participants grows accordingly, as does the governmental bureaucracy involved—two areas of service which its proponents contend would be minimal.

Health Care

The growing need for adequate health care is undeniable, especially given our aging population and the exorbitant rise in costs for much of it. In addition, the multiplicity of diseases and afflictions besetting modern individuals numbs the mind, and staff shortages exist for some of the most necessary medical and psychiatric programs. The health care field involves a number of different agencies, including senior citizen care, hospital and clinic work, drug and alcohol dependency programs, mental illness hospitals and homes, hospice work, and paramedic services. As we shall shortly see, it may also involve "laboratory" work.

The services provided by NSPs can be numerous and potentially valuable. Moskos believes that the most promising avenues for service here are in nursing homes and in transporting the infirm, as well as in providing some in-home services.[74] Danzig and Szanton add that "in inpatient facilities.... NSPs might provide information and referral, transportation, groundskeeping and maintenance, telephone reception, health education, child supervision, and recreation and craft activities."[75] Similar tasks can provide for outpatient services, and even in facilities which are largely private.

Danzig and Szanton make the very good point that national service participation in this field opens it up to public scrutiny. The window effect that occurs as former NSPs rise to positions of responsibility might prevent abuses within the system. National service, then, can provide a check on the nation's public and private health care system.[76]

Nonetheless, unsettling problems remain concerning the use of NSPs in the health care field. First, there may be a danger in giving people easier access to prescription and over-the-counter drugs.[77] Preventing resultant drug abuse would require both tighter security and surveillance methods at health care institutions, and a thorough investigation of the backgrounds of the potential service-givers. This raises costs to the system, and requires that participants be treated as objects of investigation, research, and analysis. I discuss the implications of this in the next chapter.

Furthermore, such participants become functionaries of a bureaucratic regime, not decision-makers or individuals asked to use judgment on even the most trivial of issues.[78] And if some of them decide to enter the health care field, it would probably be from their observations of others at their place of work, not because they were allowed to participate in the care of individuals.

This may open up health care centers in the future, as Danzig and Szanton suggest, or it may alienate young people from the health care field. For, as Albert Hirschman argues, one powerful force that turns people away from public participation toward private gratification is their encounter with corruption.[79] Such exposure may lead to alienation on the part of those idealistic service participants who suddenly discover the seedy side of the organizations in which they work. Under these conditions, civic service could become civic disaffection.

Thirdly, participation in modern health care programs often means participation in private, corporate, for-profit enterprises. This assists those corporations that are already profitable, and furthers their hegemony over the health care market. This is not a public good for a few reasons: (a) NSPs will promote an essentially private-sector industry, (b) the increased labor force in some of these organizations might make them even more profitable and competitive in relation to smaller firms; thus (c) the service given might assist large companies to buy or merge with smaller firms. If this occurs, community-run hospitals become even fewer, with fewer individuals and towns retaining financial control over their health care systems. Thus individuals might not take pride in their community's health care services, because they alienate themselves from those services. Ownership and control would be in the hands of outsiders. All this is not to say that national service participation must lead to this, but in an age of the corporatization and bureaucratization of health care systems, the additional (and essentially docile) labor available by the program abets the economic alienation of health care from the community.

Finally, national service participants could become vital parts of health care research. Both statements from contemporary proponents of the plan and evidence from the CCC demonstrate that medical experimentation may become an element of the national service program.[80] For instance, Donald Eberly conducted a survey in which he asked young people in what sort of tasks they would be willing to engage as national service participants. One of his categories was "guinea pigs for medical research," and a surprising fifteen percent of high school youth, and nine percent of college youth, responded positively to this option.[81] At the same time Danzig and Szanton do not specifically mention medical experimentation as part of the responsibility of NSPs, but they do suggest that health care, defined broadly, includes "medical research and public health activities," and they estimate that sixteen thousand NSP positions could be available in "research, planning, etc."[82] The mere sight of medical research as an option, and/or the failure of proponents to deny it, indicates that national service planners consider it "viable."

Criminal Justice

A number of proposals for national service provide for public safety corps. These involve police, highway patrol, and border patrol corps, and their proponents hope that NSPs might contribute to the internal security of the nation. The Nunn and McCurdy bills discussed in the previous chapter provide for these, and the Democratic Leadership Council contends that participants would perform "unspecialized tasks in support of our overtaxed criminal justice system: police, prisons, the courts, and border patrol."[83] Danzig and Szanton estimate that 250,000 positions could be created for participants in this area, which also includes parole and victim assistance programs.[84] There has also been one suggestion made to involve them in a sort of prereform school, a "youth academy," that functions to discipline and educate teenagers from broken homes to prevent social ills.[85]

Indeed, some proposals suggest that the participants themselves could be involved as security forces. For instance, some representatives propose the establishment of a police corps (Senate Resolution 1299), which offers participants ten thousand dollars a year in educational vouchers in exchange for four years of police service after they graduate from college. Supported by liberals and conservatives alike, the plan hopes to increase the number of college-educated police officers. Such a program also addresses "the very high level of violent crime and neighborhood deterioration afflicting communities throughout the Nation."[86] Moreover, the regular infusion of fresh talent could bring new spirit to the alienated squad room subculture that feeds cynicism and burnout, even protects the brutal or corrupt. And graduates of the program, returned to civilian life, would spread understanding of the police.[87]

Thus, a police corps provides a check on the activities of police forces throughout the country.

Charles Moskos also argues that participants could act as prison guards.[88] And James Jacobs has studied the feasibility of employing national service participants in correctional institutions.[89] NSPs could do clerical work, run educational programs, assist in visitation programs, and even conduct routine searches if necessary. Jacobs contends that such participation aids in due process by making record-keeping and procedures more efficient. It also professionalizes the guard system, by bringing more college-bound youth into the system. Finally, national service helps democratize the prison: "If a broader cross-section of the American population imposed punishment, both the public and prisoners themselves might perceive it as more legitimate, and, more important, prison reform might be easier to accomplish."[90] As in the day care and health care systems, NSPs could be watchdogs against abuses in the system. This could be a sort of education for the participants themselves by opening their eyes to many things. Ultimately national service could "focus attention on the legitimacy of punishment in a democratic society and the question of whether punishment is too isolated from society's mainstream."[91]

These arguments are powerful ones, and where NSPs educate prisoners or provide a check on abuses in the system their efforts would be greatly rewarded. This would be even more true where participants council prisoners on their legal rights, and inform them of the options they possess both in and out of prison. Thus, participation in the corrections system might be particularly appropriate for lawyers or future lawyers. Indeed, one might insist that this be required for law-school, to give future attorneys a firsthand look at the criminal justice system.

Nevertheless, problems remain with the participation of national service enrollees in the system of public safety. First, the vast majority would be engaged in clerical work, so it is difficult to see how they will develop a sense of civic spirit, or learn job skills, from such routine tasks. There are also physical dangers to the participants in this sort of program and extra training and cost will be necessary to prepare them for whatever they do. Third, there is evidence that this training will be at state centers, thus adding to the expenses of the states. For instance, the bill proposing a police corps calls for the creation of state police corps training centers.

Furthermore, there is some problem as to where, exactly, participants would serve. Some suggest that individuals serve near their homes and communities. This makes sense especially if one wishes to inculcate a sense of community in the participants. But it may also cause a problem to those participants in areas where "security officials" are looked upon as repressive. Most proposals, like the bill creating the police corps, suggest that participants be assigned to those areas "where there is the greatest need for additional law enforcement personnel."[92] Certainly, with prison workers and border patrol guards this is a necessity, because most prisons, and borders, are located well-outside cities. Yet if this were to be the case one might question the civic content of the program. How does one develop a sense of community and citizenship outside of the city, or even the region, where one grows up? Moreover, this would require camps or barracks for the participants, and this runs into the problems afflicting the CCC.[93] Finally, this suggests that the choice by individuals to work where they want is further restricted, and the service program itself becomes that much more constraining.

Such a proposal also directly threatens unions that currently supply labor to police forces, prisons, and parole systems throughout the country. The problem is endemic to all areas of service, but especially severe in the security field, where unions are well organized. Some proposals have tried to appease the unions by setting limits on where the participants would work, and the police corps bill even offers the same benefits to children of officers without their participation.[94] Nonetheless, well-trained service workers could be used to break-up strikes, or otherwise prevent union members from bargaining for a decent wage.

The ironic problem remains of who would discipline lackadaisical workers—the service program, or the criminal justice institutions themselves. Would the police have the authority to penalize those workers who did not abide by regulations, or who did not work up to their capacity? Would the national service program have to take on disciplinary powers and procedures in order to retain its sovereignty over the participant in this regard?[95]

Most importantly, service in this sector, and in institutions such as mental hospitals, is qualitatively different from services in the other sectors. Not only do participants serve the community at large, but they work for institutions which "work upon" individuals.[96] That is, the service they render involves the violation by the state of the sovereignty of some individual's body. Such individuals contribute in whatever way to "the intensification of the body—with its exploitation as an object of knowledge and an element in relations of power."[97] They become part of a system that extracts information from individuals, and uses that knowledge to exercise power over them. In this sense, they serve institutions that both represent and impose particular strategies of power upon their subjects.

Indeed, these institutions are ones that constitute subjection and subjectivity, for they repress individuals (their avowed purpose). But they also generate knowledge about them (often in order to resocialize them). Through experimentation, research, and investigation they compile dossiers about these people that define them within the institutions. They generate the knowledge about those individuals they wish to incarcerate, deport, or arrest, and in doing so perpetuate a system where people are perceived thus. This is both an indignity to those individuals, and a technique by which they reinscribe their hegemony over those individuals. In this way, NSPs participate in a system that does not treat certain individuals as ends in themselves. Moreover, it substitutes for community a regime where bodies are analyzed, regulated, and interrogated, and it substitutes for public discourse a projection of state power onto the individual.[98] Consequently, NSPs, in even their clerical functions, are part of a system that does more than serve. National service in institutions of criminal justice becomes a misnomer, because the intent of those institutions is not simply to serve the public, but also to generate information, and apply power onto subjects.[99]

Furthermore, there is some evidence that, while such programs might serve a public by providing for a democratic check on the institutions, national service participants might accept the organizational ideology promoted by the various members of the criminal justice system. The authors of the Police Corps bill hope that training centers:

> provide basic law enforcement training, including vigorous physical and mental training to teach participants self-discipline and organizational loyalty and to impart knowledge and understanding of legal processes and law enforcement.[100]

"Organizational loyalty" could extend beyond the limits of the law, and so the needed check against corruption may never surface.[101] Moreover, where would a participant lodge a complaint against a public safety institution? At the local police station? At the local national service office?

Such organizational loyalty suggests a kind of bureaucratic rationality that may deny the sorts of new or diverse experiences that national service proponents claim as an advantage. The NSPs, in these sorts of organizations, may be fitted with a particular sort of groupthink and/or organizational logic that closes their minds to either new ideas or new social arrangements.[102] Thus, a member of the border patrol corps might accept unquestioningly the institutional perspective of the immigration service in thinking about the problem of illegal aliens. Such a corps necessarily denies its participants the opportunity to discuss the problem of illegal aliens in its broader geopolitical context, and so does not help them understand the implications of federal policy in this area.

Such a practice may not improve individuals intellectually, nor does it necessarily enrich their civic life, because they are not be challenged into defending their actions. The function of service in a border patrol might not be to discuss reasonably the merits of American policy toward illegal aliens, but merely to contribute to the administration of that policy.[103] And where national service becomes the mere administration of policy, it does not contribute to the national debate over that policy, and it does not offer individuals the intellectual challenges helpful in enlightening them about their country.

Civic service means learning about the *civitas* through service, and working toward the end of that *civitas*. But to work toward it means to understand what its possible ends are, and to come to a reasoned judgment about which end is preferred. Tasks that do not encourage reasoned judgment on the purposes of the national community do not encourage individuals to engage in a philosophical relationship with that community. For respecting the ideas of a community—those it stands for, those it wrestles with—justifies its reproduction. Service tasks ought to reproduce these intellectual commitments.

CHAPTER FOUR

Registering and Training Service Participants

The proper functioning of a national service program requires different elements working together to effectuate the program. Individuals must be registered, selected, placed in the appropriate tasks, and supervised at those tasks. Most plans also monitor participants after their term of service ends, to ensure their success in the "real world." The techniques suggested by program planners and evidence from the CCC and contemporary programs help highlight possible procedures a future national service organization may use.

National service could be the largest system of registration developed by federal planners in the past two decades, and could be organized to maximize the production of services. It would provide social scientists and government bureaucrats with a large pool for the testing of social and psychological theories. Finally, it could be the means by which many aspects of the private service sector are brought under further federal regulatory control. In short, the mechanics of a potential national service reveal a means by which the state can not only improve the condition of its citizens, but also intervene more fully into the activities of those citizens.

In this chapter, I examine the registration and selection processes by which individuals are categorized. In the next chapter, I consider programs designed to improve the employability of enrollees. Part of the registration and selection process will be employment counseling, and in the process of categorizing and "skilling" the individual, certain lessons are taught, and knowledge is imparted, to and about, the enrollee.

On the basis of plans made by national service designers and examples from previous programs, the registration and selection system of a national service program is extensive, elaborate, and comprehensive. This makes it different in kind from a mere program of volunteerism, for it possesses a *systematic* quality. Some of these registration proposals have the intended and unintended consequences of helping the government monitor the activities of its enrollees. Such monitoring may have questionable consequences from the standpoint of civil liberties, and does not seem to add to the program's stated goal of inculcating citizenship. To some the monitoring perpetuates their exposure to bureaucratic social organizations, to others it introduces them to such organizations. For all, it continues the testing and research procedures that have been used upon them since they have been small, and further categorizes their abilities, aptitudes, and achievements. Participants are treated equally insofar as they are equal subjects for scientific research.

The rite of adulthood may become a rite of individuality, one which signifies a person's ability to tolerate, and even combat, the impersonality of the service program. It may also become a rite of technical mastery: individuals demonstrate their proficiency in some technique of production (though most of these techniques produce services rather than manufacturing). With the use of computers, and elaborate techniques of registration and training, adulthood becomes a bureaucratic category, with service organizations certifying this in writing.

REGISTRATION AND SELECTION

All national service programs must efficiently and capably register and select potential participants. National service, according to one proponent, will "supply a system of national accounting of human resources."[1] Yet it will be an accounting that is fully computerized in order ensure its thoroughness. The computer not only registers volunteers or applicants efficiently, but it also stores enormous amounts of information about them in its microchips. This is necessary for vocational counseling and testing, as well as for aggregating data about the enrollees.

Thus, the computer can process data about these applicants and the program in general. Consequently, each application or registration form becomes not only a means by which registrants inform the state about themselves, but a means by which the state can generate further statistics about the demographic composition of America. Thus, registrants become participants in a sort of universalized research report, for they can give the state information about themselves that it cannot glean from census reports.

This has two implications. First, upon registration, people are treated as subjects for research, and not respected as private individuals (who may not wish to reveal particular facts about themselves). Second, such information can, and most certainly would be used by other agencies of government for state purposes.[2] There may be occasions when this results in some indignity suffered by the individual at the hands of the state.

One could also argue that the computer itself, by accumulating and processing data about the registrants, contributes to their homogenization. The computer violates the integrity of the individual identity; it recodes that identity to fit into preconceived categories.

The ways that computers can be used for storing and transmitting information can only be ways that increase the tempo of the homogenizing process. Abstracting facts so that they can be stored as information is achieved by classification, and it is the very nature of any classifying to homogenize. Where classification rules, identities and differences can appear only in its terms.[3]

In this way, the use of computers determines the terms upon which the identity of the registrant will be formulated. This is significant because that identity breaks with the identity they construct as a part of their original communities, and forces them to think about their new identity in terms other than those in which they learn about themselves (traditionally).

This, I argue, destroys community and the citizen, because it imposes upon that citizen a truth about him or herself that he or she may have difficulty understanding. With registration for national service comes a new identity (especially for those young people who have not been registered by an agency before), symbolizing a break with the communities where those registrants were nurtured. National service might be the first time young people are removed from their old communities—especially in cases of criminal justice tasks—and assimilated into the larger American community.

Categorization (by computer) is a crucial part of the registration process. This is indicated both by plans for national service, and by the experience of the CCC's registration process. It is implied by the statements of sociologists like Amitai Etzioni, who claims that "at least 10 percent of the cohort can be expected to be mentally or physically unable to participate."[4] But a number of planners for national service also specify it and have done so for at least twenty years.[5]

For instance at a conference on national service in 1966, a number of conferees suggested uniform registration, testing, and training programs. Future futurist John Naisbitt recommended that service provide basic training and basic education uniformly to all participants, and that all trainees demonstrate their acquired knowledge through multiple choice tests.[6] Moreover, an entire workshop at the conference devoted itself to "preparation for service"—an examination of selection and training procedures for a potential national service organization.[7]

One paper proposed "summer training camps" to prepare participants, possibly modeled on the Outward Bound program, with urban variants.[8] Another paper detailed a model for "placement centers."[9] In this paper, the author suggested that "men choosing nonmilitary national service would be required to observe some form of disciplined camp life in a National Service Placement Center."[10] This meant "having them learn new modes of behavior and modify old ones," and done through manual labor.[11]

This author detailed the technological imperatives which would govern the program of national service.

In order to cut operating costs of the centers to a minimum and to create the best possible training and job environment, the assignment of all personnel to National Service Placement Centers and National Service Work Agencies would be almost wholly determined by computers. Under such conditions, computers would be called upon to determine the "proper mix" insofar as travel costs, cross culturalization, and job assignments are concerned. Although every effort would be made before a national serviceman began his basic training course to ascertain what type of work assignment he not only preferred but was best suited for, no final decision would be reached until he completed a battery of aptitude tests given during his initial training period. The information collected at this time would serve national service needs and in addition would provide a valuable source of information for a wide range of future national planning objectives.[12]

Twenty years ago, then, the first conference on national service considered the possibility of extensive data collection and testing on participants in a future program. Moreover, in order to achieve this, functions, operating procedures, and training at all camp sites had to be standardized.[13] All participants in the workshop agreed to this, regardless of the actual placement process imposed.

All concurred that national service necessitated testing and standardized operations.[14]

These proposals have not changed much over the years, as a survey of more recent plans reveals. An armed services committee report of 1977 states that "registration, evaluation, and counseling" is necessary for each enrollee. This means: (1) identifying and assessing the skills and deficiencies of young Americans, (2) prescribing remedial or skill-enhancing activities for individuals to consider, (3) offering information on service and training opportunities, (4) helping channel resources into "critical areas of national need," and (5) providing a basic registration system for a backup draft.[15] The report recommends that the registration system "be utilized for medical and vocational diagnosis," as well as counseling and advice.[16]

The Congressional Budget Office also suggests that all national service programs regardless of their voluntariness have extensive registration, mental and medical testing, and counselling services.[17] In all programs, youths at age sixteen would be registered and subject to mental assessment tests, and those enrolling would be subject to thorough medical examinations. Finally counsellors would be available in the voluntary programs, and counselling would be mandatory in the mandatory program. Such a program would invariably require a very extensive system of recruitment, registration, and placement, and standards would have to be set by the federal government. The report also suggests that the service bureaucracy work with other federal agencies in acquiring information about the individual.

A national service program could obtain its information from other governmental organizations that are already conducting registration-like activities, for example, the Social Security Administration, the Internal Revenue Service, state motor vehicle departments, and state and local boards of education.[18] Seattle's Program for Local Service exemplifies the procedure in identifying potential volunteers through the State of Washington's computerized list of licensed drivers.[19]

The report also suggests that the military help organize the plan. For instance, the service agency might test individuals via the Armed Service Vocational Aptitude Battery (ASVAB) as an "aid in career guidance counselling."[20] And the Selective Service System can maintain and process the data, with help from the Employment Services Administration.[21]

The Nunn-McCurdy bill discussed in chapter 2 also involves

fairly extensive state intervention in the registration and selection process. The governor's office, regulated by the federal government, approves service plans in every locality. The governor certifies local councils, comprised of local community service workers and representatives of local governments, agencies, and labor unions, and they in turn select NSPs. The councils recruit enrollees in accordance with a plan approved by state and federal officials (to ensure nondiscrimination).[22] Yet the bill does not forbid federal monitoring of the program, nor does it forbid the collection and processing of data about the enrollees at the federal level. It merely requires that service be *administered* at the local level. The recruits remain subject to federal testing and examination.[23]

Private schemes for national service involve extensive government involvement in the registration process.[24] For instance, Eberly and Sherraden's voucher plan requires a number of federal and state bureaucracies to participate in the search for recruits.[25] The authors favor giving all eighteen-year-olds a service voucher that "entitles the holder to a full year of financial support and medical coverage in exchange for a year of civilian service." They recommend that voter registration, draft registration, and motor vehicle agencies locate these eighteen year olds. Finally, all participants must interview for a position and sign a contract with the participating agency. The contract is approved by an official of the service organization, and individuals can be rejected for a number of reasons.[26] Despite the "voluntary" or "decentralized" nature of the program, the federal and state governments are slated to play large roles in the investigation, monitoring, and regulation of all service participants, and possibly all 18 year olds.[27]

Interestingly, Charles Moskos ignores the recruitment and registration process for national service.[28] His estimated budget for national service shows sixty million dollars reserved for advertising and federal administration, but he fails to specify how the money will be spent, or what mechanisms will be used to recruit and register the participants. He does make a few comments about recruitment procedures for a "voluntary" service, but he is silent about how people will be registered, and what sort of information the government will acquire about them.[29]

He suggests that one requirement be "sophisticated, admittedly expensive, advertising of the type, if not the scale, used for military recruitment."[30] Thus large advertising firms are to be enlisted, none of which are presumably willing to donate their services as part of a civic gesture (because of the federal money allocated for this purpose). Moreover, such advertising by its very nature exaggerates the virtues of national service, and the participants might be as disappointed with their experiences as military recruits are found to be after they enlist in the army.[31] If advertising is similar to that used in military recruitment, it highlights individual benefits the participant receives. This may reinforce the instrumental thinking I discuss in the previous chapter. If so, advertising itself may not even concentrate on the civic aspects of service, but on the private benefits to be awarded, and occasionally with the message "be all that you can be." In terms of civic duty, Moskos has no other advertising ideas beyond a "resort to those old stand-bys, guilt and shame."[32]

Registration, whether compulsory or voluntary, is thus more than a means by which the government accounts for volunteers or selectees, rather it is a complete system of guidance and prescription.[33] Unlike selective service registration today, national service registration is far more complex, because it must provide vocational guidance and fulfill "areas of critical need" across the country, and not merely in the armed forces. It also involves twice as many people, because women now register.

I return to the guidance aspects of national service below. Let me now turn to a concrete example—the CCC—to demonstrate how the state compiles information about individuals and categorizes them systematically, and in the process redefines their rights and capacities as citizens.[34]

THE REGISTRATION AND SELECTION PROCESS
IN THE CCC

The most remarkable fact about registration and selection in the CCC is that, despite its rhetoric to the contrary, the process was not geared toward the participant. Rather, registration was used to select and place individuals most efficiently for the types of jobs the program wished to fill.

The most significant aspect to the process of selecting enrollees was that one had to *qualify* for entrance. That is, one had to "make oneself competent for something, or capable of holding some office, by fulfilling a necessary status." Similarly, one had to make oneself "legally capable; to be endowed with legal power a capacity; to be given a recognized status to."[35] In other words, not everyone could enroll in the CCC. Only people with certain attributes could apply, and only a portion of those could be accepted. The most basic qualifications were that the person be: (1) an American citizen, (2) male, (3) between seventeen and twenty-three years old, (4) not in prison or on parole, (5) needy, and (6) unmarried.[36] By fulfilling these qualifications, the individual could at least apply, whereupon the selection board would judge him mentally and physically "competent."

But individuals had to qualify, and were qualified, in other ways. For *to qualify* also means to "invest with a quality or qualities; to describe or designate in a particular way; to characterize, entitle, or name." And these individuals were *designated*: before, during, and after their service in the corps, the young men were named, described, and given particular qualities. One not only qualified for entrance, but one qualified for things upon discharge. The CCC interpellated the individual in order to find out more about him, and to give him "direction in life." For many young men, for the first time in their lives, they responded to questions and demands concerning themselves and their private lives. They accepted this interrogation in order to be given some identity, in order to *qualify* themselves for living in modern society.[37]

The CCC simultaneously qualified individuals for enrollment, qualified them to act as adults in a capitalist society, and qualified their capacities to be autonomous individuals. Most importantly, though, individuals were designated as workers appropriate for necessary jobs. In this sense, they were not envisioned as citizens first, and they were not afforded the opportunity to exercise some control over their activities within the organization; therefore, at least in the process of registration and selection, the CCC was not an agency designed to inculcate citizenship.

The CCC's selection process went from being a localized operation in 1933 to a nationwide system of recruitment and examination by 1941. In fact, in 1941 an elaborate guidebook was completed by the agency for recruiting and selection. The first recruiting agents were generally local draft board agents or the equivalent who chose enrollees after a short interview. They were wholly responsible for recruitment and selection in the areas where they were based, and many, if not most of them, were long-time residents of the small towns in which they recruited. So the agents were familiar to some of the boys who applied, especially in the smaller towns. Initially, the only criteria for judgment that these recruiting agents possessed, aside from the basic rules limiting who could apply, was their own intuition. Most early recruits signed on because the recruiter (later called the "selection agent") believed them to be honest, trustworthy, competent, and physically capable of withstanding the rigors of camp life. Some recruiters made better judgments than others, of course, but many men signed up because they believed the recruiter to be veracious; and in the case of the small town recruit, they had confidence in him or her because he or she was a fellow citizen. In short, one initial advantage of the recruitment process in the early years of the CCC was that it was local: The agents were local, and that their standing in the community often convinced many boys—and more importantly their parents, that the CCC was a worthwhile endeavor.

But the agency became unhappy with the quality of the recruits they were getting. There had been disciplinary problems, and many of the directors felt that the most worthy applicants were not being selected. As the depression wore on, too, other options became available for the young men, and the CCC began to be considered as a last, desperate option.[38] In June 1937 the agency implemented new regulations in order to standardize the selection process. It forced each community to draw up selection plans, obtain approval by a state board, and follow the guidelines set out by a manual that was developed.[39]

Moreover, the agency became so worried about the trends that they began to take seriously warnings by social scientists concerning the impact of the CCC and the quality of the enrollees. The most influential was a study by Kenneth Holland and Frank Ernest Hill, prepared for the American Youth Commission. In this study the authors concluded that local selection agents made decisions that were often arbitrary. And they criticized the primitiveness of their methods:

Most selection agents whom the study staff encountered were unfamiliar with trends in occupations, job opportunities, and modern techniques for discovering the vocational aptitude and interests of prospective enrollees.[40]

They also criticized agents for misleading the boys, and exaggerating the facilities at certain camps, and complained that agents lacked comprehensive knowledge of the organization. Holland and Hill also tied this problem in with the fact that the camps were not standardized, so the agent could not have an accurate model from which he or she could work. Ultimately they recommended that agents be trained in the social and behavioral sciences at least enough to do their job rigorously.

Not surprisingly, the attitude of the top-level administrators toward the selecting agents caused some tension between the two groups. This emerged in debates over who exactly should be selected. The agency tried to select only boys of good character, because they did not want disciplinary problems at the camps, and they wanted to maintain the good publicity they were already getting. Many local agents, on the other hand, believed that the CCC had to accept "problem boys" because those very boys needed the jobs and the "clean environment." With the new regulations, the administration claimed victory, and so the CCC began to accept only boys who fit its image of the good citizen. The idea that anyone could join the CCC who qualified in terms of the basic characteristics had very subtly changed. Now enrollees had to qualify morally for admission. The CCC was no longer teaching them good morals so much as it was reproducing a particular morality with which the boys entered.

By 1941 the CCC agency enjoined selecting agents to do the following: (1) know CCC camp operations through observations and visits,[41] (2) "interpret to the community...what kind of a company or agency they represent," (3) "discover what characteristics of applicants seem to result in their success as workers on the job"— through keeping careful records of each enrollee, and talking with supervisory personnel about the enrollees, (4) "appraise the qualifications of each enrollee," like personnel directors do in industry, (5) select good workers, (6) monitor the enrollees throughout their stay in the CCC, and (7) help former enrollees find work.[42]

The CCC had evolved from F.D.R.'s dream of saving a generation of young men, or at least from the idea that individuals could save themselves. Now the selection agents were required to select individuals independently of the particular needs of the individuals themselves. There was no mention in any of these regulations about judging how needy an individual might be, or how much the CCC might benefit him or her. Rather the standards for selection had become the imperatives of industry and the future public relations success of the CCC.[43] Furthermore some selection agents themselves may have alienated members of their community by following the rules in selection. Though given ongoing disciplinary problems, many selection agents probably ignored the rules as best they could, and continued to use their judgment, however "unscientific" it was. Despite this, agents had to live under the regime of a different ethic: their first responsibility was to the organization, not to the individual boy.

What was this "science of selection?" What were the agents supposed to discover in a young man to determine his potential for success as an enrollee in the organization? And how could the agent monitor the enrollee to ensure that success? The most important criterion for selection was the young man's ability to adapt to camp and complete the work assigned to him. W. Frank Persons, the head of selection for the CCC, wrote in 1938:

> Through this process it has been possible in many communities to attain a broader understanding of the benefits which result from the selection of young men of ambition, purpose, and character for service in CCC camps. To a much less extent, than formerly are selecting agencies besieged by public and quasi-public officials urging that "problem cases" be enrolled in the Corps without regard to their adaptability to the Corps and their qualifications for the work programs. It is not only an unwarranted expense to the government to outfit and transport enrollees who remain in camp only a few days or weeks; it is also a loss to the community which selected such applicants and is a disservice to the applicants. The youths who are best able to contribute to the work of the Corps and most anxious to profit by its work and training opportunities are the young men the CCC wants.[44]

The most important aspect of CCC enlistment, then, was selecting young men "of character."[45] Though, ironically, one of the strongest arguments in defense of the CCC had been that it would *build* character; that it would take "drifting," "cast-off" youth and turn them into good workers and good citizens.[46] But it was also the first way the boys gained identity, for by enrolling in the CCC they, or at least their parents, could be assured that they were young men of character, worthy of being Americans.

But what, specifically, was "good character?" The "Guide" cites four relevant qualities: (1) maturity—"camp commanders and selecting agents are agreed that desertions are usually due to 'homesickness' and immaturity,"[47] (2) dependability—"this means that he must be a *willing worker*,"[48] (3) mental alertness—"the possession of *reasonable mental capacity*,"[49] and (4) interest in the CCC as a work and training opportunity, which was "the single most important criteria" to look for in the boys. With these four criteria the CCC designated the ideal enrollee and provided each selecting agent with a standard by which to judge all enrollees.[50] Such a standard concerned the productivity and personal interest of the individual; there were no platitudes about helping the community. A civic ethic was not a character trait necessary to the success of the enrollee or the success of the program. The CCC thus held particular notions about the ideal camp citizen: one who was of average intelligence, who knew how to follow rules, and who wanted to join the CCC to learn a particular skill.

The model enrollee was realized through the careful use of scientific methods of data collection and analysis. The selecting agent ensured the enrollment of quality boys, and monitored their progress by keeping detailed records about each one. Through these means, the selection and analysis of the young men became an integrated process—one that surveyed the individual throughout his CCC career. In this way, too, the strengths of each individual could be identified, and boys were then matched to the sort of work best suiting their strengths.[51] In order for the agents and COs to succeed in this task they accumulated as much data on each young man as possible, and this required relentless note-taking and careful and detailed analysis.[52]

The agent recorded everything relevant about about the boy's background, and the CO and instructors noted all his activities and accomplishments. One researcher concluded that, on average, each individual had at least a four page dossier after six months in the organization.[53] And they recorded a variety of information— from participation in the Boy Scouts to what sort of family life he had at home.[54] In fact the manual suggests that the selecting agent visit the home of the applicant to ensure his "quality." It detailed the proper method for making this visit and specified its purposes: "to determine the fitness and adaptability of the applicant."[55] And for those from "unusually poor environments," the manual suggests that this "indicates the desirability of interviewing and counselling with applicants much more thoroughly."[56] So the selection agent began to take on the duties of a social worker.

After interviewing the boy, and making a visit to the home, the selecting agent had to "verify eligibility."[57] This involved reviewing the boy's birth certificate, marriage records (where necessary), attendance records in school, physical health records,[58] court records, local law enforcement records, the records of other CCC corps areas, and the memories of relatives and dependents. In short, if a selection agent did his or her job according to CCC regulations, he or she collated all the data extant on a particular individual. So the individual became an "object of writing."[59]

Once the applicant had been approved, all this information went in a sealed envelope to the CO at the camp to which he was assigned.[60] In camp the enrollee was further monitored for health problems, physical strength, and intellectual ability. All the movements of the enrollee to and from the camps were monitored, especially on weekend leaves.[61] Finally all the records of all the enrollees were kept, usually until a year after their discharge, at the office of the adjutant general. This office served as a general communications center that contacted all camps and prospective employers if and when they needed information about a particular individual.[62]

To assist in the placement of the young men, the CCC developed production scales and personality tests to determine the aptitude of each enrollee. And the agency perpetually tested camps in order to discover more efficient and accurate methods of measuring the aptitude of the boys.[63] The results became a part of their permanent record.[64] Ironically, with this data, they "fit" the boys to the particular jobs available, and so often ignored their personal wishes.

The CCC even accumulated data on individuals after they left the organizations. Upon leaving, men completed a questionnaire detailing their experiences in the CCC and indicating their future plans and address.[65] And the selection agents engaged in "post-camp guidance," involving a follow-up visit to their residence and employer to see how they were doing (or in the language of the agency, to "help in the readjustment to their community").[66] In short, by the time the enrollee left the organization, the agency had compiled a great deal of information about him, without the assistance of computers. More importantly, it had information about individuals (and their families) from whom it would normally be difficult to get information: farmers, small town residents, rural blacks, and native Americans. In this sense, the lower orders were brought into the modern world of bureaucracy.

This brief examination of the selection and registration procedures of the CCC demonstrates that the program did not merely assist boys in need, but rather categorized them in a number of ways: by physical ability, intelligence, and mental health. Moreover it allowed the state to investigate the enrollees and collate data on them to be used for further testing or monitoring. It did so through the multifarious tests to which many of the boys were subjected. Indeed through the use of tests the directors declared the program a success.

But how just is the process of national testing, especially norm-referenced testing, which is designed to categorize individuals around a norm for the purposes of placing them in particular jobs or allowing them to enroll in particular classes? Let me turn to this issue in the next chapter, because testing will play an important role in *national* and systematized programs of service. I do this in the context of proposals which seek to promote vocational education—the kind of education encouraged in the CCC, and the kind that proponents of national service insist that program must provide.

CHAPTER FIVE

Testing and Vocational Education

One cannot separate the issues of testing and vocational education because the two are so intimately tied together: individuals in a national service program are tested largely, if not exclusively, for the purposes of determining their aptitude for particular jobs. In some instances, testing will be used for educational purposes, and to encourage or discourage enrollees from further schooling; but the program is specifically a post-high school activity, and so provides a transition into the "real world." This real world is one of material production and consumption, and national service planners want to ensure that individuals are prepared to be efficient producers and avid consumers. For the economic health of the country and the individual, then, testing and vocational education are central to each enrollee's service training. In the previous chapter I tried to demonstrate that such testing is proposed under most any program.

In this chapter I analyze and critique possible methods of testing and vocational education. The literature on testing and vocational education is so vast that I do not have the space to engage in a thorough going critique, though I refer to sources where such critiques can be found. I focus on the political effects of testing and the misuse of testing; moreover, I do so from a number of standpoints. Testing and vocational education, though justified by notions of progress and economic efficiency, have drawbacks to them that must be considered in any plan for national service.

TESTING

"World War I demonstrated that testing on a mass scale was possible; World War II fulfilled the promise of World War I by transforming Americans into the most tested people in the world."[1] Thus remarked a national committee on ability testing, of the Assembly of Behavioral and Social Science of the National Research Council; and it seems reasonable to add that the war on poverty, the war on drugs, and the battle to improve education contribute to the further testing of Americans. Consequently, a moral equivalent of war ought to provide a moral equivalent of testing. Unfortunately for millions of Americans, mostly young adults, this will not be the case, and though war may become superfluous, testing will not. The enemy is now internal (drugs, crime, teenage pregnancy, etc.), and the artillery to combat it begins with a pencil and a multiple choice response.

Such weaponry took a long time to develop, though, and still undergoes revision with each test taken. Within the discipline of educational policy analysis, testing is subjected to much critique and reform, and there is wide disagreement over the purposes and methods of all the tests used on a nationwide basis. With the exception of a few notable critics, though, like Ralph Nader and his organization, the principle of testing is generally endorsed by educators.[2] I make two arguments here: (1) that these educators are correct, testing is an imperfect science that sometimes discriminates, but (2) that the very idea of testing may work against the intentions of national service supporters. I focus my analysis on the second point because it is more controversial and less well known, and because it is in certain ways more central to the very principle of national service currently being promoted.

The political effects of improper testing—either through problems of content, construct, or reliability—are well known and have been debated for years. A wide variety of tests measure a wide variety of constructs—IQ, aptitude, achievement, employability, etc. Surrounding each of these constructs a heated, sometimes ferocious, debate flares—for example, the controversy over the claims of Arthur Jensen and Richard Herrnstein.[3] Nevertheless, testing for education and employment purposes continues apace, with no immediate prospect of termination. Thus, while deleterious political and social effects are known and testing reforms implemented where possible, the debates over testing often provide no more than a sideshow to the real difficulty: the categorization and normalization of those who take the tests (all of us). Yet one ought to recognize some important issues brought up by test experts.

First, testing imposes a cultural bias on the test-taker. Many studies show that tests for employment and education favor white, middle class, male respondents.[4] Through either the content of the test, the test site conditions, the type of questions asked, or the expectations of the test designers, tests result in the mismeasuring of those being tested. The question critics of testing ask is whether this is endemic to the process itself, whether any test is free of bias.

As one committee puts it, "the recognition of excellence, Americans have come to realize, also creates invidious comparisons and more visible inequality."[5] It also highlights the issue of adverse impact: how can test scores be used which avoid adverse impact for particular groups? Such criticisms point up that the content of the particular tests used can label and categorize groups unfairly.

These questions have afflicted employment and vocational testing for a long time, and were ameliorated only recently by the Supreme Court, in the 1971 case *Griggs v. Duke Power Company*.[6] In this case the court required employers to use tests that did not have an "exclusionary effect" on minorities, and since then a "significant body of precedent" requires that all tests conform to this standard through formal validation studies. Since 1971 the court has ensured that all employment tests contain questions and measurements determining "job-relatedness" alone. Tests could become more job related with use, and further research on political action by interested groups could ensure this. The participation of national service enrollees as political activists in this process (not as subjects for research) could go a long way in guaranteeing fair and dignified testing for all groups.

But there are political issues which are as fundamental as cultural bias in the ideology of testing. For instance, testing does not occur in a vacuum, but exists within a particular social organization and political economy; and tests influence structures and functions within those frameworks. Let me list some of the most important issues.

First, nationwide testing reinforces the sort of lock-step educational process that national service proponents hope the program combats. Testing extends the lock-step character of the young person's life under the guise of the rite of adulthood. David Harman notes the irony of this process in an era of alternative teaching methods.

At a time when individuation of instruction and pluralism of educational paths are becoming increasingly accepted educational practices, tests continue to set age- and grade-specific standards, essentially reinforcing the lockstep character of the enterprise.[7]

In this way, the very act of testing, in the name of rites, perpetuates the educational organization national service proponents blame for many of the nation's ills.[8] Rather than transforming the educational system, then, national service, as another step in the system, maintains it.

Second, tests must be developed somewhere, and in this country they are created and distributed by large corporations. This is not insignificant, given the material interests involved in the business of testing; national service requirements would increase profits for these corporations. Such interests have even more force where testing is not merely for diagnostic purposes, but educative ones. Lee Shulman notes:

> A potentially dangerous vertical monopoly, one that I am increasingly uncomfortable with, has developed in the education industry: The same companies are producing both the standard curriculum materials and the standardized tests. Therefore, what constitutes average expected performance at a given grade level in a subject area by some remarkable coincidence corresponds to what the curriculum makers have chosen to define as the content of that grade level.[9]

By "some remarkable coincidence," then, national service may provide large contracts to companies requiring service programs train their enrollees in methods developed by those service companies. National service, in this sense, most certainly benefits particular corporations, actually promotes those corporations, and this, I argue, is a curious way to foster community. A national service program thus favors large corporations, providing this sort of service over small ones, and may help concentrate wealth and power even further in the United States. Thus, while the government may not actually administer the tests, it can help private industry bureaucratize the program. Therefore, the claims that national service can be a decentralized one are somewhat misleading: the site of centralization could be, in certain aspects of the program, in private industry. In short, testing may contribute, not to a decentralized, participatory national service, but to a program run for the benefit of certain private industries.

Testing could have a bureaucratizing effect on the behavior of students and teachers alike. Harold Berlak notes that

> teachers are spending more and more time teaching for tests. Where standardized tests dominate the curriculum, they dictate the content and reduce the method of instruc-

tion to a set of routines, and teachers become mere functionaries in a bureaucratic system.[10]

In this way standardized vocational tests that certify NSPs further
routinize the program—thus centralizing it and reducing its flexibility. Michael Apple argues that insofar as teachers instruct using
educational packages or modules developed by corporate
researchers, the teacher becomes "de-skilled." The teacher loses
his or her ability to teach, because he or she merely follows the
instructions on the package, and instead becomes "re-skilled" in
"behavior modifiction techniques and classroom management
strategies."[11] This has two implications for national service: First,
instructors of NSPs within the program (say, for literacy or numeracy) who do not possess teacher skills may simply follow standardized educational instructions. At the same time, they may function
as lay psychologists or management scientists. Thus, NSPs do not
benefit from the abilities of individual teachers. This could alienate them further from the educational process, and dissuade some
from attending college or vocational school. Second, those NSPs
who wish to teach as part of their service may not get the opportunity, for the ten percent that Danzig and Szanton estimate would
teach, may merely convey already prepackaged lessons. Thus, even
the most skilled and intellectually rigorous of service positions are
in danger of becoming mechanical.

The third political issue involved in standardized testing arises from the process itself. One problem concerns the construction
of the tests. Norm-referenced tests, the sort of tests most likely to
be used on a large scale to categorize people, do not diagnose the
particular strengths or weaknesses of the learner, and the multi-
ple-choice quality of the tests can trivialize learning.[12] Moreover
the experts writing the tests are removed from the particular
atmosphere of the learner, and even where cultural bias is not a
problem, such writers cannot understand the nuances of a particular region in the composition of the questions. For instance, the
very interpretation, or even significance, of the Civil War could
take on different meanings in New Hampshire, Alabama, Nevada,
and Hawaii, and among blacks and whites. Thus, as their name
implies, they can work to normalize individuals by standardizing
their responses to questions that might be answered correctly in a
number of more subtle ways.

Testing for minimum competency, which is standard for both
academic and vocational performance, also rests on some shaky

assumptions: (1) that there exists a common and indentifiable set of knowledge and skills students must possess to function adequately, (2) that tests can be designed to assess reliably the extent to which a student possesses these skills, and (3) that standards can be set to accurately classify students into various proficiency categories (i.e., competent and noncompetent).[13] One review of the literature suggests that these three assumptions have not been borne out by empirical evidence.[14] This is significant for national service where so many different individuals gather to do so many different jobs. How can these individuals be compared fairly?

Tests also label, despite their professed anonymity. Standardized tests label with respect to some ideal (e.g., the average, the median)—whether arbitrary or well researched. This can be stigmatizing, no doubt, but the stigma itself is significant insofar as it has a psychological effect on the test-taker. This effect has political import because it transmits the message to individuals that they cannot, in fact, "be all that they can be." Standardized testing unfairly denies some students a sense of self-respect or self-worth, and only the special ones might rise above the results in order to prove themselves.[15] Moreover, at least one national service planner applauds the result because individuals can then "develop a realistic sense of their capabilities and limitations."[16] This "realistic sense" transmits the sort of messages most national service proponents wish to change. Thus, the idea that national service helps young people, or others, pursue the American dream is true only to the extent that the American dream promotes a statistical norm. Programs to test such participants do much to discourage thousands of young people from developing themselves.

To be fair, there are two moral justifications for the use of tests, like employment aptitude tests: they are democratic and they are, or at least appear to be, impartial.[17] First, tests, through common procedures, uncover talent suppressed or repressed by the individual in his or her daily life. Consequently, equal opportunity is promoted for all, because testing advances individual fortunes by demonstrating characteristics relevant to school or work, and not on skin color, sex, etc. Second, tests are "relatively inoffensive," and if standardized tests are not used "the morale of the work force and the productivity of the economy would suffer."[18] Both arguments appeal to a sense of fairness, both in the society at large, and within each individual.

But these arguments do not apply so well to a national service program. For one, the very ideals of the program ought to promote equal opportunity without the use of tests. A service program should not fit people to jobs depending on their measured skills, rather, NSPs should be able to select the work they wish to do. (This is because of the public nature of the enterprise. National service is *not* like a private firm in this respect, and planners need to be more cognizant of this.) If they choose unwisely they will learn from their mistake, but at the very least they will learn to choose. If the danger arises that too many individuals choose one task over another, then we must ask whether national service can really be justified on the grounds of individual development, or even citizenship. We must question why the "morale of the work force" (or in this case the service force) is a problem. For whom would it be a problem: the participants themselves, or the prospective employers?

Moreover this points up an ambiguity in the democratic polity.[19] In many substantive ways democratization and equalization may also mean normalization. The democratic impulses spurring the creation and use of tests also spur unintended and intended consequences, one of which is the normalization of individuals around an average. The problem is not that tests are not a democratic means of discovering talent, the problem is that other consequences of such means are either not known or masked. In this way the very act of testing establishes the individual in an educational and vocational grid, and his or her aptitudes or achievements become not individual measures of ability, but public marks of normality and equivalence. Thus, test-makers and guidance counselors ought to recognize the potential normalizing functions of the exams and either change those exams to capture the creativity of the test-taker (say, in essay exams), or counsel some individuals *without stigma* not to take the exams. However, I doubt whether this is possible in a national service program, given its size and the intent of the planners. Hence, I suggest that the program itself abolish tests in order to err on the conservative side, and guarantee equal opportunities to all by allowing the freedom of choice of occupation. This is not to say that individuals should not be instructed in a number of different skills, or informed of their choices beforehand, it is merely to state that standardized tests should not be used to ensure equality (for this can be ensured in other ways).

VOCATIONAL EDUCATION

All programs of national service possess some vocational component to them—after all, many of its supporters justify the program on the basis of how it skills its participants. Literacy programs are planned, as are training in particular trades. Almost all federal service programs in the twentieth century have a vocational component to them—the CCC, the National Youth Administration (NYA), the Job Corps, the local service corps (e.g., PLS, NYCC, CaCC, etc.). Furthermore, the military advertises itself as a sort of semisophisticated trade school, and national service will probably have to do likewise in order to compete with it for enrollees. Thus, one supposes that if national service does not begin with a vocational component, it will develop it in the long run.[20]

There are two components to vocational education in employment, military, or service programs: the teaching of literacy and training in technical skills for employment. In this section I argue that both are relevant and necessary for a service program, but not in the forms suggested or currently practiced by many educators. I assume service educational programs to be motivated by the concerns that motivate similar programs in the armed forces, because the military is the only institution in society with experience in nationwide, public, nonacademic, adult educational programs. Thus, I assume that *educational* techniques developed there (especially for vocational programs) will be considered useful for the national service program. This is even more true in service programs which have a direct institutional link to the military; where they share particular structures, and even functions. The service program may be influenced by educational techniques developed in private industry, of course, and provided with educational packages from that industry for its classes. But logistical support must come from individuals who help design and implement large-scale, standardized programs intended to train individuals with real-life skills. The most sophisticated of these originate in the military.

Literacy

The most well-developed vocational program tested by the military, called "functional literacy," is learned through "functional context training." Designed by Thomas Sticht and associates the program has been tested very thoroughly and refined, for almost twenty years.[21] Working very closely with the military, Sticht and his fellow researchers are motivated by the desire to improve the life chances of thousands of cast off youth—young men and women cast off by the society because of their inability to read and write, and their failure to learn marketable job skills. Their studies have shown that even the most educationally retarded individual can develop literacy and job skills when given the opportunity, and they intend with their work to demonstrate the need for national efforts at making all individuals literate.

They base their techniques on so-called functional literacy: the "possession of literacy skills needed to sucessfully perform some reading *imposed by an external agent* between the reader and the goal the reader wishes to obtain."[22] To "function" in this instance might be a misnomer—what it amounts to is survival—for the "external agent" is an employer, and the "goal" is a steady job. To test their theories, Sticht and his colleagues used the army, and established a program called "Project 100,000," named after their target goal. This project was designed to analyze "experiments conducted by the armed services to develop effective training for youth from the low-end of the mental quality spectrum."[23] Using the army's ASVAB test, they experimented on those recruits who scored in the lowest mental categories (IV and V). By employing innovative teaching techniques they hoped to prove to the army that even these "lower-aptitude recruits" could function successfully in the army. Towards this end, they suggested that the recruits be taught to read within the "functional contexts" in which they operated as soldiers.

Functional context training deploys a number of strategies, all of which might be dysfunctional in a national service program, though. The early studies by Sticht and associates suggest that there be a two-pronged approach to literacy training: first, to improve the literacy skills of the recruits, but second, (and more disturbing) to "reduce excessive demands for reading skills." In that study they suggest two ways in which "literacy demands for jobs" be reduced—communicate instructions orally, develop job aids, use pictures, be redundant, etc.[24] Moreover, Sticht and associates recommend that functional context training guide literacy programs in the public schools, too, to improve the future employability of teenagers.[25] Yet in the function of matching a person to a skill, the individual might learn to read very poorly because the standards for literacy would be so low. Subsequent "literacy demands" become insignificant, especially with technology—like radio, television, and photography—substituting for words.

But what of the "positive" side to the two-pronged approach? How does functional context learning help individuals read and write? Project 100,000 develops certain guidelines for such an approach: (1) "develop a learning system that uses what the individual trainee already knows as the basis for further training"; (2) identify precise learning requirements for courses and jobs, paying special attention to areas that might be especially difficult for category IV personnel; (3) delineate requirements for literacy training—"integrate needed literacy training into the skill training program or during off-duty hours"; (4) relate learning situations and materials directly to the military; and (5) develop specific course objectives that are job-relevant.[26] The program contextualizes learning, which reduces attrition and motivates students "by showing the immediate, practical value" of their lessons.[27] It also blends the learning of technical skills with literacy training, thus making each an integral part of the other. It takes learning how to read out of the classroom, and into the real world—significant for thousands of young people, underprivileged or otherwise, who are alienated by the educational system.

But there are also some troubling justifications used for the program. For instance, Sticht and associates maintain that new information be introduced into such a program only when it can be fitted into the context of the material learned already. In defense of this proposition, they quote an early supporter of the program, H.A. Shoemaker: "The method contains safeguards against inclusion of topics that lack functional significance. The relevance of a topic is readily judged when it is viewed in relation to established functional topics."[28] The danger here is obvious—learning becomes relevant only within the established context, and where the context remains exclusively technical, learning does as well. This prevents the individual from learning a wide range of topics, *especially in an educational program that focuses on vocational and service training.* For not only do individuals learn only those techniques relevant to the job, but *all* learning, because it is done within the context of vocational training, is vocational learning. This may prevent individuals from learning about the world, about politics, about themselves. I suggest that national service should employ functional-context training, *but only in political contexts. Because* politics reflects "the world," this does not inhibit learning, and a wide variety of related topics take on functional significance, including the world of work. I return to this point in Chapter 9.

What, specifically, are the functional *literacy* programs suggested by Sticht and associates? Using a "cognitive science" framework, they posit a developmental model of literacy. They conclude the following:

The point to be emphasized is that much of the acquisition of literacy is not simply learning to read; that is, it is not just learning a graphic language system that can be substituted for the oral language system. Rather, a large part of learning to be literate, and perhaps the most important part for acquiring higher levels of literacy, is learning how to perform the many tasks made possible by the characteristics of printed displays—their permanence, spatiality, and use of light—and then using that knowledge to develop large amounts of new knowledge.[29]

At first glance, the authors seem to deploy a deconstructive method of analysis: an attack on phonocentrism (substituting "graphic language" for "oral language"), a focus on presences and absences ("the characteristics of printed displays"), even on differance ("their spatiality"). But their writing presents itself as a system of knowledge, both deductive (by premising functional-context learning), and inductive (through experimentation).

Nevertheless, there is a political project to this writing, for it ironically serves to decontextualize reading and writing. Reading, by this understanding, becomes a way to "perform the many tasks made possible by the characteristics of printed displays." Reading, then, is an instrument to be employed for practical purposes, not a skill one cultivates as a means of enjoyment. The "pleasure of the text" is now functional, not erotic, and this robs the learner of both the thrill of reading and the appreciation of the integrity of the written word. Reading, in the context of "functions" becomes an appendage of those functions, rather than a good for the sake of the learner. The message conveyed? "Read for the sake of implementing some practice, not because learning is a good thing."

Moreover, such a technique implies that the context could shrink—for reading may become appropriate to only minute technical details of only slightly larger technical details. Where does the limit of the context begin and end? Sticht and associates imply that a strict outer boundary exists (the job task itself), but no inner boundary—such a task breaks down endlessly into smaller and smaller tasks. In this way, not only do they ignore the larger sociopolitical context, but the occupational context may be trivialized too. At this point, *reading* becomes unconnected to *understanding*; in this instance understanding means recognizing the ways in which "contexts" relate to each other.

Most importantly, then, literacy, even vocational literacy, is not a technique, or a method of interpreting graphic symbols. It is a way of understanding and critically appreciating the world. When one reads one does not merely decipher graphic symbols, one engages actively in analysis and criticism, otherwise the process of reading might as well be analogous to a Saturday morning television cartoon show (but not as enjoyable). The pleasure of reading ordinary texts comes not from the deciphering the signifiers, but from exercising of the skills that connect the signifiers with the signified—realizing that one has understood the connection between the symbols and the world (or even that one has understood the relationship of symbols to each other). For in learning to read one begins to understand the relationship between the text, the reader, and the world, and this is a source of pride and wonderment.

Literacy programs ought to present the written word within the context of the world in order to engage the reader with the world, to make him or her care about the world. In such literacy programs, the reader learns not only how to read, but how to appreciate the society and culture in which he or she lives. Consequently, literacy teaches people not only to read, but how to understand the world and others around them. Literacy ought to be taught not within the hermitage of a technical vocation, but within the context of politics, for this is the real world.[30] And this is how reading can advance "citizenship."

Paulo Freire, and his associates in Brazil and North America, exemplify this method. Freire and his co-workers demonstrate that peasants residing in Northeast Brazil and elsewhere learn to read more quickly and accurately when their lessons are charged with political meaning.[31] The thousands of young people and others who are functionally illiterate can be trained within the context of their socioeconomic realities—they learn how to organize politically, how to recognize the social, economic, and psychological causes of their malaise, and how to appreciate the American dream more critically *while* they learn to read and write. This is the role national service can play for our country. It is functional to our nation by generating real political interest on the part of those learning. Thus a political education does not merely reflect an education about politics, but an education about enjoying politics. This is no less than an education for community concern and civic consciousness, and would raise people's awareness of society (more so than being a clerk in a hospital or day-care center).

Of course, individuals need not read only without participating or serving, for one can read while engaging in political activity. As

Freire and others demonstrate, literacy develops just as easily, if not more so, by reading a poster from a political demonstration, or the labor codes of a corporation, as it can from engaging in technical skills for market employment. I return to this argument in Chapter 10.

The Political Effects of Vocational Training

Finally, two related issues may create problems for the participant: (1) his or her political judgment remains undeveloped, and (2) technical, or vocational, education contains within its practice particular political biases, especially a bias *against* politics of all sorts. Both issues bear directly on the civic consequences of vocational education, and both anaesthetize the learner's impulse to participate.

Vocational education does not teach people to think about their moral and political situation, and thus does not require them to exercise political judgment. Where a program of national service focuses on vocational or service education, then it can inhibit enrollees from developing skills of political reasoning, as well as discourage an interest in politics. Michael Oakeshott makes the case well.[32] He charges that education should be concerned as much with "practical" knowledge as "technical" knowledge. Yet this practical knowledge cannot be "learned," but only "acquired" through experience, in order to satisfy the "felt need." Modern society focuses on technical education—in all fields, including politics—thus individual learners fail to comprehend the "nuances" of their professions. Furthermore, it fails to inculcate "morality of habitual conduct," but teaches merely banal routine.

At this point one might think that Oakeshott's ideas coincide with those who defend vocational education: after all, it is a practice isn't it? But Oakeshott's concept of rational conduct disrupts the tyranny of vocational education. Oakeshott argues that *skill* is needed in order to conduct oneself properly and morally under particular circumstances, but this skill is not technical. Rather it is the knowledge of how to behave appropriately under the circumstances. Reasoning, then, is a matter of *conduct*, not simply intelligence. This conceptualization denies the validity of constructs like the IQ, as well as technical devices which inculcate knowledge, like functional-context learning. For Oakeshott, learning comes from participating in the world, not from being subject to devices which are designed to train individuals in particular techniques of information processing. This is most relevant for our purposes, because we can see how the learning theory described above violates "idioms of activity." Such learning uses the *ideology* of practicality to mask an essentially technical, mechanical notion of learning.[33]

In this sense, political education for Oakeshott is similar to that for Freire. Individuals must learn politics by doing it, not by reading about it. Moreover, the activity of politics helps establish moral ideals and principles, and so is the source of judgment. Unlike Freire, of course, Oakeshott denies that a specifically ideological politics is useful, for it is subject to the same rationalist constraints which afflict technical education. For Oakeshott, politics ought to amend existing arrangements by exploring the "intimations" of those arrangements, not engaging in a total critique of them. Nevertheless, political education means learning how to participate in the conversation so that individuals discover those intimations for themselves. Thus, political education is necessary for even the most conservative of theorists, for one's judgment (both individual and collective) depends upon it. In this way, judging things like contexts means judging the situation appropriately. For Oakeshott, the extension of technical education from the schools (in academic guise) to national service (in vocational guise) inhibits the ways one learns to judge appropriately, and thus to conduct oneself rationally. This is a more politically charged way of saying that the lockstep character of the educational process continues.

The second political issue involved in technical education reflects its inherent conservatism. While some theorists regard this as pernicious under all circumstances, I would argue that conservatism is bad only insofar as technical education conserves unjust or immoral qualities within the society itself, without conserving good qualities, like the above-mentioned capacity for rational conduct.[34]

But technical training diverts the learner from cultivating another capacity that permits the functioning of a just polity: the capacity to love politics and engage actively in it. Vocational education does not motivate individuals to be concerned with their communities, moreover it does not impart the kind of knowledge necessary to make reasoned judgments about those communities.[35] Therefore, to be civic service, national service ought to hold the attention of its participants to social and ethical problems in the real world, not simply skill them in technical (or more likely clerical) skills.[36] One ought to learn from experience and learn on the job, but that experience and those jobs ought to involve the participation of individuals in the political life of the community. National service *could* provide meaningful work and an alternative to the lock-step of education by engaging in activities that are themselves different from school or work. This is politics: working on neighborhood urban planning councils, engaging in political study groups, debating the abortion issue, teaching young people or other groups about various issues and ideas of the day, working as journalists for local papers (even establishing alternative presses), etc. *These* are socially useful and necessary tasks, for they help individuals understand the idea and practices sustaining their communities. Neither clerical work nor vocational training accomplish these goals. Serving the country need not mean merely serving the postindustrial sector; it can mean learning enough about the principles with which people live, so that one may conserve the good ones, and transform the bad. But this approach is dysfunctional to national service planners who consciously or unconsciously support the idea that service ought to train a new-age workforce.

CHAPTER SIX

The Theory and Practice of Service and Service Learning

> "A service is nothing other than the useful effect of a use-value, be it that of a commodity, or that of the labor. But here we are dealing with exchange value."
>
> Karl Marx, *Capital*[1]

Thus far I have analyzed the structural and organizational characteristics of both past and future service programs. I have argued that such organizations and their concomitant testing and vocational training procedures reveal a politics to service. In this chapter I assess in greater detail the political and educational ideology of service policy. I argue that service, while effective in some instances, is inadequate for citizenship training.

More specifically, I discuss two aspects of service: (1) the arguments for and against service learning, as well as those which both its proponents and opponents ignore; and (2) the practice of service among teenagers and young adults—what do young people learn on the job? Evidence suggests that learning through service is not always benign, beneficial, or public spirited. Participants also learn a subjectivity on the job—young service participants are taught not only service, but often servility, not only discipline, but often normalization, not only independence, but often individuation. In short, the participant who serves is politically and socially constructed, but the tools and materials come from a postindustrial political economy, and the engineers use organizational norms, not merely civic duty and Christian charity.

THE POLITICAL THEORY OF CIVIC SERVICE[2]

In the first chapter I discuss the relevance of national service to political philosophy, and I suggest that its proponents generally recommend service to socialize young people toward certain values. Service, though, is more than a particular type of work, it pos-

107

sesses a philosophy and affiliated educational program.³ Service, then, is not merely a doing, it is a thinking and a learning as well. It is an *ethic*, a mode of conduct. "If we are engaged in promoting national service, we are engaged in the subtle business of trying to shape the national ethos."⁴ Service helps one understand the moral life of the nation, and act according to its principles. As an ethic, service is something (i.e., a particular body of knowledge) to be learned. Furthermore, service-as-knowledge is treated as an unproblematic concept, one reflecting a basic characteristic of human nature.

> At different points in history, in different countries, for different age groups, and for different social issues, the same universal truth emerges. The combination of service and learning touches something very fundamental about the human spirit and its relationship to other human beings and to the surrounding culture.⁵

Service and service-learning, then, remain part of the basic human instinct of caring for others.

Service is said to be an act (or acts) done for the public good, and involves one individual (or group) helping or aiding another, with no (or minimal) remuneration. One serves by committing oneself freely and voluntarily, out of a concern for the commonweal, or public welfare, not from narrow self-interest. At best, self-interest rests in the belief that a society which serves is a good one in which to live; the individual wishes to perpetuate such a society in order to participate in the "good life." That many Americans serve others and their country in this manner no one disputes, nor can one deny that voluntary care-giving has become part of a mythical American ethos (at least since Tocqueville's day). As a practice engaged in selflessly by millions of Americans throughout the history of the country, service seems to be relatively uncontroversial. Yet the practice of service is embedded in institutions that are quite controversial, and one needs to examine these, and the very doctrine of service, more closely in order to reveal some hidden assumptions made about them.

Although no coherent, consistent philosophy of service has been successfully articulated or developed in any text or texts, it nonetheless remains the focal point for thinking about education in a national service program. Most of the main proponents of national service recommend a service education curriculum for the

program. And many professors of education support reflective components in all experiential education.[6] But what do "reflections
upon service" look like? Service organizations often held up as
model programs offer some "reflection" upon this. One can look at
the lessons taught, the rhetoric deployed, and the texts used by
these programs in order to understand this so-called philosophy.

Few, if any, service programs have experienced more success
over a longer period of time than the Center for Service Learning at
the University of Vermont.[7] Established in the late 1960s, the center has employed countless students contributing an enormous
amount of service to the Burlington community and beyond. Currently about a thousand students participate in one of three programs the center offers: Volunteers in Action (VIA), Volunteer Community Experience Programs (VESEP), and programs for college
credit on the Vermont campus. Within each of these programs, the
student volunteers in many subfields and the longevity of the center
confirm the popularity of most of them.[8] VIA relies on twenty-five
student volunteer coordinators who make the program work—their
excitement, involvement, and energy often translate into the same
for the other volunteers. VESEP works more directly with local and
state service agencies, and students are employed directly by those
agencies. The center has become so successful that some of its staff
are being hired by other colleges to start up similar programs in
other states (e.g., Mary Washington College in Virginia).

More importantly, the center has a comparatively well-developed philosophy of service learning, as well as a fairly sophisticated curriculum for the students, in both programs. The Center
offers a manual of service learning, and its coordinators require
students to read certain texts in order to give them a sense of its
purposes and goals and in order to help them reflect upon their
experiences in service.[9] What is service learning? It is

an approach to experiential learning, an expression of values—service to others, community development and
empowerment, reciprocal learning—which determines the
purpose, nature and process of social and educational
exchange between learners (students) and the people they
serve, and between experiential education programs and
the community organizations with which they work.

The discipline combines service toward the common good with
reflective learning, "to help individuals appreciate how service can

be a significant and ongoing part of life. Service, combined with learning, adds value to each and transforms both."[10] But it is more:

> Service-learning builds into the experience a reflective component which helps the service volunteer develop a focus on the needs of the client or organization. This translates into a focus on the issues that surround that service, a focus on the structure of the organization's work, and a broader understanding of that service in the context of the student's academic knowledge and knowledge of the community at large.[11]

It helps individuals establish a "personal ethic of service."

In this manner participants internalize the values of the service professional. As an expression of values, as a means of social and economic exchange, as a significant part of life, as a focus on the needs of the client or organization, as a focus on the nature of the organization, and as part of a general understanding of service in the world, the service learning experience imbues the service learner with the purpose of a sophisticated care-giver. And, as I mention toward the end of the chapter, the Center for Service Learning has established learning curricula for this.

More importantly, some conceive national service as a means by which this professionalism is universalized to some degree. Donald Eberly hopes that national service can

> exploit the potential of service-learning...[yet] what passes for service-learning is little more than remedial education unrelated to the service activity. We cannot dump service-learning on the nation's schoolteachers and college professors because they are not equipped to handle it.

Presumably they are not equipped because they have not been trained professionally in the service education field and in service education techniques. For this reason there must be continual testing of "service activities on the frontiers of human and environmental needs."[12]

Yet what does it mean to develop an ethic of service—one that is systematic, one that guides one's life, one that situates itself as a body of knowledge and practice? It means: (1) establishing philosophical principles about service that make it a form of behavior to which each individual ought to conform, (2) establishing clear rules of procedure as to what constitutes service knowledge and practice, (3) developing organizations whose sole or primary purpose is to serve and promote service, (4) establishing within those organizations norms of professional conduct which conform to the philosophical principles and rules of procedure mentioned above, and (5) employing means by which those concerned can measure the amount of service given.

Questions remain, however: Are these qualities desirable? Are they the sorts of things we should be inculcating in NSPs? And, most importantly here, do they help constitute the civic-minded individual? The answers to the first two questions seem self-evident: yes, in fact, they are worth inculcating in NSPs because that is the point of national service: to teach people that serving others is not only a good thing, but a necessary part of living in society. No supporter of service disputes this. While I doubt that these qualities are as benign or helpful as service proponents seem to assume, I do not contradict them here. This is not what I am arguing in this chapter.

The third question is more difficult, however, and while good citizens serve the public (however defined), a service philosophy and a service education do not constitute citizenship. Moreover, a service ethic actually distorts the idea of citizenship, the practice of citizenship as contestation, and it removes civic and political concerns from the agenda of public deliberation. A service ethic is antithetical to democratic citizenship. In short, a good server is a bad citizen. This is the most difficult (and probably the most controversial) argument I make in this book, and in many ways, the most important—for it rejects national *service* as a *civic* enterprise. Again, I am not maintaining that service is a bad thing, but, rather, that it does not contribute much to an understanding of the contestability of citizenship. For me to do so, I must look at service in an historical, political, economic, and social context—a situated service revealing the inconsistencies in a (deontological) service ethic.[13]

Service, as in "national service," is not simply one person serving another for the good of the community. It is a historical practice, and one existing by virtue of a particular politicoeconomic arrangement. I want to examine briefly the genealogy of the concept and analyze institutions that embody this ethic. In doing so, I attempt to demonstrate that service is not always democratic, public, and grounded in a civic ethic. Moreover, I hope to show that institutions use the service ethic and the practices of servers to serve private interests. Thus situated service becomes less a norm of caring and good civics and more an instrument for individual, corporate, and bureaucratic privilege; and as that instrument it violates the civic purposes of the ethic. When it violates the civic purposes of the service ethic, service loses its force as an ideological and rhetorical justification for a *national* (or possibly any governmental) program.

Historically, service, and the service professions, have been more than simply institutionalized do-gooding. The service professions—for example, social work, relief work—were constituted by the five characteristics of service I mention above. As such they became part of the political economy of American society. Moreover, they were a means of *socialization*: designed to help people conform to certain values sometimes at the expense of their traditional community practices.

In his now-famous account of social work, Roy Lubove argues that the profession was established as a middle class response to social dislocation caused by industrialization and increasing urbanization. In the late nineteenth century the "truly scientific charity" emerged as an instrument of urban social control. This work depended upon scientific organization: functional specialization, centralized coordination and administration, corporate managerial techniques, and an "application of biological and economic law."[14] These charity organizations sought "character regeneration" in a rearticulated social sphere.

> The charity organization ideal was to reestablish the patterns of general social interaction of the small town or village, where the primary group exercised powerful social controls. The charity society was an "artifice," designed to restore the "natural relations" which the city had destroyed.[15]

Moreover, these "natural relations" looked uncommonly like a middle -class utopia.

> The visitor saw in her client less an equal or a potential equal than an object of character reformation whose unfortunate and lowly condition resulted from ignorance or deviations from middle-class values and patterns of life-organization."[16]

As the twentieth century unfolded, though, this feeling of moral superiority was supplanted by an ethic of scientific expertise.[17] "Friendly visiting" became "social diagnosis," and the charity organizations became bureaucratic social work agencies. Servicers became experts on "family adjustment" with developed "casework techniques."[18] Psychiatry was introduced into social work, as was the study of criminology. A professional subculture emerged, and professional organizations developed. Finally, social service agencies became bureaucratized, as the principles of organization shifted from "cause" to "function."[19] Efficiency became the key virtue of the service organization (and has become more so in our time), agencies coordinated their activities more closely, a theory of supervision emerged and a supervisory function became delineated. Finally a "federation" movement further reinforced these bureaucratic and professional tendencies. Service had become less a charitable practice and more a technical means of therapy.[20]

Social service as a technique of social control has been well documented in America by Frances Fox Piven and Richard Cloward. They contend that the primary function of relief-giving has been to maintain civil order in a capitalist economic system.

> Historical evidence suggests that relief arrangements are initiated or expanded during the occasional outbreaks of civil disorder produced by mass unemployment, and are then abolished or contracted when political instability is restored.... [E]xpansive relief policies are designed to mute civil disorder, and restrictive ones to reinforce work norms. In other words, relief policies are cyclical—liberal or restrictive depending on the problems of regulation in the larger society with which government must contend.[21]

Piven and Cloward argue that this has been the primary function of relief policy since the New Deal, and they marshal a good deal of evidence in support of their claim.

Social control involves different characteristics. Some who are of no use as workers—the aged, the disabled, the insane—are treated so poorly that they "instill in the laboring masses a fear of the fate that awaits them should they relax into beggary and pauperism."[22] Low-wage work is enforced through statutory regulation and administrative methods.[23] And relief agency practices degrade the relief recipient, for example in the practice of surveillance. The client is forced to "surrender commonly accepted rights [e.g., to privacy] in exchange for aid."[24] The welfare explosion of the 1960s expanded these surveillance and regulative practices in the name of "relief." One effect of these programs has been to shift the function of relief and service agencies from the regulation of civil disorder to the regulation of labor.[25]

Service is not simply a means of social control, though—it reflects certain ideological premises. Alan Ware argues that the very concept of community service results from bourgeois political ideology. "The state legitimize[s] the middle-class ethic of volunteering by transforming it into an ethic of service for the community—an essentially classless ethic."[26] Yet the ethic of service is very much class-based, and thus situated in a particular politicoeconomic strategy. Ware's account of the growth of volunteerism and intermediate organizations is quite revealing, and suggests a number of points that refute the arguments of service planners. First, volunteerism is not an American tradition (or something that defines an American), but an ethic that has been strong historically in Britain (and presumably Canada as well). He demonstrates that there are more volunteers *per capita* in Britain than in the United States.[27] Thus, to argue that our voluntary tradition makes us special is to deploy *Americanism* ideologically.

He also argues that the political economy and ideology of service is class-based. He suggests that volunteerism had its roots in both the upper and lower classes. But, like Lubove, he contends that the working class ideals were largely supplanted by middle class ones. For instance, volunteerism arose not only from the charitable impulses of the middle classes, but also from the politicization of the working classes.[28] Yet the volunteer institutions that have eroded have been largely "low-level working-class institutions outside the workplace through which solidarity could be expressed on a regular basis."[29] Friendly societies and mutual-aid societies promoted collective solidarity, socialized distribution, and communal living—practices at odds with bourgeois ideology. But those working-class voluntary organizations were systematically replaced by middle class service organizations.

Finally, Ware contends with others such as Richard Titmuss that any current decline in volunteerism may have less to do with a change in values than we think, and more to do with the effects of a market economy on the service industry. One example might be the practice of donating blood. With the rise of for-profit plasma centers, blood donation as an act of charitable service has declined. Another example might be the appearance of for-profit recycling companies, or stores that sell "ecologically sound" products. Even huge corporations market their products on grounds of conservation—for example, McDonald's, Colgate-Palmolive, and General Motors. On a broader level, because service is a profession, more people are motivated by instrumental reasons to serve (i.e., the desire for money and status) than by charity.

John McKnight also comments on the relationship between service and the political economy of a market society.[30] He argues very persuasively that in a postindustrial market economy the service business not only provides services, but manufactures them at the same time. He maintains that this is the true meaning of the *service economy*: an economy which not only fulfills need with certain remedies, but defines what those needs and remedies are. At times the service economy generates needs to fit preconceived remedies.[31] Ultimately, politics is reduced to deciding what service to render, and this (falsely) renders politics itself apolitical.

McKnight contends that the service ideology mystifies the dilemmas of traditional politics: more guns or more butter? more wheat or more steel? The new service politics is a debate over more doctors or teachers, more lawyers or social workers—the kind of politics possible in a relatively abundant society. But, paradoxically, this makes politics ostensibly impossible because services are not goods, and as such they are not political choices *per se*, they are services. We do not need services like we need guns or butter, for the latter may be essential to our survival. Put another way, services do not generate losses: if one trades education for conservation, one hasn't lost anything, but one has gained education. Politics apparently emerges again where services are traded for goods. For instance, where a government chooses to pursue conservation policies at the expense of industrial production, that government selects a service over a good.[32]

Consequently, politicians see national service as if it is uncontestable ideologically. That is, they sense that national service, in principle, is something anyone could support regardless of their political or partisan affiliation.[33] This motivates most, if not all, of its supporters to lobby for it in Congress as a nonpartisan issue, because it makes good political sense to support service. It can be a program that supplies jobs and benefits to people and areas needing them, at relatively little political cost. After all, service is provided (theoretically in unlimited amounts), but at what expense to other services? Furthermore, it is an additional (i.e., new) federal program, and so does not compete ideologically with other programs for funding, but is established in its own right.[34]

All this is deceptive, however. Services are so essential to our

economy that lawmakers *treat* service tasks and organizations as
if they were apolitical. "The apolitical nature of service is so perva-
sive that it is difficult for the public and policy makers to recognize
that services are the central political issue in many modernized
economies."[35] Service can be treated apolitically because its sym-
bolic referent is the notion of love, or care. Its apolitical nature
reflects the universality, or potential universality, of love. Everyone has the capacity to love, or care, so the argument goes; thus, in
theory, service is boundless, an unqualified good, something
uncontroversial, a nonzero sum. Love and care are not political
issues, and thus not policy questions either. *Care* becomes a potent
political signifier, which sets off a chain of other signifiers such as
service. Service becomes a uncontestable concept—an unlimited,
unquestionable, unqualified good—and where *service* merges into
citizenship, that too becomes uncontestable.

But the apparent uncontestability of the concept of service on
the part of politicians, theorists, and servers alike masks the servicers and their systems, techniques, and technologies. Service is a
business in need of markets, "an economy seeking new growth
potential, professionals in need of an income."[36] The discourse of
service obscures a critical political issue in postindustrial societies:
the demand to manufacture needs in order to rationalize a service
economy. Thus where national service proponents declare that the
needs are there or that the opportunities for service are unlimited,
they not only express care, but they reflect the demands of an
economy which depends upon the fact that there *must* be an
unlimited set of needs.

It is very literally a means of generating clients to fulfill the
requirements of a business—the business of service. With national
service, this business can be accomplished at wages below the federal minimum. The business of service is business—the financial
health of nursing homes, day care centers, educational testing
units, uniform manufacturers, zoos, museums, etc., etc. However,
many if not most of the businesses profiting from any service, and
national service in particular, are corporations—for they have the
resources, technical skills, and size to supply servicers with their
instruments.

McKnight takes the argument one step further. "The central
political issue becomes the servicers' capacity to manufacture
needs in order to expand the economy of the servicing system."[37] In
this system, the client is less the person in need than the person
who is needed—he or she is needed by the service industry to

allow that industry to recreate itself. Thus service industries perpetuate themselves. Moreover, where services fail to provide, new
services are created to manage them and protect the political support for them. The service manager brings to the business four
techniques of systematization: budgets (cost control systems), personnel (training systems), organizational structure (delivery systems), and technology (innovations). Furthermore, service man-
agers have developed a fifth technique—marketing—to convince
people that such a service is necessary. Service is a system of techniques, and those who serve are not simply caregivers, but appli-
ers, and targets, of techniques of systematization and efficiency. I
have tried to make this argument already regarding national service in chapters 2–5 of this text.

The ideology of service is antithetical to citizenship here for a
few reasons. First, service reinscribes an individualist, atomized
society. A professionalized service ethic legitimates individuals
whose capacity is to see their neighbor as somehow deficient, as
personally deficient. The deficiency is placed in the client, and the
remedial practice isolates the individual from the context. Thus
the *theory* of service is (simply) persons serving persons—persons
without a history and without a position in a particular class or
ethnic group. The server and the served become deontological
beings, where the service being performed is an act between individuals. While this may not always be true in voluntary organizations, it would more likely be true in a national service where
NSPs serve with people they do not know, and service clients they
have never seen before. Many NSPs and clients, then, will be "pro-
cessed," in the worst sense of that term.

Moreover, in theory at least, servers specialize and render service in a systematic, technical manner. The teenage, drug-abusing,
pregnant runaway is often treated by different agencies, as a
teenager, as a drug-abuser, as pregnant, and as a runaway.
National service ideology neglects this: when NSPs serve, they
may be serving only *part* of the problem, and thus learning only
part of the so-called solution. This effectively atomizes the client
into a number of different parts, submits that client to different
servers and different technologies, and forces the NSP to specialize
in a particular type of care. The NSP thus does not learn only service, but a specific type of service with certain technologies associated with it. The NSP is not learning "service" here so much as a
particular application of caregiving. This seems incompatible with
a philosophy of citizenship that demands an understanding of

diversity about its citizens. In serving a senior citizen, is a national server serving a citizen, or applying technologies to an elderly client? Or is it something in between? Even if something in between, the ideology of service masks an incomplete or flawed civic experience.

Furthermore, as I have argued, the remedies of service often dictate the needs of service. That is, the technologies and systems employed by the service business (e.g., marketing techniques) can be used to assure clients and servers alike that needs can be professionally identified. Thus needs are forever being named, and services are forever being created to meet them.[38] Yet in doing so, service becomes further professionalized and further removed from the hands of the ordinary citizen. The capacity to define the problem becomes a professional prerogative.

The privileged definition of *service* is, I would argue, antithetical to citizenship because it translates political problems into technical ones.[39] Thus, helping the environment becomes an uncontestable service which can be accomplished through the judicious application of national server labor. But helping the environment also involves knowing what interests do not want to help the environment and why. Conserving nature involves fighting corporate polluters as much as it does planting trees. Making homes energy efficient means lobbying against utility rate increases as much as it does weatherstripping houses. Yet national servers may not get the opportunity to do the former, and will spend many hours laboring over the latter.

Here the apolitical ideology of service disables the civic. The server is told to do his or her duty by universalizing the sense of care or love in his or her job; yet that duty is not held universally. The utility company does not provide home heating because it cares or serves the community; it provides heat for a profit. And that same utility implements conservation measures only if it is profitable to do so. Therefore, political disagreements over what constitutes service to the nation emerge—because "service" is a contestable concept, because "the nation" is a contestable concept, and because "citizenship" is a contestable concept. Service, and national service, neutralize the contestability of these concepts by masking their politics, and by generating needs to meet the requirements of a service economy. If we want to serve the needs of the nation we ought to be providing for those in need at the same time that we limit the power of service "to disable the capacities of all citizens to perceive and deal with issues in political terms."[40] In this way we can politicize service and generate debate about good citizenship.

SERVICE ORGANIZATIONS AS SOCIALIZING INSTITUTIONS

In the previous section I argued that the very premises of the concept of service belie a politicoeconomic context in which it flourishes, and that this distorts the practice of the civic. For in this context, civic practices entail pursuing ends that privilege some interests over others. This violates the premise of equality upon which accounts of democratic citizenship, and defenses of national service, are often based. But, *more importantly,* service rhetoric and ideology close down discussion about its necessarily political nature, and in doing so, the citizen is silenced. In this section, I examine the actual practice of service groups that have been established by federal and state governments. I argue that these practices reflect a socialization toward instrumental reason, individuation, and atomization. Service agencies established by government often reinscribe the very practices national service proponents wish to abolish or transcend. Furthermore, these very same offices help institutionalize organizational regimes of normalization and discipline. Socialization toward instrumental, individualist thinking and normalization inhibits the development of the civic as I have defined it in Chapter 1.

The practice of voluntary community service demonstrates goodwill toward others, contributes to the community in which one lives, and develops a sense of social responsibility. Certainly countless examples exist which confirm these beliefs, and the very logic of these sorts of programs assume it. I cannot nor do I want to disconfirm these: volunteerism builds associational life. However, government-sponsored, systematic programs of voluntary service do not teach selflessness, open discussion, community concern, and, ultimately, good citizenship very well. Government reinscribes the same sort of instrumentalist logic and individualist vocabulary upon which critics of the contemporary American community (such as Bellah, Barber, or Moskos) focus. The government is not necessarily at fault because agency directors reflect the dominant and popular values of the day, and because they often implement technocratic methods of service developed in the private voluntary sector. Rather, the problem rests with systematizing service in bureaucratic form—tailoring organizational procedures to deliver services efficiently. But I speak of governmental programs because national service is a governmental program, at either the federal, state, or local levels.

Thus, I premise the following discussion on the fact that, however decentralized, service programs have a systematic, regulated quality to them, and that the agencies involved do not teach the participants to *challenge* that systematization and regulation. Along with everything else service participants are taught, they will also be taught to conform to organizational behavior—its instrumentality, technocracy, discipline, and normalization. This is a part of service learning that proponents choose to ignore, and it is the part obstructing civic education. One can argue that learning organizational behavior is endemic to participating in any organization, and this may be true. But service programs will not even teach individuals to recognize organizational behavior when they see it because they believe they are apolitical, because they do not even recognize themselves as political organizations. This deception bespeaks the uncivic practices of community service. For, quite simply, it violates the sort of independence of mind that all those who privilege the civic (from Thomas Jefferson to present-day communitarians) demand of the citizen. A democratic, citizen-run national service might develop its own organizational norms and standards, but one of them ought to be self-criticism. Here is where service moves away from socialization and toward education, and where national service can reflect "American" skepticism toward the government.

Historically, service institutions sponsored by the government have socialized individuals toward the values I mention above. I have argued elsewhere that this characterized the Civilian Conservation Corps.[41] William Graebner also demonstrates that voluntary organizations helped engineer the consent of their participants to the American polity.[42] I want to show how programs since the 1960s have done similar things. While the Peace Corps, Job Corps, and other service programs may or may not have engineered consent, they have promoted an uncritical acceptance of certain organizational and behavioral norms—norms that contradict the civic requirements of an independently minded, participatory citizenry.

For instance, the politics of the Peace Corps have revolved around its function as a socializing institution. T. Zane Reeves argues that, since its inception, the Peace Corps has been a bureaucratic, rather than a deliberative body, and that this has inhibited the free and open exchange of ideas.[43] Founded as an ideological weapon against communism, the corps developed a commitment culture that forced it to avoid controversial issues.[44] It was a relatively activist agency until 1968, when the Nixon administration reorganized it under the Office of Management and Budget. This, Reeves argues, depoliticized it and its activist culture. In its place, the Nixonian ideology promoted service, volunteerism, and achievement orientation as important values to inculcate into its participants. The administration even established "programming institutes" to ensure indoctrination.[45]

The corps was repoliticized temporarily under Sam Brown in the Carter administration.[46] But the Reagan administration sought to dismantle the program, by cutting much of its financial base. More importantly, Reeves argues that the administration's policy essentially killed whatever activist culture remained.[47] The Peace Corps was to be a service organization, rather than an advocacy one.

The Peace Corps also embodied disciplinary organizational tendencies.[48] It regulated the sexuality of participants, it conducted constant security checks on the volunteers, and it set out behavioral guidelines in systematic form.[49] Sargent Shriver wrote the booklet *The Social Behavior of Volunteers* in which he laid out guidelines on dress, language, drinking habits, and the use of leisure time.[50] The guidelines expanded to the point that some of the staff and volunteers even complained outright of the administration's attempts at behavioral control.

The corps developed a comprehensive testing system under Dr. Nicholas Hobbs, a psychologist who became the Peace Corps first chief of selection. It subjected participants to "continuous testing and review," and compiled an "assessment survey" of their "progress." This raised tensions among some volunteers who resented a process that was "clandestine, inhumane, and arbitrary."[51] A uniform training schedule was instituted. Some participants believed this training program to be like "boot camp,"[52] and many critics recognized that these training institutes were not successful in teaching foreign languages and cross-cultural education. Finally, in training, individuals could be categorized and deselected if necessary. "Poor performance during training, health problems, psychological instability, or general unsuitability were all potential grounds for 'deselection.'"[53]

Similar tendencies can be found in the federal youth work and service programs of the 1960s. As a number of supporters testified, an early, unrealized version of VISTA, the National Service Corps, was designed to spontaneously generate voluntarism.[54] It was not supposed to be a "political" organization.[55] Nonetheless, domestic service programs in the early 1960s placed political and social limitations on participants. In both the Senate and House bills, enrollees were deemed employees of the federal government, who were required to undergo "security checks" in order to ensure that their enrollment was "consistent with the national interest."[56] The President's Study Group on a National Service Program recommended to the committees that comprehensive selection and testing procedures be implemented (for "aptitudes" and "attitudes") by trained professionals. "Selection will continue throughout the training period: a Corpsmen's [sic] performance will be assessed by the instructors, by trained psychologists, and by the NSC and local project personnel."[57] The study also recommended background checks and fingerprinting of all enrollees.[58] Finally, the study advised that a dossier be kept on each individual.

> Applicants will be invited to begin training on the basis of their detailed questionnaire-application; responses to reference-inquiries by those who have known them best in work, school, and community activities; the results of their aptitude-placement test, medical examination, and civil service background investigation.[59]

According to the account given by Michel Foucault, the dossier is one important criterion of the disciplinary society, for it brings the participants under the gaze of the agency.[60]

The Job Corps also was designed to discipline and normalize its corpsmembers as much as it was meant to give them marketable skills. This is evident from the *Residential Living Manual* produced by the Department of Labor for the program. However, such discipline was not particularly harsh, and the authors of the manual implore the residence directors to involve the enrollees in the discipline and to be "flexible" in meting punishment.[61] In this sense discipline was democratic: the community, not just the director, disciplined the offending party. Consequently, social control was most effective as a means by which the individual could regulate his or her *own* behavior.

The manual also suggests that the government was interested in inculcating the apolitical ideology of service. Instead of promoting discipline toward rigid norms, the Job Corps attempted to depoliticize corpsmembers, or reinforce their political passivity and indifference. This, in turn, could make coercive discipline unnecessary, and deflect any contestation on the part of the enrollees.

First, they were to "direct behavior patterns and attitudes into constructive channels" by modifying "character and personality traits" where necessary. The Corps emphasized "flexibility," "creativity," and "humanization," and tried to nurture "supportive relationships."[62] Yet they isolated the individual by establishing a one-to-one relationship between the corpsmember and a residential advisor (RA). The RA was "the one person in the Center who [was] closely familiar with the individual corpsmember as a total and unique person." The RA was the "mentor," the "concerned friend"—and this was the RA's institutional duty. Like the National Service Corps and Peace Corps before it, the Job Corps demanded that a dossier be compiled by the RAs, marking down everything related to that person in order to compile a "total" record. The Labor Department proposed that corpsmembers be monitored regularly by constant attendance-taking (at each part of the day), and frequent day time dormitory checks.[63]

Rigorous testing and evaluation were also recommended and put into place. Why? So the corps member could

a. develop realistic training, employment and human relations goals, b. understand how his performance and behavior are enhancing or impeding achievement of these goals, and c. understand how his behavior affects the other corpmembers and the general welfare of the Center.[64]

Note what is implied here. The individual was taught to be "realistic," not to pursue, for instance, the American dream. The RAs and staff directors were also urged to place any failure of the corpsmembers on the corpsmembers themselves—in this way the problem was individuated. Furthermore, this kind of discourse designated the corpsmembers as instruments of the center, and not vice versa. Finally, these problems were resolved by counseling. Yet counseling was not a public or participatory means of resolving problems, it was individual, focused, and sought the source of enrollee distress in psychological, rather than political, terms. In this way, problems were resolved through therapy rather than deliberation. In group counseling this focus on the individual was not so acute, but even there the emphasis was on the problem of the individual. Group discussions sought ultimately the cure for an individual's psychological or sociological pathology, and they did not treat group therapy and the corps camp as political settings.[65] Like service, both forms of counseling masked a politics of atomization and individuation or promoted nonpolitical solutions to what might have been political questions.[66]

The Job Corps member was also taught to reason instrumentally through a required "comprehensive incentive system." This system really represented two different sub-systems: the Phase System and the Maximum Benefits System. The Phase System offered a series of graduated rewards and services offered in exchange for good behavior, hard work, and retention. By the last phase, the corpsmember was expected to demonstrate an "ability to regulate his own behavior." This was to be rewarded by more privacy and more freedom.[67] The goal was to encourage "self-study" and "individual projects." It is clear, then, that the Phase System was designed not to encourage critical thinking, but to adapt the behavior of the participants to a norm of individualism. What was taught here was not greater independence, but greater individuation. The Maximum Benefits System encouraged "progress" through personal, on-on-one discussions with staffers, and was fairly similar to the counseling system already in place.

Was the Job Corps successful in its employment and behavioral goals? According to at least three reports, it was not. The dropout rate was very high, and relatively few individuals stayed beyond three months.[68] Twenty percent of the participants left within thirty days of entering the program, and in 1967 sixty-seven percent dropped out within six months. Much of this was due to the fact that residential centers were placed at an average distance of 943 miles from the homes of the participants. Stripped of access to their homes and communities, the participants could not tolerate the artificial conditions of the residence community.[69]

Finally, let's return to the Center for Service Learning at the University of Vermont to see how service is currently being taught. Not surprisingly, the center teaches service as an apolitical ideology, but more paradoxically, it also teaches service as an exercise in individuation. This is evidenced by the sorts of books employed in its curriculum.[70] Moreover, because the center is at the forefront of establishing reflective components to service experiences, it may inculcate a service ideology well, though that fact does not necessarily foster good citizenship. In fact, it may do just the opposite. If good citizenship is to be a goal of service, and if concern for the political community is to be part of this goal, then service organizations ought to encourage their participants to reflect upon social, political, and economic topics.

The center teaches the philosophy of service, and its central text, Ram Dass and Paul Gorman's, *How Can I Help?*, reflects this clearly. The text promotes the sorts of ideas about service upon which I have already commented. For example, service is "a timeless inquiry of the heart," and "caring is a reflex."[71] In this sense the activities are presented as "natural and appropriate." "You live, you help." They assert, but do not argue, that service is natural, habitual, and instinctual, but most importantly that it is essentially an *individual feeling*. Service triggers questions about the self, such as "Who am I?" And service means looking within oneself—"to be of most service to others we must face our own doubts, needs, and resistances." The text coaxes the student to discover his or her inner obstacles to service in order that his or her "generosity will flow more spontaneously."[72] It focuses on the effects of the service "experience" on the student, and the capacity of that student to "experience" greater "unity" with others.

The psychological premise upon which Dass and Gorman rest their analysis is that modern individuals have "relatively real" multiple identities.[73] They contend that moderns must unite these identities into "Helpful Being," a new character trait and a sign of a new human being. To achieve this character, though, individuals must go through a diacritical process of "self-transcendence," and the two suggest forms of therapy for the self—for example, meditation and "engaging suffering."[74] Most of the book discusses those practices in which individuals ought to engage to change their "inner" life through self-transcendence.

They offer one chapter on "social action," but it still emphasizes the individual and individual feeling. They define social action as a "personal instinct" and a "state of mind."[75] Furthermore, the purpose of social action is nonpolitical:

We're an environment, not an argument for social change. Our aim is to awaken together and see what follows, not to manipulate one another into this action or that. We do so by recognizing the integrity of one another's experience.... We're out to share, not convince; action follows.[76]

They conclude that "the basic social institution is the individual human heart" and that "any of us who choose to enter the arena of social action must go deep to the plane where we are One."[77]

Dass and Gorman obviously reinforce the kind of individualistic, apolitical conception of service I have criticized previously in this chapter. And the text intimates an inappropriate model for citizenship, because citizens must convince as well as share. When individuals are taught that service does not do the former they are stripped of a civic lesson. I cannot and will not contend with Dass and Gorman's text, because they do not defend their points, they assert them as "natural" and "true." But I take issue with service programs that choose to use this text as representative of *the* philosophy of service, or even *a* philosophy of service. For the text totally ignores the political, social, and economic context in which service is given, it privileges a certain definition of service by asserting it instead of arguing for it (and thus belies any claim to philosophy), and it promotes the idea that one can have a coherent and justifiable philosophy of service. The book is appropriate for one narrow conception of service, and completely inappropriate for any program wishing to include the civic in its definition of service.

The workbook used by the center, Timothy Stanton and Kamil Ali's *The Experienced Hand*, is little better. It, too, asks the student to approach his or her "experiential education" with "a look at yourself" first.[78] And it helps reinscribe an atomistic, instrumental society through the classic liberal device of the contract. The authors contend that the service learning process begins with a "learning contract," which describes what the student intends to learn and accomplish while on the internship.[79] Many different programs deploy service contracts—not only the center, but nonuniversity programs like Seattle's Program for Local Service, and the New York City Youth Corps. Contracts reinscribe the Lockean conception of society from which most civic republicans and communitarians distance themselves, but the actual contract signifies more than this.

For the contract is a means of self-discipline. According to Stanton and Ali the participant draws up the terms of the contract by which he or she essentially regulates his or her own activity. The participant sets out the job description, the type of supervision expected, the evaluative criteria employed, and the learning activities pursued. Through the learning contract one renounces the ability to judge for oneself the worthwhile nature of the service experience. It binds unequals: the student is forced to surrender certain rights—the right to judge the service experience, the right to assess one's own progress—to the service agency, in return for an evaluation. Yet it is done with the full and active participation of the students themselves—for, as Stanton and Ali put it, they must "monitor themselves, their learning and their internship experience."[80] In Foucault's terms, the normalizing gaze turns inward.

There is little mention of monitoring the agencies under which they serve, or the particular bureaucratic and contractual routines and practices which they are learning. When Stanton and Ali do discuss monitoring the organization, they reflect the bureaucratic ethic I have been criticizing. They enjoin the student to "learn about" the organizational environment without criticizing it. They encourage students to collect facts through a series of information-al questions, and "assess" its behavior on grounds of efficiency and effectiveness.[81] They do not advise the student to assess organiza-tions morally or politically. Yet any civic service program ought to have its participants ask not only if their agencies are efficient, but whether or not they are good, useful, and of benefit to the pub-lic. It should teach students to ask the question, "does this agency serve any other purposes beyond service?" And then, "why is this so and how are these purposes accomplished?"

"Reflecting" on the service internship denotes "obtaining feed-back" on "work performance" and its "learning aspects." "Many programs have designed forms for this purpose," and the authors provide an example of this.[82] In it, participants' qualities are "eval-uated" inventory-style. Work habits, skills, attitudes, and "human relations" are all judged, and the student's "growth" is charted. The criteria seem to apply across any task: the participant must be "punctual and dependable," "conform to expected organization norms," "dress neatly and appropriately," "have a pleasant and positive demeanor." That punctuality and conformity renders iron-ic further suggestions that the participant "have an open mind" and not "rush into judgment." Openness here signifies acquiescing to "the necessity of some dull or repetitive tasks" and recognizing and accepting of one's own "limitations."[83] In the end, Stanton and Ali assure students that they can "celebrate": "After months of arduous and sometimes anxious work, you deserve a good time.... Have one!"[84]

Again, I am not criticizing service learning in toto, for it can provide a constructive alternative to "book learning" for some peo-ple. I am only indicating that the issue is far more complex than its philosophy admits. What is learned on the job and in service learning programs is usually service, but, as the above language connotes, it may also be servility. Servility and docility have little place in *democratic* civic education, though they may serve important functions in producing and reproducing a postindustrial economy. Before service proponents celebrate that they have helped the community, they need to look at their organizational practices and ask whether those practices engender confidence, intellect, and moral integrity in the citizen. Service theory and practice educate participants in many more ways than most service proponents are willing to concede. But do service organizations educate the individual in *explicitly* political ways? In this chapter I have recounted the unintentional political lessons service programs transmit; in the next, I discuss the intentional ones.

CHAPTER SEVEN

Political Education in Service Programs

I want to examine how past prototypes of national service educated their participants politically. This chapter relies on evidence from the CCC, because that agency developed the most systematic program of political education of any service organization in the United States. The agency developed manuals and pamphlets to instruct camp leaders and educational advisors on the teaching of citizenship. But I also present ideas gleaned from service programs instituted since the 1950s, some of which may provide an example of an effective program for political education.

In the first part of this chapter I contend that former programs are of questionable educational value in the making of the active citizen. Service agencies, especially the CCC, discouraged critical thinking. Indeed, many programs emphasized their *non*political nature to the extent that they restricted opportunities for participants to learn about their country and other countries, and denied participants the chance to discuss political change.

However, there have been examples of civic vitality in past programs of national service. I look at one in particular—a leadership camp established in the CCC toward the end of the program—to demonstrate that self-governing communities were possible, but also to show that such communities contravened the interests of the agency. I also present more modern examples of participatory service communities that promote critical thinking and political learning.

These programs represent possible alternatives to current national service plans. The second part of the chapter discusses alternatives developed more fully in the remainder of the text, and presents service plans that emphasize education and participation. These alternative plans also represent examples that contemporary national service planners do not consider seriously. Yet they ought to in order to help young people understand the nature and responsibilities of citizenship.

FEDERALLY APPROVED PROGRAMS OF
POLITICAL EDUCATION IN SERVICE ORGANIZATIONS

Federal agencies have recommended or imposed several weak and ineffectual educational programs. Despite the jeremiads of politicians and bureaucrats about the need to inculcate citizenship values in the youth of the nation, the programs they have devised have been either devoid of political content or propagandistic (or, occasionally, both). Such failure was quite evident in the Civilian Conservation Corps, where citizenship education either did not exist, or where it promoted a weak conception of the citizen. Moreover, it offered little opportunity for individuals to actually talk about politics the issues of the day and their possible solutions. While corps members took an interest in politics, the agency discouraged many, if not most, of the boys, from becoming politically aware. Let me examine the political content of the CCC's programs in order to assay its effectiveness as a teacher of civic virtue and current events.

The Political Atmosphere of the CCC

Immediately after becoming president, Franklin Roosevelt was determined to have the CCC camps operating within two months, however, it was mid-July when he succeeded in doing so. Following the advice of the Chief Forester of the United States, F.D.R. decided to use the army to initiate the program.[1] Working in conjunction with the departments of the interior, agriculture, and labor, and later with the Office of Education, the army headed what can only be described as the largest peacetime mobilization and organization of men in the history of America. In the first three months of the program the army established 1330 camps, and moved 55,000 men more than 2000 miles toward the Rocky Mountains. As one top administrator observed: "It was the fastest mobilization in the history of the United States, in peace or war."[2] Many military officers and civilians looked upon the task as a valuable peacetime experience for the Department of War, and suggested that it was important practice in case of attack.[3]

Just how much control the army had at the early stages and throughout the life of the CCC is a matter of debate, but it controlled at least a portion of the daily life of the enrollees. It certainly contributed to the restricted political life of the camps. "The Army is the provider and tailor, doctor and teacher, spiritual advisor and paymaster," wrote the author of a short story about the CCC.[4] One former CCC enrollee remembers that "although there was no military training involved in the program, there was indeed military discipline."[5] All transportation was regulated by the army, and wherever an enrollee went he had to have printed on his travel order: "travel directed is necessary in the military service."[6] The director of educational programs at the agency reported directly to the Secretary of War.[7] Monthly accident reports were sent to the army because it controlled the safety standards of each camp.[8] The chief of finance in the War Department directed fiscal affairs according to the CCC acts of 1933 and 1937; so the army's institutional position strengthened in that it appropriated a large portion of the funds going to both the camps and the administrative apparatus. On June 26, 1940, F.D.R. issued a directive which added to its central purposes that of being in "the interest of the national defense." Thus, the CCC directly involved itself in the growing war effort, and trained enrollees for twenty hours per week in preparation for an attack. Finally, the rules and practices of selection and discharge reminded all of the military influence in camp. The uniforms were standardized to military regulation, an oath was required from all new enrollees, and discharges were given according to military procedure ("honorable," "dishonorable," "administrative").[9] One could even go AWOL in the CCC.

The involvement of the army worried some observers that young civilians would be militarized in more discreet ways. Certainly, the army had its own ideas on how to run the organization, and it sought to free the CCC from left-wing interference. Indeed, one officer proclaimed that the army would prevent "radical and leftist infiltration of the camps...[by] long-haired men and short-haired women."[10] One editorial suggested that this kind of attitude endangered the nation, because it justified the militarization of the CCC in the eyes of those very radicals.[11] Some contended that the army controlled all aspects of the organization, and one writer suggested that Robert Fechner, the director, was merely a "puppet" of the generals. He claimed that the army "by and large have ruled and continue to rule by force. To teach obedience is their primary task."[12]

The army also tried to prevent the circulation of certain books and pamphlets in the camps, and often its officers prevented particular ideas from being discussed.[13] And army regulations concerning information about the camps were particularly harsh. One regulation prevented the taking of any private movies at the camps "which might create a false public impression of conditions and activities under the Emergency Conservation Work Program."[14] There were rather strong regulations concerning the control of adverse publicity; the Company Officers were required to notify the district offices of all instances in which a particular case might generate adverse effects in the hands of the public.[15] Finally, explicit regulations prevented military officers, like the CO, from engaging in "political activity."[16] Therefore, the leaders of the camp were legally prohibited from teaching politics or political ideas. Thus the army contributed to a daily regime in the camps where deliberation and discussion were curtailed.[17]

But the military did not control the organization. Regulations limited its involvement, and explicit orders tempered the militarism of the commanding officer.[18] One regulation limited direct military intervention in the camps.[19] Moreover, enough people worried about the powers of the army that the assistant secretary of war, and others in the military bureaucracy, had to apologize publicly for statements implying that its militarization would be a good thing.[20] Other departments and agencies were responsible for some very important functions. For example, the departments of agriculture and interior selected the individual work projects and sites, and supervised that work. They were also responsible for job-related training. In fact, the army was only responsible for the welfare of the enrollees during the time they were in camps. At the work sites, they were technically the responsibility of these departments. And the Office of Education developed the educational programs pursued in the camps, though the director of those programs did report to the secretary of war.

The role of the army in the CCC is not irrelevant because some highly respected academics in our day have called for the participation of the military in the construction of a national service program, and have used the CCC as an example of a successful civilian program of military organization. They do not only suggest that the military be an option to civilian service, but they argue that the military must help organize the civilian aspects of a general national service program.[21] Yet the very structure of the military, and military regulations and rules, do not serve as examples of a participatory society. In this way, any military intervention into the civilian aspects of the national service would, if not curtail the free expression of ideas and rational deliberation of political issues, then represent a political organization antithetical to the practice of democracy within the service program itself. Even if the army did not curtail free speech in the CCC, or enforce unreasonable discipline in the camps, it hindered the self-governance of those camps, and it represented a sort of order that denied civic engagement and a participatory ethic.

Beyond the role of the army in daily camp life, the agency limited the political beliefs of enrollees and employees by both policy and ideas circumscribing the political universe of the enrollees. The organization and the camps prevented the complete freedom of ideas and expression. The rules governing such freedoms were delineated by codes derived from the military, so such regulations were harsh, even by civilian standards (and even for the 1930s).[22] Moreover the common practices of the camp employees inhibited the intellectual growth of the enrollees. For instance, one researcher found that some camps "discouraged frank discussion" and feared "outside agitators." He also told of one supervisor who complained that any political discussion was subversive of authority.[23] While this policy was not endorsed by the vast majority of COs and agency staff members, the agency itself demanded that good enrollees "need to believe in our form of government."[24] Curiously, in 1934, one government pamphlet praised the CCC for allowing its enrollees and educational staff to engage in totally free discussion. But within a year, the agency published a handbook recommending that group leaders "keep discussion away from dangerous topics."[25] The director, Robert Fechner, barred a left-wing journal called *Champion of Youth* from camp libraries in April 1937, and later the *New Republic* and *Nation*.[26] The most common journals found in the camp libraries were *Life, Newsweek,* the *Saturday Evening Post,* and *Farmer's Digest.*[27] None of these journals offered a wide variety of political opinion, and they rarely presented new political ideas, though at least *Newsweek* gave them the "facts."

Even more troubling than the constraints under which the exchange of ideas operated, though, was the fact that most camp commanders, educational supervisors, and enrollees, were indifferent to political ideas.[28] I have already noted that the army prevented its officers from being political, but even the civilian employees displayed little interest in raising political issues with the enrollees. And, with the exception of partial enrollee self-government in some camps, there were no programs offered at the camps which offered the enrollees an opportunity to learn political ideas beyond an elementary notion of civics. In short, the opportunities to discuss politics were, if not restricted by agency regulation or practice, unavailable to most men given the general temper of the camps.

Inculcating Citizenship in the CCC

Yet despite appearances, the CCC played a very important, and very ideological, political role, and this role became crucial in the education of the good citizen. The CCC was justified originally on the grounds that it helped inculcate citizenship and instill a sense of patriotism into the young men. This was especially important given the ideological dangers emanating from Europe at the time.

> The human body of the growing lad, if neglected, is even more susceptible to disease, to crime, to "isms" than is the tree in the forest susceptible to the diseases which may attack it. In this human problem the army looks beyond the veil into the future, visualizing these lads finally returning to over a million homes, bringing better discipline to each, better respect for government, better appreciation of the responsibilities of life, and the eradication of the various "isms" which are destroying many a family tree today.[29]

The prevention of "isms" largely meant communism in the eyes of the leaders of the corps, and of the military personnel involved.[30] But some worried about the danger posed by Hitler, too.[31] And much was done to keep both communist and fascist forms of organization out of the camps. Thus the CCC was very conscious of its political role, and felt that it needed to educate its enrollees correctly about political issues.

Consequently, the enrollee had to act in certain ways, according to one corps educational advisor.[32] This meant: (1) becoming a productive member of society, (2) functioning as part of a coordinated whole, (3) "learning how" to work and play, (4) learning to respect the rights and property of others, (5) developing a love for nature, and (6) developing one's physique. These injunctions were aspects of corps citizenship that many individuals admired.[33] It was in the love for nature that the CCC distinguished itself from other programs designed to inculcate citizenship. Here the CCC taught the enrollees particular sorts of qualities the leadership hoped would enhance their capacities as citizens. The CCC appealed to the mystique of the forest and of the frontier, two themes which have always been important in the myths of this country.[34] Some have also suggested that this quality was important to the corps because it was personally important to Roosevelt, who fancied himself a woodsman.[35]

More particularly, CCC citizenship demanded "woodsman-ship"—a politics of nature. Woodsmanship was the virtue of the CCC, it was the way individuals learned their responsibilities to their community and the surrounding natural areas. It was a romantic idea which represented the individual being uplifted through a communion with nature and his fellow man. It was also the quality which marked the enrollee as part of a select communi-ty, as a "senator of the woods," and it harked back to virtues like prudence and courage. It was a form of knowledge—the "homely knowledge of the forester."[36] And it was celebrated in CCC festivals and parades.[37]

Robert Fechner, the CCC's first director, developed this notion most fully in a pamphlet.[38] It helped teach young enrollees from the city the way of life of the "woodsman," in the hope that they would be pioneers like their forefathers. Woodsmanship was "the ability to live and work safely, to conduct yourself in accordance with your surroundings, and to adapt yourself to your environ-ment." The woodsman conducted himself in the following ways: (1) he was careful with fire, (2) he was clean, (3) he obeyed wildlife laws and did not kill animals for the sake of killing animals, (4) he observed while traveling, (5) he stayed calm if he got lost, (6) he did not imagine "fantastic tales of savage wild beasts and danger-ous reptiles," (7) he watched out for rattlesnakes and poisonous plants, (8) he was safe and skillful with tools, and understood first aid, and (9) he understood the meaning of conservation and forestry. "By doing your part in helping to conserve and protect our forests you are working for the national welfare."[39]

At the same time, a manual was developed by the CCC to teach the enrollees the very sorts of things Fechner mentioned. Called *CCC Forestry*, the manual defined both the forest and the forester more precisely, yet did so in two somewhat incompatible ways. On the one hand, it was very pragmatic and mindful of sci-ence: "The forest is an association of trees or shrubs or both, grow-ing on a considerable area, upon which it is possible to practice forestry."[40] And forestry was treated as a science throughout the book—indeed new techniques were explained to the enrollee in detail.[41] Moreover it valued the forest for its material yield, for the sorts of products that one could extract from the forest.[42] In this sense the work perpetuated a technological domination of nature.

On the other hand, the "scientists" speculated about the mysti-cal properties of the forest. They personified the forest. "Trees in the forest are comparable to human beings in a social or economic community, except that the trees' inherent savage struggle for existence is more openly ruthless than man's subtle diplomatic schemes to get ahead."[43] Here the authors took liberties with human nature, and most certainly treated a Machiavellian ideology as fact. They also mentioned an important mystical value, provided by the forest.

> There is another value, often called spiritual, that may be secured by everyone. Something deep within us urges us to get out of doors where in the quiet of the woods big troubles become little ones; we orient ourselves with the general scheme of things, and are refreshed and rested.[44]

This was particularly perplexing from a book purporting to treat forestry as a science, for it attributed to the forest powers that clearly could not be explained through the scientific method. By fetishizing the forest the CCC mystified itself in order to appropriate an aspect of citizenship special to the organization. For the CCC not only sought to train people in the skills of the forester, but wished to do so within the context of an American myth.[45]

The values of the woodsman and the forester appealed to the virtues of the pioneer.[46]

> It should be remembered that camps and work in unsettled areas were an American inheritance three hundred years old. America had grown from cabins and sod huts pushing into forests or prairie, from surveying camps and railroad building camps, from emigrants from the settled East living in wagons while they erected their new homes. America had seen boys' camps, camps of militia, camps for private families and social groups. Living in and working from temporary shelters and pioneers battling with the wilderness were both experiences in the American blood. The CCC called on both, as well as a fund of practical knowledge, when it planned and set up its thousands of forest, mountain, and desert centers.[47]

It was like times of old, even invoking the myth of Paul Bunyan. In fact, MacArthur saw the program as a movement for a national folklore.[48] And such a national folklore maintained national morale and prepared young people for "normal community life."[49] Thus, woodsmanship was a central aspect to the CCC's conception of citizenship, and through it the agency imparted various myths of America to the enrollees.

Citizenship, however, meant more than simply the values of the woodsman. Indeed woodsmanship was often merely the means through which the agency imparted the real lessons of citizenship. But their version of citizenship suggested a passive acceptance of existing institutions and an obedience to bureaucratic authorities. In the words of one critic, the CCC's definition of citizenship meant no more than "to be profitably employed."[50]

Yet it did mean more than simply being profitably employed, because an ideology surrounded the kind of citizenship one learned in the CCC: "conforming citizenship."[51] For the enrollee, this meant: (1) the ability to earn a living for oneself and one's family "in some useful occupation," (2) good health, physical and mental, "to the extent that an individual is neither a public charge nor a source of danger to other people," (3) observance of laws and moral conduct to the point where "he ceases to be a menace to others," (4) the ability to live and work with others so he is "not a public nuisance" and does not infringe on other people's rights, (5) to provide, as a parent, a home where children can follow these same guidelines, (6) to read and write well enough to achieve the first five objectives, and (7) "the ability to understand and carry out instructions in which disciplined action best serves society."[52] The CCC provided all these vital elements to citizenship, according to the most extensive study of its programs.[53]

Only rarely did civics classes go beyond the teaching of these particulars, to teach what Holland and Hill called contributing citizenship.[54] One element of contributing citizenship was participation, though this was only very rarely taught, and where it was taught it was done so by a subtle means of coercion: the bulletin board. In many camps bulletin boards (swathed in floodlights at night) displayed the participatory activities of each individual by means of stars.[55] The more stars one collected, the more merits one received. Participation, then, was encouraged by rewards and the public shame of the bulletin board.

How did the corps teach "conforming citizenship?" First, as I have mentioned, there was a general lack of discussion of political ideas and issues, and the agency removed any controversial books from the camps. Moreover, the evening programs, in the educational hour after dinner, also contributed to civic education. Occasionally the CO summoned the enrollees to hear a speech on good citizenship. Usually, though, they learned good citizenship while learning to read, write, and count. At least by the late 1930s, the CCC employed its literacy and numeracy programs to gently impart lessons in good morals. The learning texts became the central organs of propaganda for the agency.

In the late 1930s the agency developed a series of workbooks designed to help enrollees read, write, and do arithmetic. But they also transmitted moral lessons in each of the exercises, so reading the book was more like confronting a secular, capitalist Sunday school teacher. For example, the arithmetic workbook was arranged in twenty two lessons of increasing difficulty; each lesson connected to the previous one.[56] By the eighteenth lesson, the book had progressed toward a practical application of the arithmetical principles. The titles of the last five lessons included: "Banks and Checks," "The Checking Account," "Using a Checking Account," "Bank Loans," and "Installment Loans." While these lessons were useful, they transmitted concealed messages: (1) that paying by credit and checks was an acceptable, and good, practice; (2) going into to debt was normal; but (3) loans were the personal responsibility of the enrollee. These lessons were "harmless" instructions for managing one's money, but they also endorsed consumer credit practices.

The reading workbooks needed no such subtleties; they blatantly relayed messages. Most of the subjects in the workbook related to camp life, with titles like "My First Night in Camp," "My First Pay Day," and "The First Joke on Me." But they also served to deliver sermons about morality and behavior to the enrollees: "Health—keep your nose clean...take a bath daily...drink plenty of water," etc.[57] In fact many of the sentences the enrollees learned employed the imperative construction: "Follow the rules!" "Know how to take orders!" "Be on time for everything!" "Develop yourself—learn hobbies!"[58] Simply by reading these lessons, individuals were "hailed": the CCC enjoined them to be the sort of subjects that "got along." It was as if the agency asked its enrollees to shed the character traits with which they came to the program, in order to reform them completely from within. These workbooks, then, were a source of regeneration—a site where individuals recreated themselves under the watchful eye of the text. Yet it was more like a de-creation, for the enrollees were taught to remain passive in their political and social engagements.

Workbook 4, published in 1940, was the most explicit, and it concerned itself with all the moral lessons the CCC inculcated into the future citizen. It began atomistically enough, with the task "I

Must Know Myself," and concluded with two narratives which exemplified "good work values." In between, the enrollee learned about cleanliness, sanitation, social diseases, getting a job, managing one's personal finances, and using leisure time wisely.[59] Among the most interesting lessons were lessons concerning community— the camp community, communities in general, one's responsibilty to one's community, membership in the camp community, and patriotism and membership in the American community.[60] All of these lessons reinforced the goal of "conforming citizenship" discussed above. The first few lessons considered mythical ideal American communities. These involved neighbors helping each other, and a discussion of the economic origins of the community. But they did not criticize or question the values or history of the communities. So such infantile presentations as "in a community, laws are made to help the majority of families in the community— You must obey these laws yourself," offered a simplistic vision of the political world to twenty-year-old men.[61] And the workbook enjoined the enrollee to "look out about and see what undesirable things must go from your community—you have a job in ridding the community of factors that are harmful to it."[62] In fact, the only specific reference to politics in the entire series was a two-sentence injunction to vote regularly—and to "remember to give the officials all your cooperation."

The workbook also enjoined the enrollee to be a "good camp citizen." This meant that "you must live peaceably with the other members of the camp. You must be a gentleman. You must take care of the property entrusted to you. You must give a day's work for a day's pay."[63] The lesson went on to describe the benefits of being in camp: learning the "values of a well-ordered life," and "learning to be a more useful citizen," etc. Finally, the workbook championed the importance of *American* citizenship. It emphasized the greatness of the country, focusing on the Bill of Rights, and it presented a biography of the model citizen—Henry Ford. It concluded with an atomistic, market-like vision of society and government:

A nation is made of many individuals. I am one of those individuals. I receive many benefits from being a part of the nation. I must do my part to earn those benefits. In a nation individuals exchange services. That is the only way we could hope to progress.... [Each man works] to satisfy the needs of other persons.

Moreover, government was "a means by which persons cooperate in providing benefits for themselves which they could not have if they acted alone."[64]

In these short definitions, we see the sorts of attitudes that contribute to an atomistic mentality: a vision that society is constituted by individuals who precede the collectivity. But it also points up other ideological constructions (many, if not all, of which contribute to the contemporary search for community). Society thus depends on individuals selling themselves and buying goods and services in a market exchange relationship, and on a utilitarian description of government and the governing process. Citizenship education in the CCC taught a particular notion of community, and did not conceptualize society in ways that would discourage atomistic individualism. Rather, it taught a radical politics of rights, benefits, and individualism, presented as "fact," and "demonstrated" to be the constituent units of a nation.[65]

Moreover, this was the sort of information being presented to twenty-year-old men, (as well as veterans!). It was a pedagogy that assumed that the men were not only illiterate, but completely docile, and that they exercised none of the critical abilities that individuals, no matter how illiterate, possess at that age. Some may argue that the workbooks were not designed to enlighten these men, but only to teach them how to read. But this is impossible: (1) every lesson had to be about something; (2) the particular lessons were chosen for their relevance; and (3) there was unabashed political content to many, if not most, of the lessons. The directors simply chose to include the sorts of banalities about America that college lecturers ask their students to question.

CITIZENSHIP EDUCATION SINCE THE 1960S

More recent (non-school-based) service organizations do not promote good citizenship or educate their enrollees politically. The Program for Local Service (PLS), VISTA, and the modern day conservation corps programs do not include citizenship education in their budgets.[66] In fact the only educational programs budgeted for most of the contemporary programs of service are technical ones. For instance, the Seattle area's PLS provides four days of "preservice training," virtually all of this concerned with the technical details of the tasks to be done.[67] Many service proponents argue that education should be largely or exclusive technical.[68] I have discussed my objections to this in Chapter 5.

The clearest example of what might be called civic education can be found in the Job Corps.[69] In the residential camps, corpsmembers were encouraged to establish dormitory government, though this was not required. A "leadership training program" was required, though, as was a community participation program. But these were not specified, and were left up to the individual residence directors. Citizenship training was not a central part of the corpmembers' experiences (as it was for the CCC), and it is difficult to judge the success of this aspect of the program because of high attrition rates.

This does not mean that citizenship education is not on the agenda of service planners, though. A conference on the "Citizenship Education of the Young Worker" was held in 1966 with participation from national service proponents.[70] Interestingly, the conference, composed largely of business, political, and academic leaders, set aside much of the discussion for an analysis of citizenship in the corporation and the schools. Not surprisingly, their conclusions mimicked those of Holland and Hill for the CCC: conforming citizenship ought to be the norm.

Nevertheless, national service planners have not thought about, or designed, lessons that teach people the virtues of citizenship. While they *talk* about the need for this, none have offered a comprehensive plan to inculcate citizenship, probably because national service and smaller service programs are concerned with youth employment and productivity. Nowhere is this clearer than in Moskos's estimates for the annual costs of a national service program, where there are no outlays for citizenship education, though he allocates thirty million dollars of federal money for advertising.[71] Until more service proponents discuss the nature of citizenship education and provide money for it, it can only be a hollow ideal used to advertise the program.

THE PARTICIPATORY IMPULSE
IN SERVICE ORGANIZATIONS

Service programs in North America, including the CCC, have demonstrated that there is room for participation by the enrollees. Here I want to examine a few such programs which have developed over the past fifty years. I begin with an analysis of a little-known program that emerged from the CCC, Camp William James, and afterwards I discuss nongovernmental versions of service work. I conclude with an analysis of Katimavik,a successful program in

Canada. The two themes of this section are that participatory service work is possible but that federal service directors and planners seem to exclude that possibility through policy or ignorance.

Participatory Democracy in the CCC

Citizenship in the CCC meant participation, at least in the eyes of some. For instance, many educational advisors called on the enrollees in the camps to use their newfound knowledge to protest against poverty, and to contact their representatives in order to win approval of poverty-relief programs.[72] And the founders of a leadership training camp, called Camp William James, demanded that active citizenship in the CCC meant learning to participate, not simply learning information about one's country; the tasks of active citizenship "defy purely bureaucratic solution."[73]

Some camps were models of direct democracy, and in all there was at least some semblance of community life. James McEntee, the second director of the CCC, claimed that "every CCC camp [was] a small town."[74] And CCC informational pamphlets advertised that

> the CCC offers a real opportunity to young men who are willing to work, and who look forward to being self-supporting and progressive American citizens. We want young men who believe in our form of government, who love their country, who share the desire to develop its resources and keep the spirit of independence and self-reliance alive in all its people.

As part of the idea of the self-reliance,

> each CCC camp is a small town of about 200 men. It has a commanding officer who acts as "mayor" of the town. Just as a town has its local laws, a camp has its rules and regulations.[75]

Of course, the description was inaccurate, because the CO had far greater disciplinary powers than a mayor, and more importantly, he was not elected. Nor were the rules and regulations formulated in the same democratic style as laws were in the small town.

But the myth was necessary largely because most of the enrollees could relate to it. After all, the majority of them came from small towns and communities, and the CCC helped perpetuate a Tocquevillian idea of America that many of them had internalized from their youth. As I mentioned, though, there were camps which governed themselves, at least in part. These camps functioned as autonomous units of production, making their own decisions concerning the procurement of food and other items, their relationships with nearby communities, and the internal behavior of the enrollees. Some of the more successful camps developed schemes by which the enrollees themselves monitored their own behavior and sat on disciplinary hearing committees when necessary.[76] Self-governance also helped campers work together to make camp life a tolerable, and sometimes even enjoyable, experience.[77] Camps that practiced even a modicum of self-governance were more successful at retaining boys, and keeping them satisfied, than those which did not.[78] Finally, many camps allowed the boys to run their own newspapers, in which they wrote, edited, and published a wide variety of articles. Some of these articles demonstrated quite a bit of knowledge about the outside world, and a sophisticated understanding of the depression.

Sometimes self-governance was a political necessity, as in the case of native Americans, for the CCC left the administration of these camps in the hands of the Bureau of Indian Affairs. And the bureau often allowed the enrollees themselves and their appointed leaders to make decisions about camp culture and education. Some of the programs in these camps developed in conjunction with tribal councils, and much of the work done by these camps was on the reservation.[79]

Toward the end of the term of the CCC, F.D.R. and the directors, along with some of the most enthusiastic and capable young men in the program, tried to establish a leadership school to train some of the enrollees to run their camps. Named Camp William James, this school was established in rural Vermont by a group of young Dartmouth students led by a professor of philosophy, Eugen Rosenstock-Huessy. Camp William James was founded in Sharon, Vermont, as "an experimental leadership training camp whose purpose was to explore the means for turning the CCC into a form of national service."[80] Its founders wished to train college boys to lead the CCC and to convert it into a permanent school of national service. Soon Camp William James became more inclusive, letting in women, and training rural and working class boys for leadership positions too. The camp's founders designed Camp William James to be the first CCC camp to integrate work and education in a program accessible to all young Americans. They also wished to elevate the intellectual standards of the camp, after complaining about the intellectual life in other camps.

> I can see very definitely, however, that without the stimulus of contact with a group of boys educated as I am, and without the drive toward a worthwhile objective, I could very easily be lulled into the perpetual routine of chores, meals, jobs, sleep, and so on.[81]

The young men involved believed that they were fulfilling the goals of William James's "war against nature." They believed that they were bringing the upper and upper middle classes into the CCC in order to toughen them up, and enlighten the other enrollees to particular political and social ideas.[82] The camp based itself on socialistic principles like self-government, work-sharing, and moral enlightenment. They hoped to create the moral equivalent of war that James had prophecied, in contrast to the moral complement to war favored by CCC directors.[83]

The camp was founded, in the words of its director, because the CCC was becoming an appendage of the army. "Boredom, playing cards, loafing are the results of being an adjunct to the Army.[84] And other founders complained that army rule and bureaucratic regulations inhibited the spirit necessary to foster an enlightened and spirited community of involved men and women.[85] With some fanfare, Camp William James opened on January 11, 1941.

Unfortunately, the camp was doomed to failure almost as soon as it began, for it could not sustain an integrated and democratic structure *and* remain simultaneously within the administrative sphere of the CCC. A week before its establishment, the Department of Agriculture imposed a certain structure on it "in order to give [it] direction." This meant: (1) unified control by the Federal Security Agency, (2) unified command within the camp (the director, Rosenstock-Huessy, would be in charge of the whole camp like a typical CO, despite his objections), and (3) local groups would participate in the planning of the projects.[86] This third requirement was significant in that it involved local residents in some of the decision-making of the camp—something that was missing from other camps. But it also obstructed the camp leadership from choosing projects because this contravened the imperative of productivity. Yet the camp never received the opportunity to prove itself as a democracy. These and future regulations prevented the camp from becoming an autonomous political unit and community.

At the same time, the camp developed a bad reputation. The *Boston Globe* published a report that the camp trained "Nazis," largely due to Rosenstock-Huessy's ties with German work camps in the 1920s.[87] McEntee, the director of the CCC at the time, worried that this would cause problems for the organization, especially at a time when he needed to convince Congress of the CCC's value in fighting the approaching war. So he withdrew his support for the experiment on February 17, 1941. Bureaucrats within the CCC and its oversight agencies followed suit, claiming that it was a "dangerous experiment," and an "assault on bureaucratic standards."[88] In the meantime certain congressmen, mostly Republican, concluded that the camp was a center of socialist activity, and began hearings and investigations into its operations.

On March 6, 1941, a genuinely radical event occurred: twenty-four men within the camp severed their connection with the government and set up an alternative Camp William James in Bellows Falls, Vermont. This began, in the words of one of them, the "interim" camp phase. The bureaucracy had defeated the attempt to establish a CCC camp on truly democratic grounds, so the enrollees established their own private cooperative.[89]

Meanwhile, the Sharon site was shut down, disappointing many of the participants.

The democratization of the CCC, the training of leaders for it, the aid to local farmers in their work, the inauguration of a reception center to encourage resettlement—all of these things were well-known in principle. But there was admittedly not much to show for the almost two years of work and sacrifice which had been given to the attempt to translate them into reality.[90]

Instead, the new private camp got private funding for a time from the Goodwill Fund and other private charities. A woman's auxiliary camp formed, as did like-minded camps in Alaska and Mexico. And plans were made to establish similar camps in Europe and Asia. But after a few months the funding dried up, and the men dropped out. Finally, with the inception of the military draft, the camp lost all its current and future manpower. On December 12, 1941, only a few days after the United States entered World War II, the experiment known as Camp William James ended.

Rosenstock-Huessy, in a eulogistic letter written after the demise of the camp, blamed F.D.R. and the bureaucrats for destroying the camp for political reasons. He commented that "we failed because the President, who felt that his definition of citizenship was momentarily *challenged* by ours, had to choose his definition *over* ours."[91] Rosenstock-Huessy complained that the bureaucratic organization of the camps superseded the imperative of teaching one the power of self-government, and the justice that one learns working within an independent community.

The democratic involvement of the enrollees was an important aspect to some camps, but one that was, unfortunately, not practiced with the kind of regularity necessary to involve all the men in the democratic process. Too few men actually had the opportunity to make decisions in the camp, and too many of them were simply told what to do. This is not surprising, given the bureaucratic nature of the organization, the age of the men, and the attitude of the administrators and camp commanders and instructors that these boys needed direction. But in Camp William James many men, given the opportunity to govern themselves, took to it with good cheer and competence.

The political order of the CCC and its camps, then, precluded the sort of democratic participation, individual initiative, and communal development that may have offered an alternative to the ethic of conforming citizenship. The CCC was a worthwhile institution in that it temporarily employed thousands of desperate young men at a time when the future of all America looked bleak. But the political structure of the CCC did not necessarily permit changes in the political or intellectual development of the young person, nor did it capably set an example of participatory democracy. And the times when enrollees tried to take matters into their own hands and govern themselves with complete autonomy, the federal government quickly prevented them from acting further.

The Encampment for Citizenship and AFSC Camps

In the 1950s and early 1960s, Algernon Black and others developed a program, under the aegis of the Ethical Culture Society, which sought to train young people for the responsibilities of citizenship. The founders criticized the CCC for organizing its camps "for labor, not for education," and claimed that it passed up a great opportunity to explore social issues with young people.[92] As an alternative they established camps that emphasized learning, participation, and international community. These camps differed from CCC camps in that (1) enrollees governed themselves to a remarkable degree; (2) the camps were co-educational, and involved young people from all over the world; (3) the educational programs were philosophical and political, indeed lessons were given in political activism; and (4) the program was not a creation of the federal government.

At the core of the camp program rested educational practices focused on political and social problems, economic problems, and international issues. Each educational unit encompassed a lecture and question-and-answer session, a small discussion group of ten to twelve people, and then a specialized workshop on a particular problem. At the same time, each camp governed itself through weekly town meetings. The most important lesson taught was citizenship in the community. Along these lines, participation was taught as a process for its own sake, regardless of the actual content involved in civic engagement.[93]

In 1962, Berkeley researchers published a study of these camps, and their findings were very encouraging. The study showed that the camps attracted a diverse and heterogeneous lot, but that many if not most of the participants were already liberal, democratic, and tolerant in their beliefs.[94] Virtually all the campers enjoyed their summer, and attendance at all events was excellent. There were very few disturbances or incidents of discontent, and those exceptions were "idiosyncratic."[95] The results of the experiment strengthened the democratic character of the camps. Campers became more tolerant of each other's views and of racial diversity, they retained a service-work and activist orientation, and they became slightly less susceptible to prestige symbols and propaganda.[96] The researchers argue that the educational and democratic nature of the camps contributed to this, and that it also led to an increase in the sense of community, as campers began to see their peers as "reference groups."[97]

In follow-ups to the study, the researchers determined that the camps had relatively strong immediate effects on the campers, and weaker long-run effects. In the short-term, campers remained tolerant and politically active, and they moved away from individualism toward more group-oriented activity. They also became less willing to stereotype the average American.[98] Most importantly, they became more open in discussing controversial issues, especially at their colleges and universities, though it did not affect their performances at these institutions of higher learning. In the long term, the only effect that seemed to remain was sustained political activism.[99] In sum, these politically engaged work camps seemed to have been very popular with campers, and successful in democratic education. It behooves planners of national service to look more closely at Black's creation.

These planners should also review a study written by Henry Riecken, then professor of psychology at Harvard University in the 1950s. Riecken examined a number of work camps established by the American Friends Service Committee (AFSC). He noted that their structure differed from other work camps of the past, including the CCC. First, they were democratic, egalitarian, and oriented to the community (both the camp community, and the nearby local communities). Second, the enrollees were individuals devoted to public service for religious or humanitarian reasons. Third, technological efficiency and economic productivity were sacrificed in these camps for the achievement of "absolute values" accompanying Quaker beliefs.[100]

These conditions had some important implications for the young people who worked under them. Using survey and observational methods, Riecken noted some important long-term and short term effects of these camps on the participants themselves. In the short run, the participants had become more democratic, less prejudiced and less authoritarian. They had also become more tolerant of other people, yet at the same time began to judge the average American more harshly.[101] They had also become more socially concerned, and more communal, yet they displayed an increasing need for autonomy, and for a "defiance of social conventions."[102] Finally, they had become more self-confident, and looked upon new opportunities as means of achievement.[103]

These results are not as paradoxical as they seem, and they indicate the effects of service organizations designed to educate individuals politically, and to allow them to participate significantly in the decisions of the group. For at the same time that enrollees felt closer to other members of their camp, and to the nearby communities, they also realized that their lives were not typical for most Americans. They not only learned to treat their fellow human beings with more kindness, but they also learned to critique the fundamental values of their society. And they began to understand that American values were not necessarily the sorts of values that one ought to promote without deliberating about them. They discovered that the lifestyle of the average American is not something to be emulated, yet they also knew that those beliefs could be changed only through tolerance, and an appreciation of otherness.

Riecken resurveyed the participants some months after they

had finished their terms in the camps and found a "high degree of durability of the changes induced by work camps, even ten months afterward."[104] Beyond this, he noted some additional results: (1) an increased desire on the part of the former participants to enter the teaching and social work professions; (2) those who retained the changed beliefs tended to go home to communities that reinforced these new beliefs; and (3) those most affected by the experience had had a more romantic rather than scientific view of it.[105] Finally, Riecken noted a curious effect in terms of individuals' perceptions of others as well as themselves.

> The effect of a work camp summer is not to make campers perceive and understand their fellow citizens better; rather the experience seems to develop a kind of self-conscious common sense of one's difference from his larger society, and to make him even more aware of being a member of a selected group that does not agree with the views of that larger society.[106]

This might indicate that community comes from an understanding of otherness—that a service experience may not help someone understand others better, but it may create a feeling of otherness in the individual. Individuals, rather than being inculcated with a set of values common to all, may accentuate their own differences after engaging in service. This contradicts the position argued by Janowitz and Moskos, and points toward the possibility of a critical national service experience. For the understanding of otherness may foster a critical eye in each participant. This requires conditions under which individuals can express that critical eye, under which they can return the gaze of federal and social authorities.

Riecken concluded with four recommendations for future work camp experiences: (1) the camps must be democratic, and the leaders must share responsibility with the participants for the governance of those camps; (2) the camps must create a good rapport with the local communities they service; (3) do not force group solidarity onto a camp, for this alienates some members; and (4) follow up the experience by providing similar lessons within home communities.[107] None of these recommendations are, at present, being considered by national service planners, at least in those programs which require camps. But the last problem is especially acute, for despite all the rhetoric over national service, these planners have presented very few ideas about how the participants will conduct themselves civically. One should not have to remind planners that civic service is not a problem only for the young.

Katimavik

Finally, national service planners should also examine a very interesting, federally sponsored service program in Canada called "Katimavik" (an Inuit word meaning "meeting place"). Created in 1977 out of a plan by Jacques Hebert and others called Youth Camps for World Peace, Katimavik fell victim to budget cuts in the spring of 1986, and has not been revived since. Yet over its nine-year existence, it hosted over twenty thousand participants, and was considered popular throughout Canada. Its two central purposes were the promotion of community services, and the development of a sense of Canadian national identity. Given the historic make up of that country, though, this latter goal was somewhat controversial. Nonetheless, Katimavik methods reflected the multicultural composition of Canada, and planners and enrollees attempted to accomodate as many different ideas about Canada as possible.

To this end, the structure of the camps was rather unique. Each group's home was located in a residential neighborhood of some city or town in Canada, and was composed of twelve individuals and a group leader. Of the twelve, four were Francophone and eight were Anglophone. Participants committed themselves for at least nine months. Every three months each participant changed homes and provinces, so that by the end of the nine months everyone lived in two English-speaking provinces and one French-speaking province (Quebec or New Brunswick). Within these homes, the participants all worked and made decisions collectively.

Each participant traveled independently to the home, and did not have to go through any training or educational centers. Each was paid a stipend of one dollar per day, and given a thousand-dollar bonus at the end of her or his stay, though room and board were free. They were expected to work on projects helpful to the local community, usually the renovation of public facilities or social work in the community. Some were even allowed to enroll in the military as a means of fulfilling their commitment. The code of conduct was minimal, especially in comparison to the CCC: no drugs or alcohol, no sex with fellow volunteers, and accept a fair share of the work load. Beyond this, all other rules and regulations, including those governing the daily routine, had to be agreed upon by the house residents.

The educational opportunities in the homes were tremendous, especially the teaching of second-language skills. Most participants spent two or three weeks every trimester living with a local family to broaden their language skills, and to understand the community. Evenings were devoted to group discussion, and the group leader occasionally taught general education classes. They discussed issues in international development and related them to particular needs of the community. Many homes also grew their own food, and each home recycled, and so taught conservation.

All of Katimavik's components "were viewed in terms of their ability to contribute to the development of a participant's sense of social responsibility, citizenship, and self-confidence."[108] And its success in these contributions remains unparalleled in the history of service programs in North America. An astounding seventy-five percent of all participants stayed the full term, and fewer than twenty percent of those who dropped out were gone before the end of the first month.[109] Eighty-six percent of its 1985 participants recommended the program as "useful" or "very useful."[110] An evaluation report praised the program for "giving participants a knowledge and understanding of Canada."[111]

Nevertheless, some proponents of national service in this country dismiss the accomplishments of Katimavik and focus on its shortcomings. They complain that it was not an appropriate model for national service here for a number of reasons. Charles Moskos faults it for demonstrating that a "national service program with multiple objectives creates a fuzzy public image." Moskos contends that its emphasis on personal development, social services, and Canadian cultural identity sometimes worked at cross-purposes in the minds of politicians.[112] There is evidence, however, that the budget for Katimavik was cut for other reasons: The military was against it (despite its military option), and the Mulroney government was on a budget-cutting spree.[113] Bernard McMullen and Phyllis Snyder, in a study for Public/Private Ventures, claim that Katimavik was not ended because of "program failure, mismanagement or serious design flaws," and imply that it was the ideology of the program that offended the public.[114] However, the founder of Katimavik, Senator Jacques Hebert, went on a hunger strike for twenty-one days in the House of Parliament in Ottawa in an effort to prevent those cuts, and he attracted widespread support for his cause. Though he ultimately lost the fight, he demonstrated that the Canadian public had a fairly clear idea of the ideals for which Katimavik stood.[115] Sherraden and Eberly thus suggest rightly that "Katimavik was as much a movement as an organization."[116]

McMullen and Snyder criticize the plan for two essential reasons: Katimavik did not "emphasize the development of mature work behavior, discipline or the acquisition of skills," and it was inefficient and unproductive.[117] Yet these criticisms are unfair. First, the authors of this study—the only one in the United States—do not support these claims with a single piece of evidence. They present no statistics on any aspect of the productivity of Katimavik, and they offer no evidence that participants did not develop "mature work behavior"—they simply assert it.[118] Second, the tenor of their criticism indicates that the agenda for American national service is different, concentrating on productivity and discipline. Throughout this study I have tried to argue against this mentality. In fact, it could be argued that Katimavik was so successful among its participants precisely because it did not impart a productivity ethic or discipline "wayward" youth. Concerning Katimavik, one should emphasize not why members of the administration did not like the program, or what the politics of the budget cut were, but rather what the young people involved in the program had to say about it.

Furthermore, Katimavik was one of the few service programs to offer a genuinely *moral* equivalent to war. Katimavik brought the "gilded" youth into contact with the people, and helped those youth educate themselves about the social problems afflicting Canada. At the same time it accomplished this through participatory and peaceful means. Most importantly, it sought to raise the educational level of these individuals, and did not relegate them to the status of day laborer or servant.

Within various past programs of civilian service one sees the potential for a participatory program in which individuals enlighten themselves and engage freely in the civic life of communities, but planners of service programs do not seem to want these participatory programs to flourish. Either they have actively sought to destroy such practices (like Camp William James), or they have ignored other examples of participatory service organizations (like the Encampment for Citizenship and the AFSC camps), or they have recommended that educational or participatory programs be turned into programs emphasizing work and production (like Katimavik). Finally, the narrow yet pragmatic CCC conception of citizenship is aimed at a conforming citizen, who may not be the type contemporary proponents of national service admire. Thus, supporters of national service must look elsewhere if they are to develop democratic, participatory, and civic, ideas about how to engage people in civilian public service.

Part II

A Democratic Alternative to Service

CHAPTER EIGHT

National Service in Institutional Perspective

Thus far, I have criticized the theory and practice underlying contemporary proposals for national service. In the previous chapter, I suggest that participatory, political community service is possible, but that service planners choose to ignore particular institutional structures contributing to such a program. In the remainder of this book I formulate an alternative argument around which debates over national service ought to focus. That is, I offer the kind of argument one must make *if* one were to imagine a national service program which focused on civic education. I do this for two reasons: (1) to demonstrate that it is possible to think about alternative institutional arrangements for national service, and (2) to highlight just how difficult these alternatives would be to achieve. The political difficulties in achieving this institutional change weakens my support for national service as a policy instrument.

This raises some questions. First, why should Americans establish a new institution to educate people politically? That is, why don't Americans try to inculcate citizenship and educate individuals politically through more traditional means—through parties, the media, a citizen-militia, and schools? Second, what would the organization of this new institution be? How should national service be implemented so that citizens fulfill their obligations as human beings and political animals? The following chapters offer answers to these questions.

CONTEMPORARY AMERICAN INSTITUTIONS
AND CITIZENSHIP EDUCATION

If, as proponents of national service argue, America is in need of citizenship education, to what extent do its current institutions provide it? Moreover, to what degree can those institutions which may not educate citizens be reformed in order to do so? Most contemporary political institutions claim responsibility for educating some sector of the American public politically. Political parties and interest groups have become training grounds for political leaders and specialists, and a party education is invaluable in understand-

157

ing both the possibilities and the vagaries of political power. The media is the means by which many, if not all, Americans are informed about the world. The military offers discipline and a code of honor for those who wish to defend the modern state, and it trains its leaders in political negotiating. Finally, the school system is often responsible at all levels for the democratic education of future citizens—a position held by American educators since John Dewey.

However, none of these institutions educates Americans sufficiently or equally for the responsibilities of active citizenship, nor is political education their first priority. Moreover, where they do educate individuals politically, they often impart particular political viewpoints and intellectual methods, often reinforcing the individualist ideology dominant in America. These institutions fail to cultivate either a participatory ethic or political enlightenment in the modern citizen. Let me examine each of these a bit more closely to see why this is so.

Political Parties

Since the earliest days of parliamentary democracy, political parties have held a special role in the political education of the citizens—a role which they continue in more or less the same form today. They socialize elites, put political ideas into practice, inform members about political issues, and bring election messages to the general citizenry. Some of them occasionally try to teach the virtues of collective participation, and to instill in their members a sense of the public good.

One could argue that political parties are a vital means, if not the primary means, by which citizens educate themselves about politics and society. Party competition informs citizens of their immediate political choices, the general conflicts within their society, and the range of alternative means for ameliorating those conflicts. In this way, parties shape political reality for the citizen, and simplify that reality to make it easier for the average citizen to grasp.[1] Especially in the twentieth century, parties have accepted distinctive roles in political education. Mass membership parties, in the early part of the century, were often comprised of issue-oriented members who wanted to educate the general electorate toward their ideas (as opposed to, say, party machines, which distribute patronage positions). Even today, political activists educate citizens not only about party preferences but the general issues of the day. Consequently, parties contribute not only to partisan education, but also, more generally, to political education.

Political parties are among the most important mediating institutions between the individual citizen and the state.[2] And they effect participation, for people can channel their interests through the party and influence policy in a democratic manner. Thus individuals learn politics together—they can participate in a political structure which gives them some sense of collective solidarity, rather than petitioning government as individuals seeking to make policy. At the same time, the party teaches the citizen the mechanics of political activism, and presents that citizen with clear and distinct policy options and political ideas.[3]

Furthermore, some argue that the political party ought to be a stable pillar of civic unity in a democracy. The political party not only channels particular interests (through interest-group influence, for example), but it also supports the state. Indeed it expresses the political aspirations of a particular segment of the citizenry of a nation, which in turn reproduces certain political traditions.[4] The political system, comprised of a variety of political parties, defends the democratic honor of the nation, and expresses some of that nation's most cherished principles publicly. Political parties, then, can be more than a means of democratic participation, they can be a source of virtue. In Burke's terms, they are bodies "of men united, for promoting by their joint endeavors the national interest, upon some particular principles in which they are all agreed."[5] Parties embody the ways each democracy chooses to govern itself, and they signify how each republic arranges its institutions. Thus, if the nation is virtuous, they represent its virtue; and they symbolize a standard about which individuals ought to be educated.

Finally, political parties often help stir political interest among many citizens. They focus the energies of political activists and bring them together with like-minded people. During election campaigns they interest the general electorate in broad political issues. Most importantly, though, parties involve people in political affairs and decision-making, and so are an appropriate vehicle for the politicization of citizens. They are assumed to be more appropriate than pressure groups, for example, because they channel citizen activity across a wide range of issues, rather than into only one or two causes or interests. In short, political parties provide an important impetus to political education—namely, the interest required to pursue political ideals and put them into practice.

But these arguments, while in part true, do not tell the whole story. For political parties have changed throughout the years, and more importantly the *justifications* for them have changed as well. In the first place, their primary function is not necessarily the political education of the citizen or member. Epstein argues that their basic function is to help the political system structure the vote.[6] Outside of this basic function it is difficult to determine what, precisely, political parties should do. Political parties often function differently in different polities, according to the varied self-understandings of their members.[7] So political parties do not necessarily educate the citizens of a country.

Moreover, the educative function of parties is no longer considered as important as it once was. In the late nineteenth and early twentieth centuries, theorists envisioned parties as vehicles and forums of political deliberation and learning. Such theorists meant by education something more than simply informing voters of their choices or trying to sway their vote. They argued that parties were the public system by which individuals had the opportunity to make their voices heard. In this way, citizens teach and learn from other citizens. For instance, Woodrow Wilson believed that parties "should produce a high order of debate and thereby both encourage popular interest in public affairs and educate public opinion upon the issues of the day."[8] Henry Jones Ford maintained that parties ought to permit direct participation of the people "by popular interest in and discussion of public issues and officers."[9] The purpose of this educative function was to make government more responsible to the people, and parties were seen as the best means by which to do this.[10] These early theorists saw the need to reform parties, and use them as instruments of democratic control, not of bossism. Thus, education was a crucial link between the political leaders and the voters.

Yet education is not a function of political parties anymore, according to the analyses of many political scientists. In fact, it is almost impossible to even see the issue discussed in the literature on the subject today.[11] For instance, Martin Wattenberg lists eleven functions of political parties, excluding education.[12] David Price, in making a case for parties, does not defend the party system on grounds of education.[13] These and other political scientists consider political organization to be the most important issue surrounding parties today. They argue that parties today must think in terms of how to lead, how to be more responsible to the people, and how to win elections. Yet effective political organization requires an educated citizenry. Moreover, it demands a citizenry that has confidence in the parties both to teach them about political ideas and issues and provide them with a forum where they can make their voices heard.

It could be simply a matter of laying emphasis on different aspects of parties. For example, one very famous function of parties is to socialize conflict—to provide an organized means by which conflicting interests can talk to each other with civility.[14] From another perspective, to socialize conflict could also mean to generate discussion—to provide opportunities various interests to participate in discussion. By focusing on the socializing aspect to parties, theorists emphasize the control that parties have over individuals and groups in society. So long as socialization and control are the focus of party theory, education cannot play an important role in justifying political parties.

Moreover, thought about parties on all levels remains ambivalent. For example, intellectuals have always been very skeptical of political parties and the special interests influencing them. This skepticism originates in the very justification for our system of government: Madison's indictment of factions in *Federalist no. 10*. Others, like John Adams or Tocqueville, viewed parties as a necessary evil of free government. Also, the logic of party competition puzzles those searching for a communitarian order to America. For parties divide the electorate as much as they unite it. In this sense, socializing conflict institutionalizes it, and one might ask how institutionalized conflict and civic consciousness are to be reconciled.

Modern political parties can also confuse the electorate in general. Catch-all parties are weak because they do not express their principles very clearly to their constituents and to the voters at large. While they do transmit clear messages, and may in fact teach people about particular issues, it is often difficult to say what any particular party stands for today. Moreover, any one party has trouble expressing the political will of a particular community.[15] Therefore, the party system cannot offer precise or coherent *arguments* to the electorate, and cannot serve as the best model of political deliberation for voters. The very function of parties to socialize conflict precludes them from taking a clear stand on many issues, yet it is this "stand" that gives the party integrity. When a party possesses integrity it transmits its messages more confidently, but more importantly, it offers the electorate a public forum for deliberation. I do not suggest that parties cannot provide this forum, but until party elites and intellectuals begin to reconceptualize parties in this fashion, it will be difficult to imagine parties as a vehicle of political education.

Moreover, the modern, catch-all party can hinder public participation in government. Its decentralized structure contributes to a certain measure of political stability, but it may also inhibit the ability of parties to generate political ideas on a national level and diffuse them among all its members.[16] At the same time it can become an institutional constraint on those who would wish to be active and influential on the national level, because (1) one can be paralyzed by indecision when faced with the many points of access, or be ignorant of the most effective point of access, and (2) because developing a sense of social solidarity in a party with such a diverse constituency as, say, the Democratic party is difficult. This can retard the establishment of integrated political communities necessary to the political self-understandings of the electorate. I have already argued that coming to self-understanding is a part of what it means to be educated politically.

The national parties are not always forums for political ideas either. Bureaucrats formulate most policy, and many, if not all, of the political ideas which parties present on their platforms are developed in think tanks either associated with the party or only nominally independent of party governance.[17] Politicians are rarely the source for innovative or systematic political thinking, and individual citizens often contribute only to local party discussions. Furthermore, the ideas presented within political parties, either for discussion at the national level or in party platforms, are often so vague that one would be hard pressed to call them ideas at all. Alan Ware argues that this weakens the educational role of parties.

> Conflicting messages, ambiguous stances and the obliteration of political issues by transforming them into some other issue are all ways in which the party can create "white noise," which can both distort immediate electoral choice and fail to contribute to longer term political education of the electorate.[18]

This is especially true during political campaigns, when the party mobilizes to educate the citizenry on the virtues of its candidate.[19]

Also, political parties may not yet be the model of democracy one would want other organizations to emulate.[20] Parties do not always allow for equal participation by all individuals who wish to join them. They privilege certain groups at the expense of others (e.g. labor unions at the expense of consumer groups). This segregation is usually a function of the money that certain groups, or individuals, contribute to a party. The subsequent influence of interest groups on political parties can inhibit the participatory possibilities of political parties.[21] Certain regional party structures remain which do not even pretend to be participatory—for example, the local machines in some big cities. Parties themselves are also being run less by interested and active citizens, and more by party professionals: experts, technocrats, and media specialists who want to mobilize all party resources for the efficient election of candidates.[22] As the "experts" gain in power, the purpose of parties as *public* forums for political education and activism declines, because this purpose is no longer part of the electoral logic of the institution.[23]

On the contrary, an organization could be developed that harnesses the political virtues of parties—their ethic of political activism and their basic interest in political enlightenment—but that transmits those virtues more consciously. National service could politicize individuals (i.e. raise their interest in politics)—not for any partisan reasons, but to generate enthusiasm in them for all sorts of politics, and to teach them how to intervene politically in order to make institutions more participatory.[24]

Media

Some have argued that the media serve to educate citizens adequately in late-twentieth-century America. Either they claim that the improved technology of the media helps people become politically aware or active, or they argue that the institutional structure and practices of the media educate citizens. The first group contends that the new technologies, along with a proper organization of information, help inform and mobilize thousands of voters who would otherwise remain apathetic toward, and ignorant of, the political process.[25] For instance, Benjamin Barber contends that new media technologies enhance the possibility of citizen participation through electronic balloting, initiative and referenda processes, the dissemination of information, and "TV democracy."[26]

The empirical evidence for this appears to be mixed at best. F. Christoper Arterton, in a study of thirteen attempts to increase political participation through the use of modern technologies, concludes that new technologies do not enhance democracy so much as do the political purposes to which those technologies are put.[27]

More specifically, the new media fail where direct participation is encouraged or where plebiscites are staged to increase citizen power. The new media are successful, however, where efforts are made to "bring citizens into contact with government officials."[28] Arterton takes this to be an encouraging sign for democratic participation, but one can argue that even with these media, citizens cannot influence politics and policies directly. However, though these technologies do not enhance the participatory capabilities of individuals by any great means, they can bring them into contact with people who can enlighten them (i.e., "representatives"—political, media, and otherwise). In this very limited sense, then, teledemocracy may sustain republicanism, rather than expand democracy.

Kenneth Laudon, in his study of technology and political participation, argues that communications technology will not increase the participatory opportunites for most people. After testing the impact of such technology on a League of Women Voters organization in New Jersey he concludes that modern communications technology will not be cheap or simple enough for most ordinary citizens and groups to use; though he suggests that if they could use it, such use would have some constructive political consequences. New technology will be appropriated by certain groups:

> The appearance of a new political resource in the form of citizen technology—regardless of how it is organized or what technology is used—is likely to be utilized by the most politically skilled and organized groups in the population.[29]

These groups are, of course, large corporations and trade organizations. In fact, the new technology will not be "interactive," but rather "ersatz versions attached to very profitable mass participation media."[30] Thus, new technologies could increase corporate profit, and extend the gap between classes of individuals even further, rather than offer all individuals an opportunity to participate in politically meaningful forums.

There are also philosophical arguments against relying on media technologies to increase political participation. One is that such technology reproduces the atomistic society, and that the new technologies are individuating, bureaucratic, and incapable of engendering true community. Amy Gutmann makes this case well, regarding the influence of technology on children:

Pressing keys in response to messages that appear on the screen is not likely to develop moral understandings or commitments of the sort stimulated by face-to-face associations with family and friends. Nor is technological interaction a process by which children are likely to learn how to translate their moral understandings or commitments into politics by arguing, negotiating, and compromising with people who have conflicting commitments.

Furthermore,

by sitting in front of a television set, children learn that it is normal to listen, but not to respond, to absorb information but not to inquire, to be loyal or to exit but not to raise their voice in criticism, and so on.[31]

Children grow into adults; thus, television may foster uncritical acceptance of the world as it is presented. The possibility of a two-way media that enhances participation is very slight, and even were it to be developed it could transform a public, communal process—politics—into a private affair. The notion that TV, or any other advanced technology, activates citizens may be true only at a loss to the civic practices of the nation.

Moreover, technology is not a neutral mechanism for human interaction. Television and computers are not impartial toward the particular sorts of societies that employ them. On the contrary, they fit only into certain forms of community—large corporations, military bureaucracies, centralizing capitalist states—while they exclude others—local communities, neighborhood churches, grassroots organizations. The very nature of high technology advances means that larger numbers of people can be brought together more efficiently. The computer and the television deny the possibility of small communities because their design and use presuppose that they aggregate ever larger numbers of individuals. So they are not merely technologies, they are not merely means by which diverse ends are pursued, but they imply certain ends over others in their very application. Thus, arguments for the uses of the new media as means to inculcate participatory values or even civic virtue are wrong, because they perceive technology incorrectly. Technology is the product of an atomistic society seeking not only to reproduce itself, but to do so more efficiently.[32] The community that produces modern technology need not be a particularly participatory one, and the technologies themselves do not remake it into a participatory community; rather technology serves to further the interests of the institutions and groups in society that benefit materially from it. It enlarges the society where the individual citizen feels powerless, and so it is antithetical to decentralized political structures.

Beyond the technology of the media, the actual practices of the contemporary media are problematic. Despite the contentions of its members, the form and content of the print and electronic media are not objective.[33] The members of the media have particular political positions, and newspapers and television stations play a very important role in agenda-setting.[34] Even the most public and enlightened of networks—public broadcasting—contributes to what Michael Robinson has called "videomalaise."[35]

The activity of political commentary—which, in theory, offers a diversity of ideas and examples of reasoned political argument—does not necessarily function as a source of political enlightenment. For instance, Sheldon Wolin argues that political commentary interprets "the system so as to render its nature unproblematic."[36] Political commentators select the forms of the issues and set the agenda, and serve as counselors to politicians. Furthermore, political commentators do not cultivate the independent, informed citizen, but rather help perpetuate the passive, ignorant, alienated individual. Within the context of a society constituted by passive individuals,

> political education by commentary is not intended to galvanize the citizenry into action but to keep it gently oscillating between resignation and hope. Commentary accomplishes this by purveying an illusion that when the citizen reads or listens to a commentary, he is deliberating about politics. He is encouraged to believe that he is being asked to make up his mind on an issue or to indicate his policy preference. Among the functions of commentary one of the most important is to establish limits beyond which deliberation ought not to stray. For the commentator, politics is typically the art of the possible within the limits set by the existing political economy. His task is not to combat the unthinkable, but to avoid the unutterable.[37]

Thus, even those most responsible for the direct political education of the citizenry fail in their duty to open up the public space to free inquiry. Indeed many argue that this is inevitable in a political economy that works best without participatory or communitarian values.[38]

This is wrong not because the media are value-biased, for lively political debate should depend on a variety of media offering a wide range of political positions.[39] But the American media, in its illusory quest for objectivity, helps contribute to political passivity and indifference. By not staking out particular political positions, and by not allowing the alternative media a larger say in the political debate, the mainstream media reproduce a citizenry that imagines objectivity to be a virtue. Too often, though, such objectivity translates into ignorance, because people do not care to know about a particular issue if they are not given moral reasons why that issue is important, or if they are not challenged to defend their own position by political analysts. At the same time, they are not offered alternatives to the existing political economy, and so, falsely believe that the range of political debate is presented fully by the dominant media. Many people perceive this range of debate insufficient to stir them to become active: the limited alternatives do nothing to affect the essential problems of society, and so they hesitate to accept any of the alternatives. Even more sadly, such disaffected citizens do not even know how to think about the fundamental problems of their society, because news media analysis is relatively superficial.[40]

The structure of media organizations also hinders the teaching of participatory values, because they are bureaucratic organizations employing a rigid chain of command whose ownership is in the hands of a very small number of people.[41] In other words, being a member of a media organization is not necessarily conducive to learning a participatory ethic. And where employees try to buy out of the organization (like the employees who sought to purchase the Gary, Indiana, *Post-Tribune*), they have often been blocked by large media corporations (like Knight-Ridder). Thus, at times journalists and other employees wishing to learn the virtues of self-management have been stymied by a centralized and powerful system of media organization. In short, neither the public who consumes its products nor the employees who work for it benefit from corporate media practice.

In conclusion, both the technology of the media and its institutional organization often do not offer individuals oppportunities to participate in their political education. Beyond this, they can actually inhibit citizen interest in politics. An institution ought to be available for citizens to develop both an interest in politics and a desire to participate in it. Unlike the media, this institution should not be based exclusively on modern technology and its atomistic implications. Rather, such an institution ought to instill in Americans an appreciation for their local communities and a desire to become active with other people. The institution should bring people together in equal standing toward a *collective* search for public excellence not individuate their political activity, or force them into a bureaucratic organization which operates under a hierarchical structure. A properly constructed national service program might succeed in promoting this collective, participatory search.

Indeed an institution like national service might bring participatory values to the media. For example, through it people could learn how to run their own newspapers or television stations. People so educated would be more informed about the political life of their communities, and they would learn techniques of publishing or television production. Moreover, such a program could use certain media technologies to create local community awareness on issues, offering alternative newspapers or radio service to towns and villages.[42] Finally, national service participants might come to a greater global understanding by participating in short-wave radio programs and informing their neighbors about ideas and issues discussed elsewhere in the world. In all these ways, individuals empower themselves through the use of various media technologies, and learn to organize those technologies on fundamentally different grounds. Most importantly, they learn that technology and the media are not neutral instruments for the transmission of information.

Military

Can the military serve as a moral training ground for the citizens and future citizens of America? A number of sociologists and politicians seem to think so. They argue that the military can educate individuals toward civic virtue if it sustains the ideal of the citizen-soldier.[43] Indeed, some authors often tie in a program of national service to the military, maintaining that individuals must have the option of learning the virtues of the citizen-soldier.

From the American Revolution to World War II, military training was basic to citizenship education. The traditional ethos of the American military was grounded in the individual citizen-soldier. From the minutemen and the days of the earliest militias, the

American soldier was first a citizen who received discipline and nationalistic training through his participation in the military.[44]

Planners contend that the citizen-soldier learns the same basic lessons the national service participant does.

> Both citizen soldiers and citizen servers display a commitment to undertaking the duties of citizenship: both have agreed to spend a period of their lives for a civic purpose that is not going to be a lifetime career; both, for the common good, have temporarily stepped outside the cash-work nexus of the marketplace.[45]

The citizen-soldier, then, contributes to the civic possibilities of a nation because he is not a professional, because he remains a citizen first.[46] In contrasting this with the professionals in political parties, interest groups, the media, and the civil service, one sees democratic possibilities for citizenship training in the military. At least in theory the military treats all individuals equally.

Sociologists, like Moskos and Janowitz, contend that the military needs the citizen-soldier precisely because its growing professionalism endangers the civic nature of that institution. Janowitz, especially, laments the growing technocracy within the military and hopes that a program of military service, in conjunction with a mandatory program of national service, will diversify the military and restore an ethic of self-sacrifice and civic honor to the profession. He blames the all-volunteer force for helping erode the ethic of the citizen-soldier, and wishes to replace this program with a more universal requirement for citizen and military service.[47] In an ideal form of military service, soldiers will be trained for civic consciousness.

But what sort of training will this be? Moskos suggests that soldiers should receive "civics instruction stressing factual knowledge of American political forms."[48] But is this sufficient to a political education? At its worst the simple teaching of facts about American government can be jingoistic propaganda of the sort transmitted by the CCC. At its best, it perpetuates a kind of unreflective quality to American political life. In any event, one can debate what counts as a fact about American politics.[49] Citizens need more than "civics instruction," "factual knowledge," and "knowledge of American political forms." A civic education that develops the free citizen ought to nurture the ability to deliberate and criticize and to understand not just America but the world and America's place in it. As passive recipients of commonplaces about American government, the citizen-soldier acquires neither.[50] Indeed, such education functions as television does, by teaching people to be uncritical and to accept America and its place in the world.

Furthermore, other aspects of the military do much to inhibit rational thinking and the participatory ethic necessary for good citizenship. First, the military does not cultivate egalitarian or even participatory values.[51] The elements of its structure are the antitheses of a democratic community: This structure is hierarchical, operates under authoritarian decision-making, and subordinates deliberative reasoning to rule-following. Such a structure is anathema to the education of free citizens for it prevents them from learning how to make independent judgments. It is, in many ways, an example of the "disciplinary society."[52] Foucault argues that the citizen-soldier was possible only because of the particular disciplinary technologies available at the time regulating the individual. The myth of the militia, with its sense of independence and esprit de corps, belies the reality of a mass army: surveyed, normalized, and disciplined down to the most trivial motion. The autonomous and virile comrade-soldier is no more than a docile body upon whom thousands of physical, social, and intellectual regulations are placed.

At the same time, the military virtues—gentlemanly conduct, personal fealty, brotherhood, and the pursuit of glory—are no longer civic ones, at least in the professional military.[53] Such traditional virtues have been transformed over the past forty years by the bureaucratic state to such a degree that their original intent as supports for a community have been distorted. They now sustain a highly centralized and concentrated bureaucratic polity. Janowitz argues that the virtue of gentlemanly conduct has become much more vague in the military ranks. Personal fealty, originally offered to a particular individual (like a king or a prince), is now given to an office (the president or the commander-in-chief). In this sense, military loyalty has been displaced from individuals to an impersonal bureaucratic structure. Brotherhood has been worn down by bureaucratic procedure, and soldiers today care not so much about their fellow soldiers as they do the efficient administration of things. Finally the pursuit of glory has become a myth to sustain the institution. The glory of the battlefield as represented in military history now serves as "an idealized interpretation of past events designed to inspire the professional."[54] And those who perpetuate the myth of the valiant soldier to the public (Oliver

North is a recent example) often justify illegitimate military intervention in other parts of the world. Most importantly, where the
professional military falters, one cannot expect the citizen military
to learn from it; thus all these shortcomings could have counter-
parts among enlisted men.

Arguments for military reform and the extension of the citizen-
soldier concept reveal a sort of reasoning one could call "reverse
discrimination." The nature of the American economy forces many
blacks into joining the army to escape the ghetto.[55] Consequently,
as Moskos argues, civic education becomes all the more pressing,
because the all-volunteer force is "less representative" in terms of
social composition, and thus does not reflect the "civic culture" of
America.[56] Morris Janowitz argues that the military must increase
its "social representativeness" and the "educational qualifications
of its enrollees." More precisely, he states that "soldiers with heterogeneous backgrounds supply broader linkage between the military and larger society...[and] mixed educational units will have
higher standards of morality and personal conduct."[57] Translated
from sociological discourse, these social scientists argue that the
disproportionate number of blacks in the military is politically and
morally dangerous, because they do not reflect the values of the
average (i.e., white) American citizen. Civic education is vital,
therefore, in order to keep those blacks politically quiescent and to
assimilate them into white culture.[58]

Furthermore, for our purposes here, the military discriminates
in terms of age. That is, not everybody enlists in the army, only
those between the ages of eighteen and twenty-seven. So the vast
majority of people over the age of twenty-seven who lack the same
civic and democratic values do not have the opportunity of being
enlightened. For the problem of civic virtue, however defined, is
not a youth problem, but a problem that affects all adults, and
adults of all ages should be eligible, if not required, to serve in a
national service program. Civic deliberations demand that all people understand political ideas and issues, not a select few, thus
national citizenship education ought to be just that—national, no
exceptions.

Finally, the military would educate individuals inadequately
for civic participation because it is not meant to be a deliberative
body. It is not an institution designed for the discussion of the
goals of a community. It is the means by which the community car-
ries out already agreed-upon ends. Moreover the military requires
people to carry out ends with which they do not always agree, and

which they may think to be fundamentally unjust, thus making the institution even less a means of expressing oneself and understanding the purposes of one's community. In sum, the military, and the concept of the citizen-soldier is not the way to instill a participatory ethic in individuals, nor is it a way to enlighten those individuals as to the justice of their society.

Yet a national service program could provide a moral equivalent to the military. For instance, those who choose to enter the military could be obligated to enter national service also, in order to be educated civically and politically, and in order to appreciate the benefits of political participation. National service could thus serve as a means by which the former citizen-soldier could think critically about the political community he or she believes is worth defending. Or soldiers themselves could be required to serve on "literacy brigades," thus making them use their intellectual skills to serve this nation and others. At the same time, army units could be sent into this nation's troubled spots to keep order, not by armed violence, but by teaching residents the virtues they have learned as part of the armed forces.[59] In this way, the prestige of individual soldiers could be based on the fact that they are educated and skillful, not simply that they are soldiers. This would change the whole basis of how the military achieves prestige in a democratic society. And the military could participate in civil society, and not seem to be a unique or alien organization. Thus, it could be modernized and integrated into society, appeal more to all groups in society, and satisfy the intentions of sociologists like Janowitz and Moskos. In a rapidly changing international political context, where the logic of the Cold War must be reexamined, this idea of a socialized military takes on new relevance. In short, national service could be a vehicle through which the military becomes an agency of public political education.

Schools

Finally, the institution often given the responsibility for citizenship education is the public school system.[60] Ever since John Dewey's *Democracy and Education* educators have been arguing that their responsibility is to train students to be good democrats. Amy Gutmann's *Democratic Education* is the most recent, and sophisticated, philosophical defense of this position. Yet schools are not necessarily the appropriate vehicle for civic education and they do not address the problem of the civic education of *adults*. In this sense, an argument for national service might extend these sorts of arguments beyond the education of the child.

Gutmann contends that the public school system must nurture and develop "democratic virtue" in young citizens, by teaching them to deliberate and reason well.[61] The aim of a democracy is "conscious social reproduction"; thus its members must capably perpetuate their own ways of self-governance.[62] This is only possible where values of participation, association, self-respect, autonomy, and moral judgment are instilled into all people equally. Education is a democratic practice that asks all citizens to participate in their own education.

> The policies that result from our democratic deliberations [over educational policy] will not always be the right ones, but they will be more enlightened—by the values and concerns of the many communities that constitute a democracy—than those that would be made by unaccountable educational experts.[63]

Democracy in education, then, does not mean solving every problem, it means attending to those problems in a just manner; it means creating the political conditions for the training of the democratic citizen, and treating all citizens as actors in the educational process.

Gutmann maintains that democratic character is vital to both society and the individual. It fulfills a necessary condition of moral freedom: people must be robust enough morally not to tolerate injustice. At the same time, it is good for children not only to learn the conditions of moral freedom, but also to identify with their communities. Gutmann argues that the development of such moral character is possible through a concerted effort of state officials, parents, and educational experts. There must be a balance between these three groups in order to create the sort of educational policy which can inculcate democratic virtue. Democratic virtue can be achieved only where certain enabling conditions are fulfilled, where these groups agree upon fundamental political values in order to set the context for democratic learning. The first of these enabling conditions she calls "nonrepression," where neither the state nor parents may use education to restrict the rational deliberation of competing conceptions of the good life.[64] The second is "nondiscrimination": simply put, educational opportunities must be equal for all. The remainder of Gutmann's book maps out the limits of authority between the three groups in line with these two conditions for democratic moral character.

Gutmann enjoins schools to inculcate moral character and teach deliberative reasoning, but she recognizes that democratic education does not end with formal schooling.[65] While schools can provide an important start in the moral education of the democratic citizen—indeed the most important start—a participatory society ought to be concerned with higher education and adult education, in order to engage in "conscious social reproduction." Universities are particularly important institutions in this process because they educate social and political officeholders, foster associational freedom, and serve as sanctuaries of nonrepression.

Gutmann argues that primary schools are the most important means by which young citizens be trained because that is both their intellectual and social purpose. School is a means of democratic education not only because it trains people to think rationally and deliberatively, but also because its social end is to create the kind of citizens that reproduce the democratic society. It is not a political institution in the sense that its aims are to teach people the justice of their polis *exclusively*. Schools treat politics and political education as one part of a broader education that, in theory, develops the good person.

Yet this policy suggests some problems. First, in treating politics as one subject among many, it often construes the political very narrowly. Politics becomes a topic: the science of government. Civics classes are treated as particular training for acting within governmental institutions. Moreover, schools often detach themselves from the practical activities of the community. Adults perceive schools as instruments of pedagogy, not as an integral part of community life. While debates over curriculum or school board members may be considered political by the local community, the daily functioning of the institution is often not so. Thus, neither the child not the parent may develop a sense of the polis—the idea that political life is a whole way of being, that democracy is a vision of the good society, and that political debate reaches not only into the halls of Congress, but in the daily activities of each citizen. In this way, schools circumscribe the content of political education narrowly, and misrepresent the centrality of the political regime in the life of the students. Thus, to students, politics becomes something "out there," for students, something they do not perceive as part of their understanding of themselves.

Second, while Gutmann argues rightly that schools may contribute to a democratic character by teaching the skills of rational deliberation, she errs in her belief that this is the most important purpose of a political education. Before students can deliberate rationally about politics or community life, they must be interested sufficiently in politics to want to do so. But this interest is something that schools cannot teach, because they are not "political" institutions in the more narrow sense of the term. Unlike parties, interest groups, or even the media, the purpose of schools is not to engage in or mediate political argument or debate, it is to teach critical thinking and social virtue. In this way, it is once removed from the central political experiences of the active citizen. The citizen becomes interested in politics as he or she acts within the political system, something which children are usually incapable of doing, but also something which schools are incapable of letting them experience. Individuals need more than the moral education imparted in a classroom, they need to experience areas where their deliberative skills have real and immediate consequences.[66] For individuals to become interested in politics, they ought to engage in political *work*, not merely democratic schooling.

In this context of political work, I want to examine how Gutmann discusses the potential for adult education to combat illiteracy. As we have seen in Chapter 4, this function is important to the proponents of national service, and it is undeniably a worthy goal for any society. Gutmann assesses whether such a program should be compulsory, and concludes that it should not, because adults are sovereign citizens who must be left to make their own choices. Government thus respects the dignity of each citizen. Also, by mandating literacy education, the government adds to the dependency and humiliation illiterates already experience. Such indignities result from being under the tutelage of the state—a condition that aggravates their already low self-esteem. Mandatory literacy training would be a kind of "political punishment."[67]

Yet one might contend that citizens should be coerced into learning how to read, or for that matter into learning political argument. How can we treat individuals as sovereign citizens when they do not have the skills necessary to be citizens in the first place? Indeed, are people sovereign citizens when they cannot even understand the conditions of their sovereignty? Without mandatory training such individuals perpetuate their own enslavement, their own disempowerment. Without basic literacy and citizenship skills, such individuals are *residents* of a particular state, but not *citizens*. Unless they can participate in the governance of their communities, they cannot be considered free citizens; the purpose of education is to *train* citizens, if we assume people are citizens by their mere juridical status then we give no moment to how education makes meaningful other aspects of the citizen besides that particular status.

Certainly we must treat individuals with the dignity and respect they deserve, but this means treating them well as human beings. Citizens are entitled to respect *as citizens* insofar as they contribute to the reproduction of the polis and the improvement of their community, and this is impossible without their learning how that is to be done. Virtuous citizenship is an acquired status, not one given to a person for having been born. Subsequently, citizens must work at being deliberative and reasonable beings, and they must demonstrate interest in the affairs of their community. Such preconditions are democratic insofar as they are afforded to all people equally, without repression or discrimination. Yet it is not enough to say that society must be nonrepressive and nondiscriminating, because we need ways by which to even understand these terms. Mandatory literacy and civic education are prerequisites for individuals to understand what the ideas of nonrepression and nondiscrimination mean in the first place. In short, what is the significance of a free society for people who do not understand what the word *freedom* implies and what the concept of freedom permits?

Finally, Gutmann's argument is also incomplete where she discusses education for all—both young and old—outside the primary schools and universities.[68] She makes a reasonable case for federal funding and regulation of educational television, and she contends rightly that libraries and museums are vital cultural resources. She even justifies governmental funding of high culture on grounds of intellectual and artistic freedom and the possible enlightenment of individuals. All these elements are necessary for an enlightened citizenry. But nothing in any of them explicitly educates individuals to be citizens, or gives them the political knowledge and participatory resources to be active citizens in their communities. Gutmann gives "extramural" and "adult" education short shrift, as appendages to the public school system, which she considers the most important institution of citizenship education. A concerted effort can be made to educate adults politically beyond the opportunities offered in libraries, museums, or adult education courses. "Extramural" and "adult" political education could become the norm of good citizenship, not limited ventures in "high culture" or night school.

Contemporary American political institutions, while educational in some senses, ultimately fail to inculcate participatory values effectively. However, an institution that combines the political activism found in party members, the public ethic held by party members and citizen-soldiers, and the deliberative skills cultivated by the primary schools, best prepares individuals for the responsibilities of citizenship. Furthermore, such an institution demonstrates and teaches participatory values, and provides a "training ground" for future democrats. Through it individuals learn self-respect, and begin thinking about transforming some of the most basic political institutions in America. Such an institution could be "national service."

In the next chapters I sketch a program for national service that has two components—schooling and work. In the first, adults engage in study groups where they can enhance their skills of deliberation and critical thinking. Such "schooling" also teaches adults the basic issues of the day, and important intellectual skills in politics—for example, how to read newspapers and political journals carefully. Even if such schooling cannot raise the average citizen's awareness toward important issues, it exposes that citizen to the resources he or she need in order to find out more about them. For those who require it, such schooling teaches literacy.

The second aspect to national service is political work: individuals choose some form of political work, broadly construed, in order both to apply what they have learned and to develop participatory skills. The workplaces of national service need not be uniform, and the goals of the workers need not be the same. They merely offer individuals the chance to "do" politics.

CHAPTER NINE

Educating Adults Politically

In chapters 1 and 7 I suggested an argument for creating a new institution—national service—on grounds of political education. I maintained that citizenship means more than socialization, it means understanding one's society cognitively, and not merely affectively, and acting to bring about justice. Through political education one can learn the subtleties of one's community and the reasons why one ought to participate in the life of that community. Political education teaches people how to think, not what to think, and it teaches them the skills of participation, not simply the value of it.[1] Service thus becomes the way in which individuals do not merely obligate themselves to their fellow citizens, but actually grow into citizens themselves.

Planners such as Janowitz, Moskos, and Eberly make the case for national service on the basis of socialization. Despite their arguments, national service may not be the appropriate institution to socialize young people. A number of studies demonstrate that young people develop their cognitive abilities and affective orientations toward a regime well before the age of seventeen or eighteen, when they would be placed in service. Researchers have discovered that individuals increase their understanding of their communities between the ages of eleven and thirteen, and by the time they are fifteen they have developed an almost fully adult mind.[2] These findings are consistent with those authors who employ cognitive development theory in understanding human learning. Furthermore, a study by the William Grant Foundation indicates that the values of adolescents do not differ markedly from those of their parents.[3] So a national youth service may do little to inculcate community values, for participants may hold ideas about these already.

By teaching critical thinking and encouraging political interest, however, national service might provide an education that helps develop (or helps practice) the intellectual capabilities of the adult and young adult. Schools help young people think more deeply about their communities, while political parties and the media do their best to generate interest in all citizens. But national service ideally binds both of these goals together institutionally.

179

In this chapter and the next, I explore each goal more closely, and offer national service planners a possible alternative to youth service—one based on education, not socialization, and one that redefines the notion of community service.

What does it mean to teach political education? Judith Gillespie describes political education as "the development of competencies in thinking about and acting in political arenas."[4] She argues that the "thinking about" must include an inquiry into problems and an ability to propose alternate solutions while being mindful of their consequences. "Acting" means doing so in and through groups—it is collective. Furthermore, the political arena includes both governmental and nongovernmental contexts—school, home, and workplace—anywhere a relationship of power exists.[5]

In this chapter I elaborate the meaning of *competencies*—especially in the development of critical thinking in adults—and suggest ways in which national service could play a role in helping each individual citizen practice these skills. In Chapter 10, I suggest practical means by which individuals may employ such thinking while conserving and transforming society. There I sketch a few programs national service ought to consider seriously—programs that allow individuals to use those critical skills, and programs that might make people more interested in participating in their communities.

As I argued in the previous chapter, the political education of adults may take place most appropriately outside of the school system; moreover most adults receive a basic political education in school. I am more interested, then, in programs focusing on social problems, critical thinking, and political involvement. I assume that adults are intellectually, morally, and psychologically prepared to discuss important issues. If they are not, then democracy is not possible.

National service, as an educational institution, ought to create regimes of conversation, opening discussions among citizens. This builds communities by creating common action—by making the actions of otherwise separate individuals into a communal action. *The* communal activity is conversation itself. Charles Taylor describes the practice well:

> Opening a conversation is inaugurating a common action. This common action is sustained by little rituals which we barely notice.... This threshold, which conversation takes us over, is one which matters in all sorts of ways and on all sorts of levels in human life.[6]

Taylor remarks that conversations help individuals share intimacy, and engage them in common concerns. People establish particular subjects as things that ought to be attended to together, and in communal concerns individuals create bonds of attachment toward others.

Community service can strengthen a democracy that depends upon citizens who can inquire into, and converse about, social and political issues. Community conversations foster associational life and adhere individuals to each other and to the republic by allowing citizens with different interests, self-understandings, and commitments to attend to problems together. In short, they establish places where contestation and cooperation among citizens can occur simultaneously; and these places may also permit individuals to work out their own understandings of "good citizenship" by listening to others do the same. As I suggest below, these understandings rest upon a critical appreciation of political community, and national service can serve these communities by imbuing citizens with the capacity to think critically about politics. A critical service politicizes citizens by actively engaging them in conversation about their communities, which improves their political judgment. Republicans and communitarians ought thus to be arguing for a program on these grounds.

TEACHING CRITICAL THINKING (ABOUT POLITICS)

Critical thinking is a necessary practice for the citizen, though no sufficient in itself to define citizenship. It helps him or her think about the nature of the givernment, about why he or she should consent to that government, and about how to judge the efficacy and morality of government programs such as national service. In teaching critical thinking, national service might imbue citizens with the skills necessary to deepen their understanding of the political and economic justifications of, and rationalizations for, such service. Furthermore, such critique can be practiced collectively, thus contributing to the regime of conversation I mention above. Critical thinking, then, can intensify the loyalties citizens have to each other, and to the community, by asking them to come to some understanding of why that loyalty is important. And it can generate new ideas about how to create a society worthy of civic loyalty if those citizens find the present one deficient.

Schools begin teaching critical thinking to young citizens, though as Gutmann points out, not always so well. Through national service citizens could engage those skills even further, thus complementing the programs encouraged in schools. Service could be an extension of the schools, but one that blends schooling and work. In this way, service helps citizens apply critical skills to real life political situations. In this section, I outline a proposal for developing critical thinking in *adults*.

This outline differs from conventional understandings about reflecting upon service, or at least those that have been implemented in some of the private and local service programs. Rather, I reflect upon political and social ideas and events. I do not articulate a philosophy of service, but only recommend a realistic understanding about social, economic, and political issues. These suggestions are not meant to imbue citizens with the desire to help their neighbors through *individual* acts of charity (though they may do that too) but to educate their neighbors and improve their opportunities in life through *collective* action.

Education for critical political thinking involves three operations: countersocialization and countereducation, the development of reflective skepticism, and the inculcation of casuistic reasoning. These skills help make individuals more aware of sociopolitical realities as well as help them come to a better understanding of their own lives within that world.

Most significantly, these skills help individual citizens appreci-
ate the very contestability of the concept of citizenship. They do not prescribe certain values or attitudes one must hold toward a polity, rather they imbue the citizen with a certain disposition. That disposition is to be both critical and tolerant: critical of pat solutions to preselected problems, and tolerant of other people's understandings of the meaning of good citizenship. Possessing both these dispositions, citizens can work toward a more open community.[7]

Countersocialization

Schools, the media, the family, and peer groups socialize Americans, especially young Americans, to the political system. Socializing agents, like the family or peer groups cannot legally—and ought not—be regulated by the government. However, government has a very important role to play in the schools. Yet, as I argue in the previous chapter, the schools, while ostensibly socializing youth for democracy, do not adequately motivate them for active citizenship. Indeed, at the end of her or his schooling, the citizen often knows slogans about democracy but cannot reason clearly about its principles, or feel empowered to participate.

A program of education encouraging individuals to assess thoughtfully the politics of their communities, while allowing them to judge the credibility of various claims to truth, helps in this regard. Political education involves practices that permit individuals to explore the meaning of their communities independently of the institutions socializing them, especially the schools. National service might create the conditions necessary for citizens to learn "facts" about America and about political ideas, while questioning the "facts" they have learned in schools.[8]

Citizens thus become countersocialized through a critical or oppositional education.[9] This countersocialization is directed at older citizens—that is, those who have already gone through compulsory schooling, some of whom have been working for a time. Consequently, countersocialization does not actually shape the ideas of individuals, for those have been formed through the schools and through living. Rather, it presents adults with alternative explanations of, and modes of reasoning about, political issues in America. Many who accept the teachings of such education will have done so at the cost of abandoning closely held beliefs, thus they transform themselves only after an intellectual struggle. Those who do not abandon what they have been taught have defended those ideals rationally, and thus have also practiced analytical and critical skills. In this way, the presentation of critical perspectives could improve the capacity of all citizens to understand and assess political issues.

Such a project suggests the creation of discussion groups, involving citizens from various regions and backgrounds, as well as discussion leaders who themselves have had experience in presenting a number of ideas in public gatherings. Citizens themselves bring their own perspectives to others in their groups, thus expanding the possibility of alternative interpretations of a particular issue. These discussion groups deliberate over ideas developed by important political thinkers, and read the texts of those thinkers, or excerpts from them. The group members come to collective decisions about which authors they ought to read.

The discussion groups analyze and criticize American politics and institutions in a reasoned manner. This may involve writing papers or making public presentations, but the goal is to engage others in a critical discourse about the ideology of America broadly construed. Participants must examine some aspect of American politics and society—for example, an institution, a national policy, or class relationships—and make a thoroughgoing critique of that aspect (with suggestions for reform).

Richard Pratte suggests that individuals should practice "persistent questioning" in order to attain "civic literacy"—where necessary, citizens must question the aims of American society.[10] However, one questions not simply to question but to communicate more openly with other citizens. For civic literacy demands not only that one understand one's nation deeply but also the meaning of democratic exchange. For Pratte, "the decisive problem is this: how to make face-to-face communication an effective force in strengthening the capacity of the public for rational judgment and free it from the control of external or built-in censors."[11] This means engaging in what he calls "counter-politics," and he suggests that all students learn such a strategy.[12] The strategy is even more appropriate to a national service organization where adults learn, because adults are more prepared intellectually to engage in a philosophy of "persistent questioning" and apply it to politics.

Moreover, such strategies of critical discourse have been successful within the schools. A number of researchers have uncovered its possibilities in the United States, Canada, and France.[13] And the famous monographs from the Birmingham Centre for Cultural Studies suggest that such oppositional practices have long been a part of the British educational system.[14]

One method employed by these potential questioners might involve the open reading of texts; that is, teaching individuals who already know how to read, how to *read*.[15] On this understanding, civic literacy improves the reading skills of all individuals by politicizing texts, and by encouraging participants to read and even rewrite them in ways schools do not encourage. This may mean applying political reading skills to the analysis of corporate brochures, government documents, or national newspapers. Participants are encouraged to read between the lines, as residents of Eastern Europe have done for years to their national presses. This hones their abilities to respond critically to the presentation of things as factual or obvious, and "knowledge of American political forms" takes on a broader meaning. Civil literacy alerts them to the skills necessary for a thorough reading of texts, and engages them even more deeply in contemporary discourse. This encourages them to pursue other lines of inquiry with skill and even zeal.[16]

For instance, national service participants (NSPs) might analyze and criticize the various texts that constitute national service.

They would critique the ideology behind the movement and discuss the policy-making process that went into the program. They might demystify the civic discourse justifying the program rhetorically. They would investigate the class, ethnic, and gender composition of groups supporting its institution, and might also ask whether national service merely assists those groups in maintaining political and cultural hegemony or whether in fact it usefully serves to build communities. In short, this form of national service might help NSPs participate in an ongoing debate over national service, instead of merely imposing its administration upon them. Consequently, they begin to act like citizens.

Reflective Skepticism

Critical thinking involves more than the opportunity for resistance, it demands the cultivation of a particular disposition toward political facts and ideas. This disposition I call "reflective skepticism," for it indicates a critical attitude toward politics in general, and suggests caution toward all social panaceas. It also disposes the citizen to demand reasons from his or her elected representatives and civil servants when they propose new policies.

The idea of reflective skepticism, Humean in spirit, has been expressed most recently by John McPeck. He argues that critical thinking involves thinking about something; critical thought must be connected to a particular topic. It also "involves a certain skepticism—or suspension of assent—towards a given statement, established norm or mode of doing things." A "judicious use" of skepticism, tempered by experience, produces "a more satisfactory solution to, or insight into, the problem at hand."[17] Reflective skepticism, then, is not mere nay-saying: the reflective skeptic approaches problems critically in order to resolve them in a manner relevant to the situation at hand. Critical thinking must therefore "include the active engagement in activities as well as the assessment of statements."[18] In short, critical thinking through reflective skepticism activates knowing, and encourages individuals to involve themselves with practical problems.

McPeck defines reflective skepticism as "the disposition and skill to do X is such a way that E (the available evidence from a field) is suspended (or temporarily rejected) as sufficient to establish the truth or validity of P (some proposition or action within X)."[19] Such a definition requires "countersocialization"—for reflective skepticism demands a critical eye, even a resistant one, to ideas, policies, or problems. Individuals must learn a disposition or propensity to be skeptical, which McPeck argues is a skill.[20]

Harvey Siegel suggests that a position of "reflective skepticism" assumes that critical thinking abilities already exist, and he maintains that, on the contrary, those abilities must be taught.[21] He contends that critical thinkers must be "appropriately moved by reasons." This demands both the ability to assess problems reasonably and a critical attitude. Such a critical attitude reflects the character of a person, as well as his or her skills, and it signifies the love of reason. In this way, the person is *moved* by reasons. Such a rationale has a number of advantages: (1) it respects students as persons by recognizing their right to question, (2) it helps students become self-sufficient and thus is liberating, (3) it initiates individuals into the rational tradition which teaches them the criteria for good argument, and (4) it necessitates democratic living.[22]

McPeck asserts that critical thinking is not a generalized skill but a thinking *about* something, and this informs a conception of national service that is a critical thinking *about* politics.[23] A service program need not teach critical thinking in the abstract but should tie it in to real political issues. McPeck does not prescribe this sort of thinking for all contexts of human endeavor but rather where there are problems to be solved. This is relevant to politics, and national service can appropriate his formula to analyze and resolve political and social problems.

Individuals need to become more skeptical about political ideas and political leaders for two reasons. First, they ought to become more interested in politics, and a skeptical (not apathetic) attitude contributes to this end. For when one criticizes governmental policy one at least cares enough to do so; the danger that national service planners lament as much as any other is indifference, and such a program helps combat that problem. Second, through this skepticism, NSPs learn to reason about politics, because they defend their skepticism from other skeptics. In this way, their skepticism becomes *reflective*. Such reflection helps individuals combat the intellectual torpor and routine they suffer in their daily lives, as well as the routine they may have suffered in school.[24]

National service could be a way for people to develop a critical attitude and be moved by reasons in *politics*. It could be a means whereby participants develop reflective skepticism, and foster a critical disposition toward political issues and ideas. At the same time, it encourages all citizens to respect political reason—engaging citizens in political ideas and ideals, and moving them to act by their engagements. It may be a way that adults are required to practice the critical skills they have learned as students, in order for them to want to act upon them.[25] In this conception, national service extends of the basic principles of democratic education inculcated in the primary schools.

Finally, critical national service helps individuals learn the judgment necessary for practical living. That is, it helps individuals apply principles to particular circumstances through the judgment they have acquired through their experiences. Michael Oakeshott notes that teaching initiates the pupil into the world of human achievement by communicating two things to him or her: information and judgment.[26] Teachers impart judgment both consciously and unconsciously (e.g., "in a tone of voice, in the gesture which accompanies instruction, in asides and oblique utterances, and by example"). But, Oakeshott asserts, judgment can be taught. Consequently, national service might teach political judgment, if not consciously, then by example. Each citizen thus learns judgment from his or her fellow citizens, as well as from sociologists and political commentators. Moreover, by closely scrutinizing political leaders, participants see how these leaders exercise judgment over the most important issues of the day.

Such judgment is also taught through real-life political work. But the tasks involved in critical national service ought to be significant to each citizen and charged with political meaning. Thus, all primarily clerical work is discouraged in such a program, and tasks such as helping the elderly or the addicted are encouraged if they include aspects of political discussion and organizing.

For instance, a national service program for democratic citizenship not only provides meals to seniors, but also helps seniors organize for their rights. So "meals on wheels" allows servers and recipients to sit together and discuss the nature of a society that relegates many senior citizens to a life of poverty and isolation. These discussions are especially valuable for young people in the program who learn from discussions with their elders. Moreover, such a program brings together recipients in a political organization allowing them to fight for greater dignity and services.

Alternatively, if NSPs are deployed as prison guards, why not employ them as prison organizers? Here they inform prisoners of their rights and responsibilities and engage them in study groups to better themselves. They also help educate prisoners in basic skills and suggest resources for them once they leave prison. Moreover, prison organizers also work with prison guards and officials, educating them and involving them in study groups, possibly with the prisoners themselves. Through the practice of politics—of prison politics—prisoners, guards, officials, and national service participants can learn to think politically, an invaluable skill for active citizenship.

Casuistic Reasoning

The final component of critical thinking about politics—and one intertwined with the previous two—is casuistic reasoning.[27] A slightly playful concept, it refers to cases involving conscience, and helps resolve problems in cases of moral conduct. But it also employs casuistry—a false application of principles in regard to moral questions. It asks individuals to accept an imaginary identity in their process of moral reasoning by putting themselves in the place of others—like political leaders—in order to get a sense of the moral choices such leaders must make when formulating and implementing policy (especially during times of political crisis). This practice might be another way service educates individuals toward political judgment and "rational conduct," as it helps "ordinary citizens reflect upon the most important matters of state."[28] Consequently, participants understand political decision-making more deeply, and appreciate the difficulties encountered by policy-makers.

Moreover, individuals are educated to take the position of the other in order to see how that person makes his or her moral decisions. This is not an experiment in phenomenology, for individuals still translate those processes through their own language and their own understanding. Consequently, it establishes some sort of common ground, or language, of understanding, and does not simply take the position of the other. Rather, it intimates what Charles Taylor calls a language of "contrastive characterization." Through such a language individuals come to understand themselves more deeply, which he contends is an essential part of being human.

By this means, we attune ourselves to others, for in understanding something, we not only comprehend it instrumentally as an object of knowledge, but in some sense we develop a sort of positive disposition toward it. We grasp the intrinsic value of an object by coming closer to that object. So understanding is not a purely intellectual exercise, it is also a practice: we *do* something when we understand something, we come into harmony with it.[29] This does not mean that we necessarily agree with others, but simply that in order to understand them more deeply we enter into a particular relationship with them. In this sense, critical thinking is a very practical activity—an activity that unites individuals.

Taylor argues that in attuning ourselves to things or others we make "strong evaluations" of them, outside of a utilitarian context, by referring to a language of contrastive characterization. The language helps us clarify our desires by articulating them. Through this language we understand what is important to us, which we previously held in a tacit form. This contributes to the processes of "self-interpretation" and community-building.[30]

> This would be a language in which we could formulate both [the way of life of the group we study] and [our way of life] as alternative possibilities in relation to some human constants at work in both. It would be a language in which the possible human variations would be so formulated that both our form of life and theirs could be perspicuously described as alternatives of such variations.[31]

Taylor calls a version of this language "play-acting."[32] Here individuals step out of their own situation and "play it back" from a different vantage point—that vantage point being a different culture or historical epoch. To contrast oneself perspicuously against others is not to adopt that person's point of view.[33] Rather, it helps individuals clarify their understanding of *themselves* by seeing themselves in a different language.

Such a language becomes particularly important when examining institutions, and all citizens could learn to read institutions hermeneutically as part of their critical education. As a text, the institution is

> a kind of language in which its fundamental ideas are expressed. But what is "said" in this language is not ideas which could be in the minds of individuals only, they are rather common to a society, because they are embedded in its collective life, in practices and institutions which are of the society indivisibly. In these the spirit of a society is in a sense objectified.[34]

In this way the resistant and skeptical reading of government complements an attuned, interpretive one. Institutions are not agencies to be resisted, but rather expressions of the collective will of a transformed community. A hermeneutical reading of institutions complements a resistant one, and the individual citizen decides which is more appropriate in a given situation. Critical national service merely *exposes* these citizens to both sorts of readings, and provides the sort of political experiences that informs their political judgment. A solid grounding in the history and analysis of institutions is also necessary for citizens both to appreciate how institutions represent the collective identity of the citizenry, and the ways in which those institutions are democratized.

In sum, a citizen ought to be prepared to understand other members of the community through their eyes in order to come to a deeper understanding of his or her own position in that country. Thus, exchanges, visits, conferences, and other collective means of learning should be made available to the participants. National service offers individuals opportunities to meet people and visit places from which they are otherwise excluded. In this way, citizens begin to understand common institutions through the eyes of these others.[35]

In practical terms, such a program means the opportunity for all citizens to meet a wide variety of people. Consequently, welfare recipients are invited to sit with CEOs, artists with soldiers, farmers with bankers, and factory workers with actors. National service provides the institutional space for this to occur by establishing study groups across class, race, and gender boundaries. It requires a diverse mix of citizens to discuss the most pressing political and social problems of the day, and it creates a site for the criticism and transformation of institutions. Moreover it helps citizens understand how their fellow citizens "read" those institutions they share in common. This improves their understanding of political institutions, especially the ways in which those institutions represent the public collectively. This, in turn, helps each citizen appreciate the traditions of the political community more profoundly.

According to Wayne Leys,

the greatest value of casuistry is in the orientation of inexperienced persons to a community in which they are going to live. Assuming that every community has some accumulated wisdom, casuistry makes available to its individual members advice that...is conducive to good judgment. Casuistry conserves and secures values to which its practitioners may themselves be insensitive.[36]

Casuistry, then, not only engages "inexperienced persons" in a collective dialogue, but does so within the context of a particular tradition. In this way, the art of casuistry preserves, and reproduces, community. It does not teach these persons to ask questions like "what is the most efficient way to do this?" or "what means will achieve the best ends?"—questions that predominate utilitarian, professionalized service ideology. Rather, the casuist asks "which alternative will conform to the ways of our predecessors?" and "how would other members of the community act under these circumstances?" Casuistic reasoning then builds on the traditions of a community, but critically, and does not disrupt those traditions through a simple understanding of means/ends calculations. This captures the idea of the civic more forcefully than a pedagogy of service.

In this chapter I have begun to think about the ways in which adults ought to be educated politically in order to make civic contributions. I do not prescribe what the citizen must learn, only how he or she is to do so. More importantly, I believe these skills cultivate an openness toward others and toward the community—dispositions that develop trust and tolerance. These skills may not be the most direct means of establishing a service ethic, but I believe them to be the most secure. If people care about their communities, they will serve their brothers and sisters. But for them to care, they must believe that their communities are their own, not the realm of corporate capital, organized special interests, or huge bureaucracies. National service helps people recapture their communities by helping adults to recapture the power they have over their own minds.

In the next chapter I present "practical" proposals for a national service program directed at citizenship, directed at fostering contestation over the very meaning of that term. I put the word *practical* in quotation marks because, while I describe practices that are economically feasible, they are politically controversial.[37] Read it skeptically, for I have written it skeptically. It smacks of utopianism and realism at the same time—its programs put into practice themes I have asserted throughout this book, but at the same time I recognize that to implement my proposals requires a political will (and an acceptance of "citizenship") that does not exist at the moment. Moreover, the next chapter presents national service not as serving the needs of the nation, but as helping the nation meet needs which the nation creates. It is service for political and social change, in the hope that the very idea of national service can be eliminated. Therefore, I write the following chapter to stimulate discussion.

CHAPTER TEN

National Service as Political Service

Let us now consider Robert Ely, that "normal human being" William Buckley so expertly presents as the prototypical national server in his recent book, *Gratitude*.[1] The "lad" in this "deglamorized" story comes from a lower middle class home (his father is an invalid on a pension and his mother is a secretary). He chooses national service because he needs to pay for college, and cannot think up a particularly good reason for getting out of it. He is "turned on" to national service by Carl Pepper, a young man working tough but satisfying days at a nursing home. He decides to sign up for service at that same nursing home, and here he learns "a lot." He also makes a bit of money and accrues educational vouchers for the university. In college he chooses to study the economics of public health, and after graduation he gives inspirational talks to future service participants at the nursing home. When people ask him how service had influenced him he is not sure at first, but then says that he is a changed man. He helped people, "without hurting himself," he likes the idea that someone will help him if he becomes incapacitated when he becomes old, and he just plain "feels better" about himself for doing so. And— "oh yeah"—he is "grateful" that he served. Cute story.

Let us now deglamorize the story a bit further. Robert needs money to attend college because his parents have not been able to make a living wage in an era of huge budget deficits, rising taxes, and cuts in government provisions for health care, social security, and welfare. His father is on a small pension because an accident at an unsafe workplace disabled him many years before. His mother works as a secretary at a local clinic because of historic discrimination against allowing women full participation in the work force: while growing up, she was never given reasons why she should be a doctor if she chose. She makes a paltry wage because, among other reasons, the job is not unionized and her pay reflects belief in the relative worthlessness of traditional women's work. Federal educational loan money has dried up because budget priorities (e.g., spending for military hardware) precluded its continuance. Fortunately, the Elys were wise and did not invest all of

193

their money in that savings and loan closed by federal investigators a few months before.

Robert is not necessarily angry about all this, because nothing has ever made him angry about these issues. Rather, he sees his parents working at jobs that "suit" their skills and ambitions. Moreover, Robert has never thought to ask why his family is living under these conditions. This is no surprise, though, because he has probably never met anyone—his friends, teachers, relatives, basketball coach, etc.—who has questioned these things either.

Robert cannot find good reasons to avoid national service because he has never really been challenged in school or outside of school to provide reasons for anything, and he has certainly never heard of any reason for not wanting to "serve humanity." He meets Carl, whose selflessness he admires, but who tells him that he will learn plenty by being in service without telling him what he will learn or why he will learn it (could it be that Carl still has not learned to reason about his experience?). So Robert enlists. But before he can actually begin working, he must fill out a battery of forms and examinations to see if he is qualified and/or suited for the task he wishes to pursue. It is determined that he is, and he immediately goes to work for a for-profit nursing home. Here his low wages and full-time hours preclude a retirement-home worker from doing the same job, and his presence has caused some dissatisfaction—not at the retirement home (where all the residents see him as kind and caring) but at the local union office, which fights to get its members jobs in the health care field. Robert's pay contributes some to the family's coffers, but they still have difficulty meeting their health insurance payments, so to save money Robert goes without health insurance for the year (his employer is not required to provide any except for full-time, contract workers). Nevertheless, Robert works faithfully day in and day out, following orders, meeting senior citizens, cleaning bedpans. When he returns home at night he is exhausted and often relaxes by having a few beers and watching television. He has no time to read on the job, and he is in no mood to do so in the evening. Moreover, most of the people with whom he lives and works do not read much either.

After his service year, he enrolls in college as a business major, studying public health economics. Here he learns how to manage health care institutions, not labor in them, and he learns how to maximize profits for his future employers. He returns to his community to lecture on the benefits of national service. When people ask him what he learned as an NSP, he can't think of anything initially. He didn't learn that the health care system is in crisis, he didn't learn to discuss the moral issues surrounding a society that dispatches its elderly summarily into retirement "communities," he didn't learn that senior citizens can be organized to fight for their right to affordable retirement and health care, he didn't learn that his own incapacity and future residence in a similar place is not inevitable. He still doesn't care to know why his father is on a small pension, and why his mother has the job that she does.

What has Robert Ely learned? He did learn to help others without hurting himself, he did learn to "feel good" about himself, he did learn to be "grateful."[2] Did he learn citizenship? Did he learn how to reason? Did he learn that life may offer something beyond feeling good about oneself, and being grateful to the country which made all of this possible? Did he learn *anything* about the politics, economics, and issues surrounding service? What purpose, or interest, does his failure to learn these issues serve?

Under a political conception of service, victims of national service like Robert Ely might have a fighting chance to work toward the conditions that make national service unnecessary. Ely will learn, first of all, that he must think about service, about why that service is necessary in the first place, and he must be able to critique it. This I have tried to argue in the previous chapter. But though teaching critical thinking and learning about politics are necessary for the education of the democratic citizen, they are not sufficient. Robert should also engage in political activity so that he may contest the conditions and expectations upon which his citizenship rests and become more concerned for his communities. This concern, though, ought to be inculcated by work that triggers political interest.

More than one author has suggested that the primary task for any teacher is to generate student interest in the material at hand. Richard Battistoni admires Rousseau who argued that

> teachers should attempt to create interest in students where none was originally present. He felt that teachers should provide information or opposition in order not only to satisfy their students' intellectual desires, but to move them beyond where they began their inquiry.

And he suggests that teachers themselves ought to behave like political theorists in order to challenge students "to examine the world around them."[3] Gilbert Ryle exhorts teachers to create an atmosphere where students love to learn.[4] In the context of national service, this means helping individuals to learn to engage in politics and be engaged by their communities.

The best way to do this, as any number of educators have pointed out, is through experiential learning. These same educators argue that participatory learning experiences offer an opportunity for the learners to reflect on what they have accomplished.[5] In fact, in a study of community service programs in American high schools, Conrad and Hedin declare that "among program features, the presence of a formal (and at least weekly) seminar proved to be the single strongest factor in explaining positive student change."[6] This reinforces the notion that community service, to be effective as a means of *citizen* education, involves not only participation in particular activities, but also in discussion groups whereby individuals can reflect upon the social importance of their activity. Only recently have service planners incorporated the idea of reflection into service proposals, and I criticize the nature of this type of reflection in Chapter 6.[7] NSPs need to reflect upon political and social problems more than the one nature of service, or on their own particular attitudes toward service, *if* the point of the program is to inculcate good citizenship. If national service is to be a form of New Age self-help, exemplified by Dass and Gorman's *How Can I Help?*, then an orientation toward the philosophy of service is appropriate. But, as I argue in Chapter 6, the political economy and sociology behind this philosophy obstruct civic practices and learning. Critical national service recognizes such civic foundations.

In this chapter I outline organizations involved in political service, and suggest examples of tasks that help participants engage in their communities and act with the critical eye they cultivate in school or study groups. These tasks are far more political and ideological than the idea of community service suggested by most national service planners. Each of these programs can be complemented by study sessions or reflective seminars, but the work itself may be thought provoking enough to preclude such seminars in every case. The need for additional study can either be decided on a case-by-case basis or groups can be organized by the participants themselves.

By engaging in politics and ideology citizens experience fundamental truths about the justice of their society. Political service helps people think while they act, community service allows them to do good deeds without necessarily making them understand how or why they are good. Political service encourages individuals to take stands, community service permits participants to deliver services without thinking about why those services might need to be provided in the first place.[8] It helps turn political subjects, like Robert Ely, into engaged citizens.

Empirical researchers have demonstrated that a politicized environment contributes to the education of young people. Roberta Sigel and Marilyn Hoskin have shown that politicized school environments contribute to the political involvement of adolescents. Furthermore, they argue that such environments do not influence affect so much as they do cognition and participation.[9] This indicates that political environments contribute to the development of political knowedge and political concern, but *not* to whether or not individuals become attached to their governments. Thus a politicizing environment in a national service program may not have a subversive or radical effect on citizens. Rather, it may merely make them more knowledgeable about and concerned for their communities.[10] Sigel and Hoskin end with a plea to "raise the relevance level of politics" for young people in order to make them fuller citizens,[11] and this is what I suggest in the following pages.

In its pure form political service ought to be coercive and universal—because democratic citizenship implies equal duties required by, and benefits afforded to, the participants. But this brings cries of unconstitutionality and authoritarianism, thus some other solution must be found. A purely voluntary system, without special rewards for participants, is ideal, though there may be problems in obtaining and keeping recruits. All these issues have been discussed repeatedly and I have nothing helpful to add to the discussion.

Let me suggest one partial solution, given that national service is a popular idea and that many people in Washington and elsewhere intend to promote the program. For any form agreed upon by the political class—coercive, compulsory, or voluntary (as I have defined these in Chapter 2)—the content of the programs offered must be questioned and altered.[12] Most, if not all, of the tasks offered by a quasi- or full national service program ought to be political ones. This does not mean dropping such programs as health care aides, senior citizen group workers, conservation workers—these tasks can be socially useful. But these programs ought not to be treated as if they are merely service tasks—they are part of a larger political and economic system and service ought to engage participants in an ongoing critique of those tasks and that system as they work.[13] For various reasons given throughout this text, political tasks inculcate the contestable nature of citizenship by engaging participants in the political and social contests that constitute their communities. Where service programs do not address citizenship in this way, they ought not to be part of a federally controlled and financed national service program.

Good citizens ought to fight against the institution of national service under its present configurations. Thus the following remarks suggest one of two possible strategies for opponents of national service as presently conceptualized. The first strategy is to argue for political service, and I have sketched out potentially relevant service tasks below. The second is to fight against the very institution of national service. In my more idealistic moments I might pursue national service as political service, but I doubt that those who reside within and around the northwest quadrant of the District of Columbia would do the same. I doubt that even if they did agree with the following suggestions (much less the entire thesis of the book), they could transform it into a nonbureaucratic, participatory reality. I offer the following, then, as food for thought, rather than as detailed policy advice, and I advise those who share my concerns to fight the very idea of national service as the federal government is devising it. Service to a nation of individualists, instrumental reasoners, corporate interests, and large bureaucracies is not in the best interests of that nation. Thus, for the moment, the most appropriate civic gesture is to contest the institution of national service. Good citizens need to resist this sort of "good citizenship." Therefore the following tasks are practical, if currently impracticable, ways in which service workers and participants can become good citizens.

LITERACY AND ADULT EDUCATION

Clearly, one vitally important area of any community service is teaching people how to read.[14] Yet in political service, literacy training assumes a whole new dimension, as people learn to read in explicitly political contexts. For instance, literacy houses could be established in abandoned buildings in the inner city or rural America.[15] NSPs could teach neighborhood residents how to read and count using texts and documents concerning the inhumanity of poverty. Illiterates within the service organization could also benefit from organized instruction by their peers. The teachers could be recruited from the literate classes, especially those who benefit from entitlements afforded them by the American standard of living. These individuals also must be taught the responsibilities that go along with the rights they have exercised as members of the business or professional communities. This helps individuals understand that citizenship demands an active commitment to the community. Moreover, they can afford to volunteer their time without sacrificing their material interests.[16]

Within literacy houses, literacy training teaches both illiterates and political illiterates.[17] It educates through problem-solving, and challenges students to respond to the world.

> Because they apprehend the challenge as interrelated to other problems within a total context, not as a theoretical question, the resulting comprehension tends to be increasingly critical and thus constantly less alienated. Their response to the challenge evokes new challenges, followed by new understandings; and gradually the students come to regard themselves as committed.[18]

Subsequently, the world becomes not so much an object of study as an object of transforming action.

A pedagogy for literacy and political engagement demands dialogue between individuals and critical thinking as a process of collective deliberation. These are established through the discussion of certain generative themes representing the conditions experienced by the participants. Deliberation then becomes a means of decodifying generative themes so that each participant articulates those concepts most basic to his or her existence. Through this articulation individuals learn to read together. Themes are drawn from the everyday issues with which national service participants and literacy students are familiar, and the class materials could be no more expensive than a daily paper, or policy statement by the government. Such a program, though, involves cooperation, unity, and organization of the individuals seeking to learn. In this way, literacy houses could be sites of political and community organization.

A number of scholars defend such programs for literacy and education. Barbara Bee argues that such a concept of literacy

> entails a quality of consciousness. It is not simply the gaining of technical skills which enable us to read and write. Literacy encourages the oppressed to speak and value lan-

guage as a tool for perceiving that society is not fixed and unchangeable; but that its structures and institutions can be challenged and transformed through concerted thought and action. Illiterates thus become not mere "objects" submerged in a silent reality, but "subjects" in and with the world.[19]

Research also demonstrates that these methods are effective in classrooms across the country.[20] One critic even admits that this pedagogy is particularly appropriate in Western countries.[21] Furthermore, these methods may be particularly appropriate for educating *adults* to read, because they have the capacity for critical thought and judgment necessary for a "liberatory" education. Such an education treats adults as such, and does not train them for simple work, or stigmatize them for being illiterate. In fact, past work in the field of liberatory literacy training has generally focused on adult peasants, thus offering an alternative program of "adult education."[22]

Beyond literacy training, though, national service can be the means by which an alternative system of political literacy and general education is created for adults.[23] It can promote discussion and deliberation and teach the awareness that citizenship is a contestable concept. It can also assist individuals who share certain intellectual interests to meet and discuss a book, a film, or a topic they have in common.[24] Service participants can serve as group discussion leaders for this purpose. Adults can thus share ideas with others from different parts of the country and with different backgrounds, and unite in a common love for a particular object of study.[25]

At the same time national service participants can be used for other educational purposes: they might organize local educational reference centers and teach neighborhood people how to use libraries and other resources in order to investigate social or intellectual problems. They can also be placed in skill exchanges, where they list their skills and offer themselves as teachers for whoever wished to employ them.[26] In this way, they are not told what to do, but choose to teach those subjects with which they are most comfortable. Moreover, free skill centers could be opened to the public staffed by service participants.[27]

Beyond this, national service might establish neighborhood "action learning centers."[28] These organizations bring people together for social and political action, community projects (such as energy conservation), or community study. Community projects might have some real impact: NSPs could survey community attitudes toward government policy, they could study local and national institutions, and they could research local history. Strong empirical evidence reveals that these sorts of projects benefit experiential learning. Moreover these same studies suggest that such programs can increase students' interest and motivation in the politics of their community.[29]

As a moral equivalent of war, political service might establish research organizations to examine military policy. For instance, its studies might suggest how service can replace national and international security agencies. NSPs might also lobby congressmen and the president, encouraging them to enact laws replacing military personnel with national service personnel in relevant tasks.[30]

Political service may also help slow learners develop civic competence, but not in the ways contemporary planners define such competence. Charles Curtis argues that historically the civic expectations for slow learners have been very low. In a literature review of this subject, Curtis concludes that

for the slow learner the primary attribute of good citizenship was that he or she be gainfully employed and possess acceptable work habits. The second most frequently mentioned criteria were that he or she respect and obey the law and have a rudimentary knowledge of local statutes. A third commonly stated characteristic was that the slow learning adult should share in the "responsibility" for the quality of life in a local community.[31]

This definition assumes certain things about slow learners: (1) that they will not be decision-makers as adults, (2) that they cannot make rational decisions about problems in their society, and (3) that even normal learners have problems learning and discussing such problems. Future NSPs, especially in a voluntary program, may be labeled slow learners and assigned tasks conforming to the above guidelines.

On the contrary, Curtis's research refutes the general consensus on slow learning and civic education. He demonstrates that slow learners can make rational decisions about problems in their society. Moreover, he shows that slow learners have successfully investigated community problems and have helped resolve them.[32] I would also argue that a national service program which allows all individuals to participate equally also helps destroy the concept of slow learner. It goes a long way in giving some individuals the dignity and respect denied to them by public schools and service planners who focus on socializing, not educational, aspects of national service.

SERVICING ADVOCACY

At the very least, national service ought to expand the definition of service to include and promote advocacy groups. Unlike service organizations, advocacy groups take stands on issues, and speak out on matters of public policy: they "serve" the community by acting upon the ideas and practices of its citizens. Of course, many advocacy organizations also provide practical services to the community: They find lawyers for those who need them, employ counselors to help victims of drug and sexual abuse, and recruit volunteers for voter registration drives.

If national service promotes citizenship it must privilege advocacy groups. It can either fund already existing organizations or it can help establish new ones. One good example of a contemporary advocacy service center is the Lowell Bennion Community Service Center at the University of Utah. The center offers a variety of service opportunities, but these opportunities concern community issues and advocacy projects, for example, Students against Hunger, Homeless Shelter Tutoring, Public Interest Advocacy, and Friends for Refugees. The center also requires a seminar so that participants reflect upon their advocacy work—its importance, its relevance to the political and economic context in which advocacy issues are raised, etc. A national service program should seek out and help advocacy centers like the Bennion Center.

National Service might also help establish or maintain Public Interest Research Groups (PIRGs) in the various states. PIRGs have been very active in states like Minnesota, New York, and Massachussetts, and national service might help create equivalent organizations in the southern states and elsewhere. Generally located in state capitals, PIRGs monitor state and local issues of concern to the community: insurance laws, environmental issues, etc. Through PIRGs, citizens persuade each other and the lawmakers of the state through open communication, reasoned argument, and community pressure. PIRGs might encourage service participants and citizens in general to learn the issues, and to articulate those issues publicly. This, in turn, helps participants engage in critical thinking, and helps them understand the language of public policy and politics. Participants thus employ skills of casuistry in order to work for the public interest.

Another exemplary advocacy group is the Farmworker Arts, Culture, and Education (FACES) program at the Board of Cooperative Educational Services (BOCES)-Geneseo, New York Migrant Center. Interns in this program teach migrant farmworkers how to read and how to enter or reenter school. They do oral history projects with the farmworkers and document their living conditions photographically. They produce informational and media resources for workers, and they advise them on political and economic rights. Furthermore, they open up different ethnic groups to each other— as a generally affluent, white student body meets poor workers of color. It is the kind of service provider that engages its participants in political issues, and does not simply provide charity to the recipients. In conjunction with farming bureaus in other states, national service might wish to establish similar programs, and states might fund the programs by taxing the profits of large farmland holders and agribusiness concerns. The program might also open up its services to small and family farm holders.

THE PROFESSIONAL CORPS

National service might coordinate a "professional" corps—groups of professional school graduates who, either voluntarily or under coercion, serve the communities where they receive their education. In political service, doctors deliver medical services to small communities without medical practitioners nearby, architects work on public housing projects or become housing inspectors for cities, lawyers provide legal services to the poor, business school graduates help small business and nonprofit organizations become financially sound, and recent Ph.D.s teach their subjects in their local communities or use their research skills to assist advocacy and media organizations.[33]

Most importantly, though, these professional school graduates ought not simply donate their services. Rather, they ought to be responsible for the *education* of their clients or patients. Thus, dental school graduates would not only provide affordable dental care to those who need them, but would organize health and public education forums at their offices. These dentists might describe periodontal disease to the public as well as current remedies, but they ought also to describe the process by which a dentifrice or a surgical device is invented and approved for use by the federal government. The recent medical school graduate might provide low-cost medical care, *and also* educate people about why the cost of health care is so high, the pros and cons of state-funded insurance, the issues surrounding tort law that contribute to the high cost of malpractice insurance, and the role of politicians in devising affordable health care regimes. Dentists and doctors can help their patients practice persistent questioning regarding the health care system to which they presently submit themselves.

Similarly, business school graduates might teach small businessmen and -women how to secure federal or bank loans, and how to invest wisely in capital goods, pension plans, etc. But they also need to invite these businesspeople and corporate executives to forums on business ethics in order to discuss the role business ought to play in assuring fair competition in the market. Lawyers might provide affordable legal services and teach the public how to monitor the legal system. They might invite judges into public forums to discuss legal ethics or lobby state legislatures on legal reform (e.g., tort law reform for medical insurance). Architects might not only work on public housing or safety precautions, but work *for* them too. They might be required to devote two evenings a week to advising tenant groups of their rights and how to investigate unfair practices by developers and landlords. And so on, and so on. National service offers professionals the opportunity to learn about, and articulate, the political, economic, and social issues surrounding their professions.

Given that these professionals are often the most financially secure they can afford to spend time educating the public. Their positions might be funded by the private firms that hire them, in a gesture of civic goodwill, or a service tax might be levied on individuals or corporations that hire the firms employing "servants" educated, in part, at the public's expense. In a coercive system, professionals might be required to do these sorts of things after they graduate, or within five or ten years of graduation. In a voluntary system, they might be recruited by national service representatives who work with the various professional school organizations, or service organizations might arrange joint programs with those schools as a requirement for graduation. But it makes sense to recruit these people, not only because they have extracted more benefits from society than others, but because they have the writing and speaking skills that make it easier for them to participate in the public arena. They can serve as role models not only in their profession, but as citizens.

PUBLIC POLICY

Political service also helps educate individuals politically through quasi-public groups and agencies. For instance, it helps establish and strengthen advocacy city planning in cities across the country.[34] This is planning that eschews value-neutrality and deliberately politicizes the planning process. NSPs involving themselves in the planning process exercise more authority over the development of their cities. They also inform the general public of alternatives open to the city, beyond the ones presented by developers or city planners. In this program, neighborhood activists and planners volunteer to teach service participants the basics of city planning, and developers fund the program.[35] Participants then affiliate with a neighborhood organization to work for the interests of that organization. This helps them understand both the problems of their local communities and the methods and theory of contemporary planning. It also makes developers and city planners justify their plans in the eyes of a more educated public, thus democratizing the planning process.

This sort of planning exists today in neighborhood planning programs. For example, residents of the west side of Chicago formed the Interfaith Organizing Project to fight the construction of a new football stadium in their neighborhood. At the same time they offered their own plan for the neighborhood, one calling for affordable housing and a variety of neighborhood improvements. They differed, then, from neighborhood organizations merely seeking to preserve the amenities of their community. Similar organizations have been established in St. Paul, Atlanta, Seattle, Baltimore, Portland, and Cincinnati.[36] And at least one planning expert has argued that low- and moderate-income neighborhoods can benefit the most from neighborhood planning programs in city government.[37] Moreover, while neighborhood planners work in an advisory role at the moment, political servers provide the resources by which they could lobby city governments to become part of the formal planning process. This arrangement currently flourishes in Italy, and national service might help create a planning process similar to that enjoyed by the Bolognese.[38]

Political service participants also open up the policy-making process by participating in state citizens' utility boards (CUBs). CUBs lobby on behalf of ratepayers in front of the public service commissions of each state (or other such regulatory agency). Legally recognized CUBs exist in Wisconsin, Illinois, and Oregon, and groups exist elsewhere that serve similar functions—like Louisiana's Alliance for Affordable Energy. These groups provide advocacy services—like lobbying for lower utility rates, educating citizens for energy conservation, and researching energy issues such as the utility of nuclear energy. A national service program might provide participants for these groups, and might provide funding for them to provide equal representation to utility ratepayers in front of regulatory boards.

Through CUBs, NSPs could engage in energy conservation work in public buildings, and teach private industry and citizens the benefits of conservation. They could also learn about, and lobby for, least-cost utility planning, and could work in national coalitions to lobby the federal government on issues such as improving automobile fuel efficiency. Funding for these programs could come from the utility companies themselves, either out of a civic gesture or from a tax on company profits, or the utilities could be required to include contribution requests when they bill their customers (as CUBs presently operate).

Organizing energy conservation through the quasi-public CUBs promises higher civic returns than does simply establishing conservation camps. First, CUBs place NSPs in local conservation efforts, thus emphasizing community problems and activity, and making citizens personally aware of energy conservation. Second, CUBs do not simply serve ratepayers, they take stands: They argue that utilities need to be supervised by the citizenry, that their goal is accumulating capital and maximizing profits. This stand puts energy conservation in a political context, for it suggests to participants that their activities do not merely serve others, but that they are part of the politics of their communities. Participants also learn civic skills: they may engage in research and lobbying on behalf of ratepayers and in this way learn the policy process. Finally, some participants can be used to canvass neighborhoods for funds and/or petition signatures. In canvassing, participants must take stands and know the issues surrounding the politics of energy. This helps them develop critical skills more deeply by requiring them to articulate these issues to others, and it helps educate ratepayers who remain unaware of conservation and energy issues.

All this can still be done in the context of service: participants can weatherstrip homes and offices, and can provide other energy saving measures to public buildings. But they do so in a politicized context: they do not treat energy conservation as simply a good thing, but as a political practice that involves, among other things, lobbying for state and national energy policies, and fighting unfair utility practices. In funding and staffing CUBs, a national service organization can encourage civic enterprise in quasi-public organizations, but on a local level.

ALTERNATIVE MEDIA

National service might also create or fund democratic media organizations. It might recruit participants to initiate community newspapers or cable television programs devoted to the discussion of contemporary ideas and issues. Participants engage in a variety of tasks, including writing, editing, producing, etc.; thus, tasks are not limited to those with an "appropriate" background. Newspaper editors, television reporters, and production crews donate time to instruct the NSPs, but not to serve as the ultimate editorial authority. That authority would be collective. Media corporations could be canvassed or taxed in order to supply the funds necessary for such enterprise, as part of their civic duty. One might make the case to corporate executives that future employees could come from such an organization. The participatory experience they receive in national service might also transform that institution into a more democratic one, by making the media more accountable for their choice of what constitutes news.

In creating media tasks, a service program might either work with the Corporation for Public Broadcasting or help fund private groups. In the former, national service might provide money and labor for public television or National Public Radio. If this route is taken, though, the participants would have to be given socially and politically meaningful tasks. Thus, they might contribute to local public affairs shows or news broadcasts, or they might do research into the arts and present stories on local music performances or art exhibits.

In the latter, national service might provide money and participants to any not-for-profit newspaper—public interest newsletters, for example—or help establish or reestablish community newspapers. This might involve using participants to restart a bankrupted community newspaper, or to begin a newspaper in communities that media organizations deem unprofitable. This catalyzes local political and social interest on the part of participants, and might stimulate competition in the for-profit newspapers to provide the sort of local coverage that they may have abandoned. Finally, it puts community news in the economic and political hands of local individuals. Local businesses might donate materials out of civic interest or in exchange for some publicity, or profits from media corporations could be taxed to provide the necessary funds. Or, like utilities, media corporations could be required to include subscription letters from these community groups when they send their bills—if for no other reason than to apprise the public that these newspapers, television, and radio stations exist.

THE NATIONAL SERVICE FANTASY

These are the sorts of tasks that a national service program based on democratic education ought to consider. They are also the programs that might best contribute to a more politically informed and respected citizenry. They are programs that call on individuals to develop skills for the community, and they include all citizens. Thus, national service becomes not a program for the young, but for all who wish to educate Americans.

The alternatives presented here, however unrealistic, have a number of advantages over current plans for national service. They treat civic education as an on-going process of discourse, and inculcate citizenship through participation in this discourse, not in particular definitions of *democracy, freedom, equality,* or *America.* They also respect the plurality of America, for they do not force individuals to accept uncomfortable ideological positions. However, they may force them to take *stands* on particular policies, issues, and ideas. This requires them to defend the positions they hold, and thus teaches them how to reason about politics in a more constructive manner. Finally, they seek to raise people's interest in politics, not force them to conform to particular standards of behavior appropriate to someone's concept of the American community.

But these ideas also transgress political reality in America, for what corporation would agree to be taxed in order to provide alternative media? Which successful professionals would leave their positions at Salomon Brothers to teach people how to read? Which members of the Armed Services Committee would fund research programs that could radically transform the military as an institution? Finally, what politician is going to want to tax his or her constituents to create a costly government program of this sort, regardless of its voluntariness or decentralized structure? These are realistic questions without, at the moment, realistic answers.

My suggestions simply indicate that alternatives are available. Implementing these alternatives takes great political will, and forces planners to reconceptualize the nature of national service, as an educational institution, not merely as a means of political socialization.

The public must understand the pitfalls involved in establishing national service—not only in practical terms, but in its very philosophy. It is easy to be in favor of service: everyone would like to help his or her fellow citizen. The question is, however, in whose service national service will be employed, and whether such services enrich the moral life of every citizen.[39] Those who wish to serve their country ought to point out to lawmakers and citizens alike the dangers inherent in a service-based program of citizen socialization.

More specifically, those intellectuals and activists on the political Left (Democrats, neoliberals, communitarians) who believe that America needs a greater sense of community, and who believe that "service" may be a way to achieve this, must look more carefully at what they mean by service. They must also look more carefully at what it means to establish community through programs of national service and voluntary organizations, and what this might mean for the individual citizen. The Left must reconsider in what form such programs are compatible with their notions of distributive justice.

Finally, it is very easy to blame those without power in this country, and young people are a natural target. But the problems of which young people are accused arise in a society created, and re-created, by their elders. The very discussion of national service in its present form neglects the responsibility of the older citizen in the making and remaking of the American political community. Young people are not going to want to serve a country where their exemplars serve themselves. If national service is to be implemented it ought to be *national,* and that means all of us. Any other policy is hypocritical.

NOTES

CHAPTER 1

1. William James, "The Moral Equivalent of War," *International Conciliation*, no. 27 (Washington, D.C.: Carnegie Endowment for International Peace, 1910), pp. 8–20.
2. Quoted in John A. Salmond, *The Civilian Conservation Corps, 1933–1942: A New Deal Case Study* (Durham, N.C.: Duke University Press, 1967), p. 13.
3. The National and Community Service Act of 1990 states that its *primary* purpose is "to renew the ethic of civic responsibility in the United States" (section 2[1]). This purpose is also the primary justification given by Senator Edward Kennedy, its chief sponsor, in arguing for its passage. Press Release, on the Conference Report on the National and Community Service Act of 1990, Office of Senator Edward M. Kennedy, October 12, 1990.
4. See, for instance, Robert Bellah et al., *Habits of the Heart: Individualism and Commitment in American Life* (New York: Harper and Row, 1985).
5. Charles C. Moskos, *A Call to Civic Service: National Service for Country and Community* (New York: Free Press, 1988), pp. 4–8.
6. Benjamin R. Barber, *Strong Democracy: Participatory Politics for a New Age* (Berkeley: University of California Press, 1984), p. 262.
7. Benjamin R. Barber, "Service, Citizenship and Democracy: Civic Duty as an Entitlement of Civil Right," in Williamson Evers, ed., *National Service: Pro and Con* (California: Hoover Institution Press, 1990), pp. 35–36.
8. Ibid., p. 36.
9. Michael Walzer, *Spheres of Justice: A Defense of Pluralism and Equality* (New York: Basic Books, 1983), p. 175–76, 182.
10. Michael Walzer, "Socializing the Welfare State," in Amy Gutmann, ed., *Democracy and the Welfare State* (Princeton: Princeton University Press, 1988), p. 22. For another argument for national service, see Robert Fullinwider, "Citizenship and Welfare," in Gutmann, *Democracy and the Welfare State*, pp. 261–278.
11. Walzer, "Socializing the Welfare State," p. 24.
12. I premise my study on this position, though I do not necessarily conclude that this is true.
13. On this account, *citizenship* fulfills the criteria of contestability laid out by W. B. Gallie and William Connolly: It is (1) an appraisive concept, (2) one which describes an internally complex set of practices, and (3) "open." W. B. Gallie, "Essentially Contested Concepts," *Pro-*

ceedings of the Aristotelian Society, 56 (1955–1956): 171–72; William Connolly, *The Terms of Political Discourse* (Oxford: Martin Robinson, 1983). Gallie states that "to use an essentially contested concept means to use it against other uses and to recognize that one's own use of it has to be maintained against those other uses" (p. 172).

14. Fred Newmann, *Education for Citizen Action: Challenge for Secondary Curriculum* (Berkeley: McCutchan, 1975), pp. 46–54.

15. I do not necessarily mean that all proponents of national service have the same definition of *citizenship*. I do mean that all proponents of national service either define the boundaries of citizenship explicitly, or, more usually, they do not even discuss the concept, and assume or imply a specific definition which emerges in their texts. Finally, almost all academic proponents of national service (Benjamin Barber being an important exception) ignore or de-emphasize the active, learning, participatory side of being a good citizen.

16. Michael Walzer, "What Does it Mean to Be 'American'?" *Social Research* 57 (3) (Fall 1990): 614.

17. Carole Pateman, *The Sexual Contract* (California: Stanford University Press, 1988), p. 6, and *The Disorder of Women: Democracy, Feminism, and Political Theory* (Cambridge, England: Polity Press, 1989). Other scholars writing in this tradition include Birte Siim and Helga Hernes. See, for instance, Helga M. Hernes, "Scandinavian Citizenship," *Acta Sociologica* 1988 31 (3): 199–215.

18. Pateman, *Sexual Contract*, pp. 93–94.

19. Pateman, *Disorder of Women*, p. 12.

20. On the ethic-of-care/responsibility argument from a variety of viewpoints, see Carol Gilligan, *In a Different Voice: Psychological Theory and Women's Development* (Cambridge: Harvard University Press, 1982); Sara Ruddick, "Maternal Thinking," *Feminist Studies* 6 (Summer 1980): 342–67; and Iris Marion Young, "Impartiality and the Civic Public: Some Implications of Feminist Critiques of Moral and Political Theory," *Praxis International* 5 (4) (January 1986): 381–401. On its relationship to political obligation, see Nancy J. Hirschmann, "Freedom, Recognition and Obligation; A Feminist Approach to Political Theory," *American Political Science Review* 83 (4) (December 1989): 1241.

21. I am not arguing here that political socialization is completely inappropriate to the goals of a national service organization. I *am* suggesting that emphasizing socialization, to the almost total exclusion of political education for citizenship (and its understanding as a contestable concept), will not fulfill the civic goals national service planners promote. According to many researchers (e.g, Adelson and O'Neil, Sigel and Hoskin, Merelman, Easton and Dennis) most, if not all, political socialization occurs at a relatively young age. The wisdom or utility of trying to socialize young adults in similar ways that one does a child is therefore questionable.

22. In Chapter 6, I also engage the argument that national service can inculcate a service ethic, and I try to show that this sort of argument is poor substitute for the citizenship one.

23. Burton Zwiebach distinguishes political socialization from political education. He states that the former is the training of citizens to accept the civic responsibilities imposed upon them by social institutions and authorities, while the latter is the education of free citizens in the practice of making independent political judgments. Burton Zwiebach, *Civility and Disobedience* (Cambridge: Cambridge University Press, 1975).

24. Amy Gutmann, *Democratic Education* (Princeton: Princeton University Press, 1987), pp. 15–16.

25. Ibid., pp. 42–43.

26. Ibid., p. 46.

27. A good example of this argument can be found in Steven Esquith, "Political Theory and Political Education," unpublished manuscript, Michigan State University, January 20, 1991.

28. Gutmann makes the argument that education does not end with formal schooling. *Democratic Education*, pp. 232–81. Moreover, a number of researchers in political socialization have also made the argument that learning is a lifelong process. These works are cited in the last two chapters of this book. Finally, common sense dictates that political learning is an integral part of any political process.

29. For more systematic defenses of the importance of participation for democratic citizenship than I have space for here, see Carole Pateman, *Participation and Democratic Theory* (Cambridge: Cambridge University Press, 1970); Amy Gutmann, *Liberal Equality* (Cambridge: Cambridge University Press, 1980); and Fred Newmann, "Political Participation: An Analytic Review and Proposal," in Derek Heater and Judith A. Gillespie, eds., *Political Education in Flux* (London: Sage, 1981), pp. 149–80.

30. Benjamin Barber calls this a kind of "we" thinking. *Strong Democracy*, p. 171.

31. Michael Ignatieff, "The Myth of Citizenship," *Queen's Quarterly* 94 (4) (Winter 1987): 968–71. This includes, I would argue, the understanding that political contestation is integral to the life of the citizen.

32. Richard Pratte, *The Civic Imperative: Examining the Need for Civic Education* (New York: Teacher's College Press, 1988).

33. See, for instance, J. Donald Moon, "The Moral Basis of the Welfare State," in Gutmann, *Democracy and Welfare State*, pp. 26–52.

34. Empirical evidence for this comes from Roberta S. Sigel and Marilyn B. Hoskin, *The Political Involvement of Adolescents* (New Brunswick: Rutgers University Press, 1981). I discuss this issue in more detail in the last chapter of this book.

35. Morris Janowitz, *The Reconstruction of Patriotism: Education for Civic Consciousness* (Chicago: University of Chicago Press, 1983), p. xi.

36. Ibid., p. xii. Moreover, it derogates, if not ignores, possible definitions of citizenship that do not "imply" a consumerist ethic.
37. Ibid., p. 3.
38. Ibid., p. 12.
39. Ibid., pp. 119, 122–28.
40. Ibid., p. 130.
41. Ibid., p. 134.
42. Ibid., p. 138, 143. Janowitz makes a similar argument in regard to the "women's liberation" movements of the 1960s.
43. Ibid., pp. 164–66.
44. Ibid., p. 171. It also very subtly suggests that women are not "doing their jobs" as mothers and teachers, and that their children now must be taken out of their hands and put into the hands of the state where they can receive "correct" instruction.
45. Ibid., pp. 175, 187.
46. Ibid., p. 189.
47. Ibid., p. 198.
48. "Individual Rights and Social Responsibilities: Fundamental Issues in National Service," *Public Law Forum* 4 (1) (1984): 241–57.
49. Ibid., p. 246.
50. Ibid., p. 250.
51. Ibid., p. 255.
52. "Why National Service?" in Michael W. Sherraden and Donald J. Eberly, eds., *National Service: Social, Economic, and Military Impacts* (New York: Pergamon Press, 1982), pp. 3–20; quote from p. 6.
53. Ibid., pp. 7, 11. Also see Donald J. Eberly, "National Service: Alternative Strategies," *Armed Forces and Society* 3 (3) (May 1977). "The same young person who before entry into national service would be tempted to steal a car and go for a joyride will be able to drive 300 miles a day in the highway safety patrol and get paid for it. And the same person he might have robbed a few months ago, he will now rescue from an overturned car" (p. 453).
    This quote assumes a number of things: (1) that "driving 300 miles a day" is somehow a good thing, instead of a drain on the economy and the ecology; (2) that being a member of the highway safety patrol will either allow that young person to contribute in a manner beyond most clerical work, or provide something significant for him to do in life beyond just driving; and (3) that the joyride is not the only way that a young person might choose to obtain the money on which he must live. It also suggests that, despite the best intentions of service proponents like Eberly, arguments for national service sometimes remain couched in the language of criminality and deviance.
54. Sherraden and Eberly, "Why National Service?" pp. 6, 4. For a similar argument that youth unemployment is a social danger, and that the "selfishness" of youth "could represent a corrosive influence within American society as dangerous as any outside enemy," see Committee

for the Study of National Service, *Youth and the Needs of the Nation* (Washington, D.C.: Potomac Institute, January 1979), pp. 61–62, 77.

55. Moskos, *Call to Service*, p. 4.
56. Ibid., p. 3.
57. "To be sure, none of these activities contains civic content; quite the contrary," ibid., p. 4.
58. Ibid., p. 9.
59. Ibid., pp. 97–99, 95.
60. Ibid., pp. 129–44.
61. Ibid., pp. 173–74.
62. Charles Moskos, "National Service and Its Enemies," in Evers, *National Service*, p. 203.
63. He employs similar rhetorical strategies for the restoration of books in the Library of Congress (ibid., p. 203), and for college student loan programs (see the next chapter of this book).
64. Ibid., p. 179.
65. Amitai Etzioni, *An Immodest Agenda: Rebuilding America before the Twenty-First Century* (New York: McGraw-Hill, 1983), p. xii.
66. Ibid., p. 27.
67. Ibid., p. 31. Despite the fact that workers "validate" their supervisors, their supervisors do much more than validate workers, they control their economic livelihood.
68. Ibid., pp. 39, 49.
69. Ibid., p. 62.
70. Ibid., pp. 168–69, 188.
71. Ibid., p. 368.
72. See, for instance, Amitai Etzioni, *Towards Higher Education in an Active Society: Three Policy Guidelines* (New York: Center for Policy Research, June 1970), p. 32; "The Case for a New Youth Conservation Corps," *Human Behavior* 5 (8) (August 1976): 13; and "A Remedy for Overeducation—A Year of Required National Service," *Change* 15 (4) (May/June 1983): 8. In the 1976 and 1983 articles he remarks that "the 'total' nature of the situation...is what promises the sociological impact."
73. Etzioni, *Towards Higher Education*, p. III–1. Note the curious way he phrases the sentence—it suggests that family life somehow contributes to, or does not tame, the animality of children. Again, this intimates the failure of women in the socializing process.
74. Etzioni, "Remedy for Overeducation," p. 8.
75. Etzioni, *Towards Higher Education*, p. 32.

CHAPTER 2

1. Alan Wertheimer, *Coercion* (Princeton: Princeton University Press, 1987), p. 172.

2. "The interesting question is not whether a given choice situation can be understood as coercive.... The interesting situation is whether A's alleged coercion nullifies B's responsibility for the normal moral or legal effects of his act." Ibid., p. 307.
3. Ibid., p. 187.
4. Coalition for National Service, *National Service: An Action Agenda for the 1990s* (Washington, D.C.: National Service Secretariat, 1988), p. 23.
5. "National Service: Action for Youth," *Synergist* 6 (3) (Winter 1978): 21.
6. Morris Janowitz, "National Service: A Third Alternative?" *Teacher's College Record* 73 (1) (September 1973): 15.
7. Timothy Noah, "We Need You: National Service, an Idea Whose Time Has Come," *The Washington Monthly*, November 1986, pp. 39–41.
8. Representative McCloskey made a parallel point at a Senate subcommittee hearing on national service, when he stated that "reasonable young men and women are [not] going to volunteer for military service unless the draft, the possibility of the draft, is in the background." Testimony on a Hearing for the Establishment of a Presidential Commission on National Service and a National Commission on Volunteerism, before the Subcommittee on Child and Human Development, Committee on Labor and Human Resources, United States Senate, 96th Congress, 2d session, March 13, 1980, p. 9. The very idea of a coercive threat compromises the use of the term *voluntary*.
9. For the reasons behind this see Robert Booth Fowler, "Political Obligation and the Draft," in Donald W. Hanson and Robert Booth Fowler, eds., *Obligation and Dissent: An Introduction to Politics* (Boston: Little, Brown, 1971), pp. 46–62. Fowler's defense of participation in relation to registration in citizen institutions is a good one, and for reasons of space I leave the reader to examine the full justification for this argument in his essay. For general defenses of participation, and its value to a democratic society and citizenship, see the works by Carole Pateman, Amy Gutmann, and Fred Newmann cited earlier.
10. Hanna Pitkin, "Obligation and Consent—I," *American Political Science Review* 59 (4) (December 1965): 999.
11. Hanna Pitkin, "Obligation and Consent—II," *American Political Science Review* 60 (1) (March 1966): 41.
12. Philip Bobbit, "National Service: Unwise or Unconstitutional?" in Martin Anderson, ed., *Registration and the Draft* (California: Hoover Institution Press, 1982): 299–330.
13. See n. 8.
14. James B. Jacobs has called this a "truly Draconian punishment, even more severe than a dishonorable discharge." "Compulsory and Voluntary National Service: Analysis of the McCloskey Bill and

Other Proposals," in *Socio-Legal Foundations of Civil-Military Relations* (New Brunswick: Transaction Books, 1986), p. 136.
15. Two previous bills—those of Senator Hatfield (R–Oreg.) and Representative Bingham (D–N.Y.)—were submitted in 1969 and 1970 respectively. Both of these were much more coercive than the McCloskey or Cavanaugh bills in their intent, virtually guaranteeing some sort of service by all young men. These bills were proposed as alternatives to the draft system at the time, and failed to pass Congress.
16. (Lexington, Mass.: Lexington Books, 1986), pp. 223–64.
17. Ibid., p. 255.
18. Nevertheless, this is an innovative way of adding to the federal government's coffers. However, such a surcharge can be subject to the same criticism that I make below for compulsory service. That is, by instituting a five percent surcharge on a person's annual income tax, the government encourages the individual to think instrumentally and to calculate the costs and benefits of that surcharge. This reinscribes a crude utilitarian ethic, which national service proponents criticize, and actually inhibits an understanding of the good of the community for its own sake. This underscores an atomistic conception of citizenship.
19. See, for example, Charles S. Moskos, *A Call to Civic Service: National Service for Country and Community* (New York: Free Press, 1988), pp. 155–60.
20. And such legal cases have indeed been made. See, for instance, the testimony of David E. Landau, for the American Civil Liberties Union (ACLU), in front of the Subcommittee on Child and Human Development, of the Committee on Labor and Human Resources, of the United States Senate. Presidential Commission on National Service and National Commission on Volunteerism, March 13, 1980, pp. 149–57; C. L. Black, Jr., "Constitutional Problems in Compulsory National Service," *Yale Law Reports* 13, (19) (Summer 1967): 9–21; George A. Costello, "Military and Civilian Conscription: Research Issues," 1980 Presidential Commission Report (see above), pp. 503–41; or Bobbit, "National Service," pp. 311ff.

Bobbit makes the argument that the ninth and tenth amendements deny the proposition that the United States is first a nation. This implies that we cannot have a *national* service program and expect it to be justified constitutionally (p. 325). Service, then, must be decentralized and voluntary. This is an important qualifier to those who wish to compare national service to youth movements in places like China. For example, Congressman Dave McCurdy, "A Quid Pro Quo for Youth," *New York Times*, June 26, 1989.

For a thoughtful defense of the constitutionality of "compulsory" service, see Thomas J. McGrew, "The Constitutionality of Compulsory National Service," *Public Law Forum* 4 (1) (1984): 259–67.

McGrew reasons that "compulsory" service does not violate the positive freedoms embodied in the thirteenth Amendment, which refer only to slavery, and serve to correct *racial* injustice. McGrew maintains that one cannot argue from analogy here, and presume that "involuntary servitude" is an elastic concept.

I agree with McGrew on this point, though some of the tasks proposed by national service planners may entail racial injustice, as well as "involuntary servitude" that discriminates against many sectors of the population (for instance, a "border patrol" corps, or a teaching corps which allows only a few, highly qualified individuals, to teach). I would argue that one could not, on principle, claim that national service violates the fifth or the thirteenth amendments, but that the sorts of jobs and functions those proponents are considering might violate those amendments. However, following Bobbit, one would have to consider carefully the constitutionality of a service that attempts to inculcate national values.

21. Here let me digress for a moment and consider one other argument against coercive service—that it is not part of the American tradition. This is Robert Bird's point in one part of "The Case for Voluntary Service," in Donald J. Eberly, ed., *National Service: Report of a Conference* (New York: Russell Sage Foundation, 1968), pp. 491–94, and is shared by a number of others. He contends that this country was founded (and achieved greatness) because of its distrust of government, and its tradition of checks and balances.

    First, checks and balances describes a system of governmental self-regulation, not a moral principle circumscribing all social and political relationships. But more importantly, national service is being proposed precisely because something went wrong with the "American tradition." Its supporters see it as an aid in remedying the problems of America, all of which are part of that tradition. So to decry coercive service as being untraditional is to tacitly accept the individualist premises of America which have caused its decline. This is paradoxical for someone who supports the concept of national service, for if the American tradition was that strong, no service would be necessary or even be deliberated.

    Finally, a number of historians have debunked the myth that America was founded on principles of strict individualism. See, for instance, the works of Bernard Bailyn or Gordon Wood. Also, many contemporary philosophers and social scientists would contend that there is an ethic of community and civic obligation in America that parallels Lockean individualism. See Robert Bellah, et al., *Habits of the Heart: Individualism and Commitment in American Life* (New York: Harper and Row, 1985), for the clearest example of this. So the American tradition is ambiguous at the least.

22. It has since become a part of the National and Community Service Act of 1990. In this section and the next, I choose examples of bills

that are ideal types of the kind supported by Moskos, Eberly, Sherraden and others. I do not describe the National and Community
Service Act of 1990 because it is a compromise bill, and does not
reflect a single image of national service.

23. For example, section 304 lists the sorts of agencies most appropriate
for agency funds—and virtually all of these are work programs,
though some include literacy training. Mikulski fails to include any
explicitly educational program, or political agencies which may train
the individual in political issues. Indeed the corporation itself is to
be "non-political" (in the sense of nonpartisan—see section 204 [c]),
which in itself is a partisan use of the term *political.*

24. Though to opponents of all forms of national service, these still
smack of governmental intrusion—and fiscal profligacy.

25. See, for instance, Robert Kuttner, "Give the Young a Better Chance
to Serve Their Country," *Business Week,* March 21, 1988, p. 15.

26. In the words of Representative Dave McCurdy: "Sure it's going to
cost more money, but think of the service you're going to get out of
it." Quoted in *Congressional Quarterly Weekly Report* 47 (12) (March
25, 1989): 647.

27. On these points see Stephen J. Pyne, *Fire in America: A Cultural
History of Wildland and Rural Fire* (Princeton: Princeton University
Press, 1982), p. 279; and for a more anecdotal account, see Ann
Marie Low, *Dust Bowl Diary* (Lincoln: University of Nebraska Press,
1984), pp. 157, 160. This sentiment remained in the 1980s—note
Representative Les Aspin's complaint: "If we send hundreds of thou-
sands of people to plant trees on the slopes of the Rockies, they
would trample more seedlings than they would plant." Quoted in
John M. Eddington, "National Service: Uphill All the Way," *Nation's
Business,* February 1980, p. 78.

28. This criticism is appropriate to all forms of national service. I return
to both these themes in Chapter 6.

29. This interpretation is reinforced by section 223(a)(2).

30. The figures I am quoting here are for civilian service, those in the
military would receive higher benefits—an incentive to join these
units.

31. As Moskos puts it, "in time, participation in some form of national
service would become a prerequisite for federal post-secondary
school assistance." Charles C. Moskos, "Making the All-Volunteer
Force Work: A National Service Approach," *Foreign Affairs,* 60 (1)
(Fall 1981): 27.

32. Williamson M. Evers of the Hoover Institute has called the plan
"indentured servitude." *New York Times,* April 15, 1989.

33. There is empirical evidence that community service programs
emphasizing the individual benefits derived from them do not lead
to greater civic understanding or appreciation. See Robert A. Rutter
and Fred M. Newmann, "The Potential of Community Service to

Enhance Civic Responsibility," *Social Education* (October 1989): 373.

34. Democratic Leadership Council, *Citizenship and National Service: A Blueprint for Civic Enterprise*, Washington, D.C., May 1988, p. 79.
35. "Sam Nunn Wants You," *New Republic*, June 6, 1988, p. 50.
36. *Citizenship and National Service*, pp. 16–18. The council's plan rests largely on the work of Moskos, op cit, pp. 160–62. Moskos reasons that federal aid is already becoming inaccessible to many underprivileged groups and that such a program would "most likely widen rather than restrict access to higher education." This reasoning, though, does not justify such a policy, for one could just as easily reverse the policies of the Reagan administration and make federal educational aid more available to all. Thus it only holds if one accepts the morality of the educational loan policy set out by the Republicans.

Moskos also claims that student aid "by its very nature is regressive." And that only half of all young people even enter college, so most of the aid goes to those with better prospects anyway. Again, this pragmatic line rests on an acceptance of administration policy; and it ignores the issues surrounding the questions "Why do only half of the young people of the country go to college?" and "What kind of a culture produces a large number of individuals who have 'dead-end prospects'?" Moskos assumes the truth and the morality of recent administration policy in arguing that educational aid must be tied in with national service, without engaging in the issue of whether higher education is a fundamental right to which everyone ought to be entitled. This indicates that the debate over what I have called "compulsory" national service does not operate in a historical vacuum.
37. Except for Richard Danzig and Peter Szanton, *National Service: What Would It Mean?* (Lexington, Mass.: Lexington Books, 1986).
38. There are some exceptions to this. For instance, VISTA volunteers help construct or reconstruct houses for poor residents, and presumably some NSPs would do likewise. Also, there may be instances where NSPs would help out in a particularly difficult harvest period. But these instances would be few and far between, and there are many special interests who would try to ensure that NSPs did not make these tasks a regular part of their program. The vast majority of NSPs would remain in service industries.
39. DLC, *Citizenship and National Service*, p. 4.
40. I justify my use of the CCC as an example in Chapter 4, note 34.

CHAPTER 3

1. For instance, the Ford Foundation or the Arthur Vining Davis Foundation. See Michael J. Nyhan and Michael Palmer, *National Service*

in the United States: Problems, Prospects, and Opportunities, Menlo Park: Institute for the Future, 1979, p. 22; and "Social Science and the Citizen," *Society* 23 (6) (September/October 1986): 2.

2. William R. King, *Achieving America's Goals: National Service or the All-Volunteer Force,* Committee on Armed Services, U.S. Senate, Washington, D.C., 1977, p. 94.

3. Gary Hart, "The Case for National Service," *USA Today,* November 1985, p. 11. Also see the prepared statement by Bishop Joseph M. Sullivan at a hearing in front of the Subcommittee on Employment Opportunities of the House Education and Labor Committee, for The Voluntary National Youth Service Act and the Select Commission on National Service Opportunities Act of 1985, 94th Congress, 1st sess., September 27, 1985, p. 51. Or see the testimony of W. E. Phillips, Chairman of Ogilvy Group Advertising, at the same hearing, p. 100.

4. "Findings and Recommendations of the Committee," from *Youth and the Needs of the Nation,* reprinted in the 1985 Congressional committee hearings (cited in note 3), p. 162.

5. *Presidential Commission on National Service and National Commission on Volunteerism,* hearing before the House Subcommittee on Child and Human Development, March 13, 1980, p. 31.

6. Amitai Etzioni, "A Remedy for Overeducation—A Year of Required National Service," *Change* 15 (4) (May/June 1983): 7–9.

7. Samuel Halperin, "What's Wrong with Youth Service," *Streams,* February/March 1989, p. 2. One could argue that current proposals for national service are not only part of a general youth strategy, but a simplistic way of attacking social problems in a general way. That is, instead of developing comprehensive policies to assist the homeless, or drug addicts, or pregnant teenagers, or whoever, national service makes quick-fix solutions easier.

8. "A Proposal for National Service for the 1980s," in Michael W. Sherraden and Donald J. Eberly, eds., *National Service: Social, Economic, and Military Impacts* (New York: Pergamon Press, 1982), p. 107.

9. Leon Bramson, "National Service and American Youth: A Proposal," in Donald J. Eberly, ed., *A Profile of National Service* (New York: Overseas Educational Service, 1966), p. 38.

10. Donald J. Eberly, from a Letter to the *New York Times,* May 1, 1989. Also, see Michael W. Sherraden and Donald J. Eberly, "Individual Rights and Social Responsibilities: Fundamental Issues in National Service," *Public Law Forum* 4 (1) (1984): 257; and *Presidential Commission,* March 13, 1980, p. 85.

11. Eberly, Letter to the *New York Times.*

12. Danzig and Szanton, *National Service,* pp. 279–80. Also, see Eberly's remarks about the Program for Local Service in Seattle, in the 1985 hearing before the House subcommittee, op cit, pp. 124–25.

13. Morris Janowitz, in the Introduction to *Teacher's College Record* 73 (1) (September 1973): 4.

14. Donald J. Eberly, "A National Service Pilot Project," *Teacher's College Record* 73 (1) (September 1973): 75. Eberly refers to Seattle's Program for Local Service in this manner: "I recommended...that we do the project somewhere in the state of Washington since its governor, Daniel J. Evans, had said very positive things about national service in his 1968 keynote address to the Republican National Convention. When something is first tested, I figured, it requires good growing conditions." Eberly claims paradoxically that this was the "purest test to date," yet it appears that he subordinated scientific rigor to politics. Donald J. Eberly, *National Service: A Promise to Keep* (Rochester, N.Y.: John Alden Books, 1988), p. 130.

15. Ibid., p. 79.

16. Ibid.

17. Even Danzig and Szanton admit that voluntary organizations could be mere intermediary stages towards compulsory service. *National Service*, p. 255.

18. Martin Anderson, "The Dirty Work Philosophy of National Service," in Williamson Evers, ed., *National Service*, pp. 236–42.

19. Such an agency has been proposed by many, if not all, Congressional and academic supporters of national service. The only plan does not include this corporation, or some form of it, is Danzig and Szanton's proposal for "school-based" national service (*National Service*, pp. 89–94). The authors do not regard this program as a particularly promising one for it is "not likely to show substantial achievements," though it may "warrant testing." (p. 117).

    I do not consider this plan in my survey of national service programs for a few reasons. First, the most important congressional proposals promote service organizations for individuals between 18 and 26. Second, school-based service radically changes the purposes of secondary education, and so requires a rethinking of the nation's entire education policy. I am not prepared to do that here. Third, school-based service would be so decentralized that it may not guarantee a truly *national* service. Consequently there is no guarantee that individuals would learn similar lessons.

    Fourth, school-based service would make no provisions for special citizenship training that do not already exist in civics programs. Yet these very programs come under attack by service proponents for inadequately inculcating a sense of civic obligation in the spirits of America's youth. Fifth, the quality of the service reflects the quality of the school, and schools in the inner city or poor rural areas might not fare so well. Thus, national service would not meet some of society's "most pressing social problems," and so a central argument by the supporters of national service would be neutralized. Finally, a school service program could very likely fall victim to what Anne Lewis has called "bureaucratic doldrums," and lose its innovative quality. See Ann C. Lewis, *Facts and Faith: A Status Report on*

Youth Service William T. Grant Foundation Commission on Work, Family, and Citizenship, Washington, D.C., August 1988, p. 16. The most extensive survey of service programs—Danzig and Szanton's 1986 project—concluded that this form of service was not promising. *National Service,* p. 117.

20. *Senate Resolution 3,* 101st Congress, 1st sess., January 25, 1989, section 202(a).
21. No "more than $10,000 in any fiscal year," SR 3, section 203(h)(3). It is ironic that the board members could earn more money for their efforts than individual participants would under the terms of this bill.
22. SR 3, section 206(a)(2). Eberly suggests that the corporation "certify" this work. See *Presidential Commission* March 13, 1980, p. 357.
23. This is how Eberly explicitly conceives of appropriate venues for service. "A beginning point for the operation of a national service program would be the establishment of basic criteria, which an activity must satisfy in order to qualify as an approved service within the framework of national service. Included in these would be the absence of political or religious prosletyzing and the assurance that the proposed activity would not impinge on the interests of agriculture, business, or labor." Donald J. Eberly, "Guidelines for National Service," in Sol Tax, ed., *The Draft: A Handbook of Facts and Alternatives* (Chicago: University of Chicago Press, 1967), p. 111. Eberly fails to discuss what constitutes "prosletyzing."
24. SR 3, section 206(b). Similar, though slightly less restrictive, language can be found in the "National and Community Service Act of 1990," Public Law 101–610, subtitle D, sections 141–43.
25. SR 3, section 206(d).
26. Steven Muller, "The Case for Universal National Service," *Educational Record* 52 (1) (Winter, 1971), p. 21.
27. John A. Salmond, *The Civilian Conservation Corps, 1933–1942: A New Deal Case Study* (Durham, N.C.: Duke University Press, 1967).
28. Most of these regulations were taken almost verbatim from army regulations, but they all had to be approved by the directors of the agency.
29. *Federal Register* 48 (35) (February 18, 1983), section 1656.1(b)(4).
30. Ibid., section 1656.6(a)(1)(II). For a listing of such "appropriate" activities see section 1656.5(a)(2); ibid., section 1656.11(a).
31. On November 8, 1991, the federal government published proposed rules concerning the National and Community Service Act of 1990, but final rules were not set to come out until January 22, 1992. Nevertheless, the proposed rules are extensive and disciplinary. *Federal Register,* Vol. 56, No. 217, 11/8/91, pp. 57404–57471. Note especially §2506.6 and §2506.8.
32. Samuel Halperin, "What's Wrong," p. 2.
33. Though a case could be made that even conservation work is something that serves humans rather than merely produces goods, and

so it, too, could have a human-relationship function. *Conservation* here means not only conservation of nature, like the CCC performed, but also means conserving historic districts and houses within a city. More broadly, it also means renovating houses to provide adequate low-income housing for the needy, though this might be blocked by the construction industry and its unions.

34. Danzig and Szanton, *National Service*, p. 40. See my critique of this ideology in Chapter 6 of this book.
35. One example of this is that compliance with the Federal Drug Workplace Act is mandatory in the National and Community Service Act of 1990.
36. Richard Coe's analysis of the Kenyan national service program in the 1960s suggests that this was exactly how it was used there. See Richard L. Coe, *The Kenya National Youth Service: A Governmental Response to Young Political Activists* (Athens, Oh: Ohio University Center for International Studies, Africa Program, 1973), p. 14.
37. See, for instance, the Voluntary National Youth Service Act of 1988, *HR 888*, 99th Congress, 1st sess., January 31, 1985, section 5(d)(3).
38. Donald J. Eberly, ed., *A Profile of National Service* (New York: Overseas Educational Service, 1966), p. x.
39. Written testimony before the 1985 subcommittee hearing for the Voluntary National Youth Service Act, p. 129.
40. Charles Moskos, *Call to Civic Service*, p. 170.
41. Ibid., p. 172.
42. Albert O. Hirschman, *Shifting Involvements: Private Interest and Public Action* (Princeton: Princeton University Press, 1982). Moskos, *Call to Civic Service*, p. 172.
43. Moskos, *Call to Civic Service*, p. 172.
44. I will also argue below that the insistence on providing "technical" work perpetuates the status quo and thus expresses an otherwise latent political stance.
45. Moskos, *Call to Civic Service*, p. 172.
46. Hirschman, *Shifting Involvements*, pp. 40–41.
47. William Serrin, "A Great American Job Machine? The Myth of the 'New Work'," *Nation*, September 18, 1989, pp. 269–72. In this article Serrin reveals the authoritarian nature of the "new work" in advanced technology industries, "despite much ballyhoo about creative, mutually participatory relationships between employers and employees." Moreover, he argues that "most of the new jobs are not high-tech but low-tech." Indeed it is these positions—restaurant workers, clerks, maids, etc.—for which national service will provide training.
48. A teacher corps is probably the closest element of national service that requires a good deal of critical and creative thinking. But even a teacher corps intends on having participants assist the teacher, and so they may not always have the opportunity to teach. See my comments below.

49. Rutter and Newmann, "Potential of Community Service," Also, see Danzig and Szanton, *National Service*, p. 106.

50. In Chapter 6, I criticize these reflective components in the name of a service philosophy.

51. Serrin, "Great American," p. 272.

52. The Congressional Budget Office reported that for public employment and training programs, "it is difficult to design the projects so that the skills gained are transferable to the private sector." *Policy Options for the Teenage Unemployment Problem*, background paper no. 13, September 21, 1976 (Washington, D.C.: Congressional Budget Office), p. 76. Also, see Danzig and Szanton, *National Service*, p. 102. They argue that benefits in some forms of service will not be from "exposure to work" but from discipline.

53. Ellen Greenberger and Laurence Steinberg, *When Teenagers Work: The Psychological and Social Costs of Adolescent Employment* (New York: Basic Books, 1986).

54. Ibid., pp. 22–24, 190–94.

55. Ibid., p. 126. Greenberger and Steinberg cite studies by Gottfredson, Shannon, and Ruggiero, as well as their own findings.

56. This is further confirmed by the National Bureau of Economic Research study that I cite in Chapter 5, note 20.

57. Ibid., p. 212.

58. Ibid., p. 215.

59. See, for instance, Danzig and Szanton, *National Service*; DLC, *Citizenship and National Service*, p. 37; or Muller, "Case for National Service," p. 18.

60. William B. Johnston and Arnold E. Packer, *Workforce 2000: Work and Workers for the 21st Century* (Indianapolis: Hudson Institute, 1987), p. 99. Also, note their comment on page 111: "the system should be much more oriented toward stimulating movement and change by workers, rather than simply protecting them against joblessness." This report was written for the Department of Labor.

61. In the pages to follow, I do not consider conservation work for two reasons. First, as the next chapters will make clear, I rely on examples from the CCC to describe procedures within a service organization. Through these means, I do, ultimately, discuss, conservation work. Second, the work I consider in this chapter falls into the category of "new work" that I have discussed, and thus provides a sort of postindustrial answer to the CCC.

62. Cynthia Parsons, "National Service for All," *Phi Delta Kappan*, June 1984, p. 688.

63. This assumes that such a program would not threaten the professional rights and privileges of teachers. NSPs ought not to be substitutes for well-paid teachers.

64. *New York Times* editorial, August 28, 1989.

65. Danzig and Szanton, *National Service*, p. 22.

66. Ibid., p. 23.
67. Ibid., p. 29. Also, see Moskos, *Call to Civic Service,* p. 148.
68. "Study Finds High Turnover in Child Care Workers," *New York Times,* October 18, 1989.
69. Largely because they are the centers which have the organizational capability of handling large numbers of volunteers, and which can meet the regulatory requirements of screening, monitoring, and training participants.
70. Deborah Fallows, *A Mother's Work* (Boston: Houghton Mifflin, 1985), pp. 66–67.
71. Ibid., p. 69. Later she savagely indicts the one corporate, for-profit center she visits: Kinder-Care; see pp. 86ff.
72. This is confirmed by Johnston and Packer, *Workforce 2000,* p. 88.
73. Note Donald Eberly's comment that women "should be allowed a maximum of opportunities to serve voluntarily in *appropriate* national service activities." Eberly, 1966, *Profile of National Service,* p. 14 (emphasis added). Or see Morris Janowitz' recommendation that national service programs "protect women as future mothers from inappropriate types of physical strains." He adds that pregnancy could be considered a breach of contract "comparable to going AWOL in males." "The Logic of National Service," in Tax, *The Draft,* p. 108.
74. Moskos, *Call to Civic Service,* p. 150.
75. Danzig and Szanton, *National Service,* p. 25.
76. Ibid., p. 27. Danzig and Szanton also make this point for the child care and corrections systems.
77. Ibid., p. 28. This is ironic considering that many people argue for national service on the ground that it weans individuals from addictive substances.
78. In the case of psychiatric institutions, I discuss below the institutional worldview that may come with participation in a total institution.
79. Hirschman, *Shifting Involvements,* pp. 123–25.
80. For evidence of medical experimentation in CCC programs, see Eric Gorham, *National Service, Citizenship, and Political Education,* PhD thesis (Madison: University of Wisconsin, 1990), pp. 248–54.
81. Eberly, "National Service Program," in Eberly, 1966, *Profile of National Service,* p. 26.
82. *National Service,* pp. 24, 27.
83. DLC, *Citizenship and National Service,* p. 37.
84. *National Service,* p. 38.
85. Samuel D. Proctor, "To the Rescue: A National Youth Academy," *New York Times,* September 16, 1989. This is a curious proposal that effectively institutionalizes young people before they have committed criminal acts. Proctor insists that "there are legal ways of finding out who they are and enrolling them." He also suggests that

"this program could be coordinated with some form of national service."

86. SR 1299, 101st Congress, 1st sess., section 2(1).
87. *New York Times* editorial, July 14, 1989.
88. *Call to Civic Service*, 1988, p. 149.
89. James B. Jacobs, "The Implications of National Service for Corrections," in *New Perspectives on Prisons and Imprisonment* (Ithaca: Cornell University Press, 1983), pp. 202–12.
90. Ibid., p. 209. Though I do not see how prisoners themselves would perceive this as more legitimate.
91. Ibid., p. 212.
92. SR 1299, section 9(c)(3)(A).
93. See Gorham, *National Service*, pp. 222–74, as well as Chapter 7 below.
94. Ibid., section 5(e).
95. James B. Jacobs, "Compulsory and Voluntary National Service: Analysis of the McCloskey Bill and Other Proposals," in *Socio-Legal Foundations of Civil-Military Relations* (New Brunswick, N.J.: Transaction Books, 1986), p. 135.
96. See, for instance, Erving Goffman, *Asylums: Essays on the Social Situation of Mental Patients and Other Inmates* (New York: Anchor Books, 1961), p. 74.
97. Michel Foucault, *The History of Sexuality: Volume I, An Introduction*, tr. Robert Hurley (New York: Vintage Books, 1978), p. 107.
98. This is especially true for those innocents like illegal aliens, who have broken the law because they want to *join* the American community. Thus, this can hold for people disciplined even without being criminals.
99. Michel Foucault, *Power/Knowledge: Selected Interviews and Other Writings, 1972–1977*, ed. Colin Gordon (New York: Pantheon Books, 1980), pp. 59, 158–59.
100. SR 1299, section 7(c).
101. In prisons or mental hospitals, this problem of "organizational loyalty," could manifest itself in a particular worldview, as Goffman describes for total institutions. "The staff tend to evolve what may be thought of as a theory of human nature. As an implicit part of institutional perspective, this theory rationalizes activity, provides a subtle means of maintaining social distance from inmates and a stereotyped view of them, and justifies the treatment accorded them." Goffman, *Asylums*, p. 87. Thus, NSPs in total institutions may not provide a democratic check, but could, if they worked there long enough, take on the perspective of the staff.
102. Foucault calls this a "carceral system" for prisons, and it involves "the production of an objectivity, a technique, a penitentiary 'rationality'." *Discipline and Punish: The Birth of the Prison*, tr. Alan Sheridan (New York: Vintage Books, 1977), p. 271.

103. By opening up the prison and border patrol systems to the participants, it also extends "panoptic" institutions further into society. It
allows everybody to observe and be observed, and in this way
deploys disciplinary mechanisms to more of the population. For
more on the panoptic conditions of a democratic society, see Foucault, *Discipline and Punish*, p. 207.

CHAPTER 4

1. Morris Janowitz, "The Logic of National Service," in Tax, *The Draft*,
p. 89.
2. This is evident from Eberly's comments in *Presidential Commission*,
March 13, 1980, p. 364. Or see *Youth and the Needs of the Nation*,
Potomac Institute, Washington, D.C., p. 131.
3. George Grant, "Thinking about Technology," in *Technology and Justice* (Notre Dame: University of Notre Dame Press, 1986), p. 23.
4. Etzioni, "A Remedy for Overeducation," p. 9.
5. Donald Eberly, "National Service Program," in Eberly, *Profile of
National Service*, p. 26. It is also required for alternative service
work. See *Federal Register* 48 (35) (February 18, 1983), section
1656.16(2). Also see Richard W. Boone and Norman G. Kurland,
"Freedom, National Security, and the Elimination of Poverty: Is
Compulsory Service Necessary?" in Tax, *The Draft*, p. 275. They
claim that universal registration and testing will "uncover education
and health defects that remain largely undetected today." Finally,
see Harris Wofford's remarks in Tax, *The Draft*, p. 390.
6. John Naisbitt, "Education and Rehabilitation for National Service
Participants," in Eberly, *National Service: Report*, pp. 285ff.
7. Eberly, *National Service: Report*, pp. 425–64.
8. Joshua L. Miner III, and Dyke V. Williams, "National Service Summer Camps: A Time for Learning," in Eberly, *National Service:
Report*, pp. 427–39.
9. David Dichter, "A Model for National Service Placement Centers," in
Eberly, *National Service: Report*, pp. 441–51.
10. Eberly, *National Service: Report*, p. 442. See also Donald Eberly, "A
Guideline for National Service," in Tax, *The Draft*, p. 112.
11. Dichter, "Model for National Service," pp. 443, 444.
12. Ibid., p. 446.
13. Ibid., p. 446. The camps model has always been taken seriously as
an organizational principle for national service. See *Presidential
Commission*, March 13, 1980, pp. 334–38. It is even used in nonresi-
dential programs like New York City's City Volunteer Corps. See
Voluntary National Youth Service Act, September 27, 1985, pp.
64–65.
14. Dichter, "Model for National Service," p. 459.
15. William R. King, *Achieving America's Goals: National Service and*

the All-Volunteer Force, report to the Committee on Armed Services, U.S. Senate, Washington, D.C., 1977, pp. 7, 61.

16. Ibid., pp. 63, 65, 94.

17. Daniel F. Huck and David S. Mundel, *National Service Programs and Their Effects on Military Manpower and Civilian Youth Problems,* Congressional Budget Office, Washington, D.C., January 1978, p. 58.

18. Ibid., p. 62.

19. *Presidential Commission,* March 13, 1980, p. 461.

20. Ibid., p. 62.

21. Ibid., p. 64.

22. SR 33, sections 221, 222, 223, 225.

23. An earlier service bill—The Voluntary National Service Act of 1985—made such testing an explicit part of its program. See HR 888, section 5(b)(3). This bill indirectly mandates testing in order to provide for extensive aggregate data on the enrollees. See section 10(b).

24. In 1989, Edward Kennedy's bill, SR 650, and Mikulski's bill, HR 1000, both involved required training programs.

25. Donald J. Eberly and Michael W. Sherraden, "Alternative Models of National Service," in Sherraden and Eberly, *National Service,* p. 102.

26. These include: (1) less than full-time work, (2) inadequate explanation of responsibilities, (3) "forbidden duties" such as religious prosletyzing or political campaigning, and (4) absence of a training program. Eberly and Sherraden, "Alternative Models," p. 102. This further points up the civic and intellectual weaknesses of the idea of national service, because: (a) vouchers reinscribe the notion of government as a system of entitlement, (b) individuals are forced to sign contracts with agencies, thus binding them to fulfill their duties (this may have juridical implications: does failing to fulfill the contract entail civil penalties?), and (c) the service program itself demands a restricted conception of what it means to serve. In this instance it is no "religious prosletyzing or political campaigning," whatever this means. Yet religion and politics are two of the most vital defining characteristics of a community. At the very least, Eberly and Sherraden are too ambiguous about the nature of the civic.

27. Danzig and Szanton suggest testing targeted groups—like health care workers, day care workers, and teacher's assistants, for both behavioral and health problems. *National Service,* p. 97. Also, see Parsons, "National Service," p. 688, for testing in educational services. For the "police corps," see SR 1299, section 6(b)(B). Finally, see Eberly's written testimony in *Presidential Commission,* March 13, 1980, p. 127, on the importance of data collection for youth service.

29. Moskos, *Call to Civic Service*, p. 157. He is not alone. Danzig and Szanton also fail to specify the processes of registration and testing in their analysis of the various forms of service programs. This is surprising, given how thorough they were in other aspects of the program. They tend to focus on program costs and size, but they do not propose the means by which individuals will be recruited and placed.
30. Moskos, *Call to Civic Service*, p. 163.
31. Charles Moskos, "The All-Volunteer Force," in Morris Janowitz and Stephen D. Wesbrook, eds., *The Political Education of Soldiers* (Beverly Hills: Sage Publications, 1983), p. 315.
32. Moskos admits this in *Call to Civic Service*, p. 163, when he argues that such advertising must be sold on the basis of the monetary value of services rendered, and postservice benefits available to the recruits.
33. For an example of a program which monitors its enrollees continuously, see the description of the Program for Local Service in Seattle in *Presidential Commission*, March 13, 1980, pp. 458–59. There is also evidence that such a program might mandate fingerprinting, which occurs in the New York City Volunteer Corps. See *Voluntary National Youth Service Act*, September 27, 1985, p. 63.
34. The CCC is not a perfect example of the structure and programming of a potential national service. First, it responded to the depression, and so initially presented itself as an employment service. But its proponents also claimed that it would enlighten its enrollees and make them more moral. The program also attempted to improve upon nature, and so all of its activities were outdoor ones, generally involving camps set off in remote areas. These camps insulated the enrollees, and removed them from their home communities. Potential national service camps will neither be exclusively rural, nor will they necessarily require individuals to move away from their hometowns or cities. (Though most programs call for a similarly constructed conservation corps and other programs which would require work camps or training camps). The CCC involved only men (generally white, though there were black and native American camps), between the ages of seventeen and twenty-three (though there were veterans' camps). Contemporary proposals for national service, on the other hand, involve all people, especially young people, regardless of gender or race. Finally, the military involved itself much more in the daily activities and organization of the CCC than would probably occur in a national service outfit.

    Nevertheless the CCC serves as a good litmus test for national service for a number of reasons. First, all proponents of national service cite the CCC as a successful citizenship and service program. They claim that its ideals, if not its particular structure, can serve as a model for future service programs. See, for example, Moskos,

Call to Civic Service, p. 33; Danzig and Szanton, *National Service,* p. 32; Donald Eberly and Michael Sherraden, "National Service Precedents in the United States," in Sherraden and Eberly, *National Service,* p. 42; and Morris Janowitz *The Reconstruction of Patriotism: Education for Civic Consciousness* (Chicago: University of Chicago Press, 1983), pp. 172–73. In short, the most vociferous proponents of the national service idea agree that the CCC was, if not an administrative model of a future program, then at least a moral prototype.

But the CCC was more than an ideal to be emulated, because its proponents used many of the same arguments to justify it as proponents of national service justify those programs. The CCC claimed to improve moral character, cure social problems, and meet social needs, and these arguments are still being made by proponents of national service. Moreover, by 1935 the CCC had expanded from a simple employment program to one seeking to educate its enrollees in a wide variety of subjects. So for most of its tenure the CCC was a service program that had high civic and cultural aspirations. This transformed it from a means of economic security into an organization for political and cultural training.

Thirdly, the CCC was the most systematic and extensive program of civilian service this country has ever seen. New Deal bureaucrats slaved endlessly devising programs and regulations designed to accomodate all the goals of service. The administrative apparatus of the CCC was independent of other government agencies, though various departments and agencies had a hand in determining its policies. This parallels the independent administrative apparatus proposed by national service proponents, and highlights the problems in creating a new federal agency of this sort. But the CCC can also "teach" service planners certain things; for instance, "the government could organize and manage a large, residential, effective youth service program" (Donald J. Eberly *Voluntary National Youth Service Act,* September 27, 1985, p. 113). The educational programs for the corps were also designed scientifically, and so we may glimpse the sorts of methods that may be used in designing national service. At the very least, we will be able to see the effects of a rationalized bureaucracy, with an ethic of efficiency and production, on a program designed to inculcate civic obligation.

Finally, within the CCC we can see the promise of a program of civic service based more on principles of political education than political socialization. There were certain aspects of the program—like a "leadership camp" organized in Vermont, and the occasional self-governing work camp—that represented the hopes for a community-oriented form of civilian service.

35. *Oxford English Dictionary,* "qualify."
36. These were only the basic attributes, for veterans' camps were set up, and some enrollees enrolled legally before they turned seventeen and

others into their late twenties. There were even reports of parolees being accepted in some of the western states. Finally, the special regulations for Native American camps allowed married persons to enroll.

37. In fact, the CCC offered qualifications in the form of an honorable discharge and an educational certificate. Moreover, some camps allowed their enrollees to receive a high school equivalency diploma. Occasionally, a camp or a corps area headquarters would also offer certificates if the enrollees passed training sessions in a particular vocation, too.

38. See the letter by Frank Davidson to Eugen Rosenstock-Huessy in Jack J. Preiss, *Camp William James* (Norwich, Vt.: Argo Books, 1978), p. 12.; and John A. Salmond, *The Civilian Conservation Corps, 1933–1942: A New Deal Case Study* (Durham, N.C.: Duke University Press, 1967), p. 184. Charles Moskos makes the point that towards the end of the 1930s the CCC came to be looked upon as a refuge for losers, and many communities did not even want the camps in their towns. Charles Moskos, "The Enlisted Ranks in the All-Volunteer Army," in John B. Keeley, ed., *The All-Volunteer Force and American Society* (Charlottesville: University of Virginia Press, 1978), p. 74.

39. Kenneth Holland and Frank Ernest Hill, *Youth in the CCC* (New York: Arno Press, 1974), p. 52.

40. Ibid., p. 53.

41. "Furthermore, since each youth will be a worker, to be developed through training, and since often he is interested in particular types of training, the selection agent should know fairly well the character of specific camps in his area. He is not dealing with training that may be given *somewhere* in the CCC but with training that the boys with whom he talks *can get at camps to which they will be sent.*" Holland and Hill, *Youth in the CCC*, p. 72.

42. *The Selection Process: A Guide for Selecting Agents of the Civilian Conservation Corps*, Federal Security Agency, Washington, D.C., January 1941, pp. 1–3.

43. "Industry wants the best trained men it can find, whereas the CCC wants the best youths it can fit to train." *Selection Process*, January 1941, p. 2. Ironically, the statement reflects the sort of thinking that ignores the needs of the young men involved. It implies that in both the CCC and in industry, the most important notions are "fitting in" and production.

44. W. Frank Persons, "Selecting 1,800,000 Young Men for the CCC," *Monthly Labor Review* 46 (April 1938): 843. Note that Persons refuses to accept that enrollee dissatisfaction might be a result of the camps or the program.

45. "Selection for the CCC," *Monthly Labor Review* 40 (May 1935): 1163.

46. For example, note the following remark found in an article entitled "At the Observation Post" in the *Literary Digest*, April 28, 1934, p. 12: "No more wholesome work could be devised for these jobless

wanderers. They have gained an average of eight pounds a man, so Mr. Fechner has estimated; have learned the value of discipline, the rules of sanitation, and how to conduct themselves self-reliantly in natural surroundings; they have developed with their own self-respect a new respect for the lavish inheritance in trees and soil and beauty with which nature has endowed the continent." And the same article suggests that the central problem of recruitment in the early years was "not to induce boys to enlist, but to create a sufficient turnover." Curiously, the agency became more selective as the number of applicants declined.

47. *Selection Process,* January, 1941, p. 12. Signs of immaturity were (a) extreme timidity, (b) unusual dependence upon parents, (c) total lack of serious demeanor, and (d) underweight, but not because of malnutrition.

48. Ibid., p. 13. "He must be willing to subordinate his own desires for freedom of action and movement to the restrictions which CCC camps must impose." That is, the good enrollee is the obedient, docile one. Signs of undependability were (a) dishonesty, (b) excessive self-assuredness ("cockiness"), (c) "previous conduct which shows a strong habit of going off at a tangent from the groups with which the applicant has lived and associated," and (d) "an unwillingness to abide by usual standards and rules of conduct." One may question the difference between (c) and what would otherwise be considered an independence of mind and spirit.

49. Ibid., p. 14. "The Corps is not interested in selecting brilliant or highly educated youths," nor stupid ones either. There were three principles with regard to judging reasonable mental capacity: (a) the number of years of schooling does not show mental alertness, (b) "Youths with extremely limited mental capacity often become real problems in the CCC camp. They may be safety hazards to themselves or other enrollees," (c) people with "superior ability" should be guided into universities, not the CCC.

50. This was confirmed and applauded by Holland and Hill, *Youth in the CCC,* p. 70.

51. "A great many enrollees discover skills or bents incidentally in the CCC; there is far less policy and common practice than there should be designed to force discovery." What is "forcing discovery?" *Youth in the CCC,* p. 144.

52. Ibid.

53. Frank Ernest Hill, *The School in the Camps: The Educational Program of the Civilian Conservation Corps* (New York: American Association for Adult Education, 1935), p. 24.

54. This statistic was so well researched that Holland and Hill could use the records of the CCC to determine the average home life of the enrollees. So, for example, they learned that 37% came from one-parent homes, and 14% came from homes which had experienced

divorce. 90% responded that they were quite happy at home to the questionnaires the selection agents distributed, *Youth in the CCC*, p. 64. This may contradict the notion that the boys came from unhappy homes, or that they needed a better environment.

Other data included the color of the enrollee's skin, so on each application, the manual instructed the agent to surreptitiously write in the word "white" or "colored" on the upper right-hand corner of the application during the interview. And this was standard according to the regulations. See *Recruiting Regulations*, CCC, Sixth Corps Area, Chicago, Ill., 1941, p. 10. Thus the most basic identity of the young man could be gleaned at a glance.

The CCC also required that each boy be fingerprinted, presumably to make it easier to identify them in case of death. Charles A. Symon, *We Can Do It! A History of the Civilian Conservation Corps in Michigan, 1933–1942* (Escanaba, Mich.: Richards Printing, 1983), p. 156. This identifying mark was put on record for future use by whichever agency required it. Fingerprinting was both a voluntary, but encouraged practice (see the Sixth Corps Area Regulations, op cit, section 72[a][1]) and a mandatory one (see *CCC Regulations*, 1937, op cit, section 24), depending on which regulations one followed. A fingerprint card was issued to each enrollee which they were supposed to keep with them at the camps and off base.

55. *Recruiting Regulations, CCC, 6th Corps Area*, Chicago, Ill., 1941, p. 23. This, of course, also offered the agents the opportunity to investigate the "fitness" of the family.
56. Ibid., p. 24.
57. "Verify the Facts of Eligibility Carefully!" the manual exhorts. Ibid., p. 27.
58. The manual also suggests that the agent "observe the physical conditions of each applicant very carefully during interview." Ibid., p. 26.
59. Foucault, *Discipline and Punish*, p. 189.
60. *Recruiting Regulations*, p. 33.
61. For example, military transportation passes were issued, and sometimes enrollees were required to transport themselves on approved trains or cars. Ibid., p. 35.
62. It became easier for employers and potential employers to learn about the enrollees towards the end of the CCC's existence. The CCC adopted what it called the "Arkansas Plan" (named after the state which first implemented it), producing a monthly bulletin filled with facts about each discharged enrollee, and sent it out to employers. The plan was implemented at the local level, but it became national policy by 1939.
63. Holland and Hill, *Youth in the CCC*, pp. 148–65.
64. The War Department's *Civilian Conservation Corps Regulations* (Washington, D.C.: Government Printing Office, 1937), section 175(c), required that each enrollee have a "cumulative record card."

65. *CCC Regulations,* 1937, section 49(b)(1).
66. *The Selection Process,* 1941. Also, Howard W. Oxley, *Education in the Civilian Conservation Corps Camps,* United States government pamphlet, May 1936.

CHAPTER 5

1. Alexandra K. Wigdor and Wendell R. Garner, eds., *Ability Testing: Uses, Consequences, and Controversies,* "Part I: Report of the Committee" (Washington, D.C.: National Academy, 1982), p. 92.
2. For an example of this see ibid, p. 237. These educators contend that testing is not the problem, though certainly techniques can be improved, but rather that tests are *misused* in ways that discriminate.
3. I refer to "tests" as national tests for educational or employment purposes. For the most thorough refutation of Jensen's and Herrnstein's arguments, as well as the general arguments over the idea of intelligence, see Stephen Jay Gould, *The Mismeasure of Man* (New York: Norton, 1981), and Stephen Jay Gould, "Jensen's Last Stand," *The New York Review of Books,* May 1, 1980, pp. 38–44. The second piece is quite a devastating critique of Jensen's methodology. Also, see Leon J. Kamin, "Heredity, Intelligence, Politics, and Psychology: I," in N. J. Block and Gerald Dworkin, eds., *The IQ Controversy: Critical Readings* (New York: Pantheon, 1976), pp. 242–64.
4. The literature here is vast. For a sample, see Robert I. Williams, "Black Pride, Academic Relevance, and Individual Achievement," in Ralph W. Tyler and Richard M. Wolf, eds., *Crucial Issues in Testing* (Berkeley: McCutchan, 1974), pp. 13–20; Robert L. Thorndike, "Concepts of Cultural Fairness," in Taylor and Wolf, *Crucial Issues,* pp. 35–45; Wigdor and Garner, *Abiltiy Testing,* p. 16; or W. Bruce Walsh and Nancy E. Betz, *Test and Assessment* (Englewood Cliffs, N.J.: Prentice-Hall, 1985), p. 380.
5. Wigdor and Garner, *Abiltiy Testing,* p. 24.
6. 401 US 424, 1971.
7. David Harman, "On Traditional Testing," in Eva L. Baker and Edys S. Quellmalz, eds., *Educational Testing and Evaluation: Design, Analysis, and Policy* (Beverly Hills: Sage, 1980), p. 231.
8. For instance, see Stephen Muller, "Case for National Service," *Educational Record* 52 (1) (Winter 1971): 18–19; or Etzioni, *Immodest Agenda.*
9. Lee S. Shulman, "Test Design: A View from Practice," *Occasional Paper Number 8* (E. Lansing, Mich.: Institute for Research on Teaching, June 1978), p. 6.
10. Harold Berlak, "Testing in a Democracy," *Educational Leadership,* October 1985, p. 17.
11. Michael W. Apple, *Education and Power* (Boston: Routledge, 1982), pp. 144–46.

12. Norm-referenced tests simply grade the learner in comparison with his or her peers.
13. For a critique of this last point, see Harvey Siegel, *Educating Reason: Rationality, Critical Thinking, and Education* (New York: Routledge, 1988), pp. 116–26.
14. Joan Herman and Jennie Yeh, "Test Use: A Review of the Issues," in Baker and Quellmalz, *Educational Testing*, pp. 219–28. The argument has also been made that many tests are either redundant or unnecessary, thus making the process not only confused or unjustified, but also somewhat inefficient. See Arthur Whimbey, "You Don't Need a Special 'Reasoning' Test to Implement and Evaluate Reasoning Training," *Educational Leadership*, October 1985, pp. 37–39.
15. See, for instance, Williams, "Black Pride."
16. King, *Achieving America's Goals*, p. 64.
17. Wigdor and Garner, *Ability Testing*, pp. 136–39, 207.
18. Ibid., pp. 139, 147.
19. William Connolly, *Politics and Ambiguity* (Madison: University of Wisconsin Press, 1987).
20. Why people believe that vocational education benefits national service remains a bit of a mystery. The National Bureau of Economic Research, in a report on youth labor, comments that, "vocational training in high school shows little, if any, relationship to labor market success, even among youths who obtain no further education after high school." Richard B. Freeman and David A. Wise, *The Youth Labor Market Problem: Its Nature, Causes, and Consequences* (Chicago: University of Chicago Press, 1982), p. 3. The bureau maintains that academic performance, more than anything else, determines that success (pp. 277–348). Their findings thus add to the case that national service ought to promote the thinking skills of participants rather than their vocational skills. The bureau also contends that the youth unemployment problem is largely an African-American problem, and in a later study they find that young black men respond to a variety of different incentives in their search for a job (some of which are not monetary). Richard B. Freeman and Harry J. Holzer, *The Black Youth Employment Crisis* (Chicago: University of Chicago Press, 1986), pp. 3–20. So again, a partial solution to the (black) youth unemployment problem might not be makework programs tied to a bit of vocational training. This solution may require building up the political awareness and self-esteem of young black men and women.
21. Thomas G. Sticht, ed., *Reading for Working: A Functional Literacy Anthology* Va.: Human Resources Research Organization, 1975), and Thomas G. Sticht, William B. Armstrong, Daniel T. Hickey, and John S. Caylor, *Cast-Off Youth: Policy and Training Methods for the Military Experience* (New York: Praeger, 1987).
22. Sticht, *Reading for Working*, p. 4.

23. Sticht et al., *Cast-Off Youth*, pp. 9, xiii.
24. Sticht, *Reading for Working*, pp. 9, 96–110. Though he makes this point most clearly in the earlier work, Sticht still holds to the second point in his 1987 study, arguing that literacy involves "improving the readability of materials, through the redesign of the graphics displays the cognitive system must deal with." Sticht et al., *Cast-Off Youth*, p. 129.
25. Sticht, *Reading for Working*, pp. 183–86.
26. Sticht et al., *Cast-Off Youth*, p. 88.
27. Ibid., p. 93.
28. H. A. Shoemaker, as quoted in Sticht et al., *Cast-Off Youth*, pp. 100–101.
29. Sticht et al., *Cast-Off Youth*, p. 127.
30. Harvey Siegel contends that competency in skills like literacy should be minimally critical, not minimally functional. *Educating Reason*, p. 125.
31. Paulo Freire, *Pedagogy of the Oppressed*, tr. Myra Bergman (New York: Seabury Press, 1970); Cynthia Brown, "Literacy in 30 Hours: Paulo Freire's Process in Northeast Brazil," in Ira Shor, ed., *Freire for the Classroom: A Sourcebook for Liberatory Teaching* (Portsmouth, N.H.: Heinemann, 1987), pp. 215–31.
32. *Rationalism in Politics* (New York: Basic Books, 1962).
33. For an example of how these ideas are a-contextual and mechanical, one need only look at the diagram of the "developmental model of literacy" printed on page 123 of Sticht, *Cast-Off Youth*.
34. See Roger Fieldhouse, "The Political Education of Servants of the State," in Roger Fieldhouse, ed., *The Political Education of Servants of the State* (Manchester: Manchester University Press, 1988), pp. 191–92.
35. Harvey Kantor argues that the very founding of vocational education programs contributed to this. "This conceptual linking of education and work had at least two important consequences. First, it reinforced the traditional American belief that occupational success or failure was the result of individual effort, not the structure of opportunity. Second, by translating fundamental questions about the nature of work and inequality in American society into policy aimed at proper socialization and training, it focused discontent about the operation of the economy on the character of schooling, not the nature of capitalism." Harvey Kantor, "Work, Education, and Vocational Reform: The Ideological Origins of Vocational Education," *American Journal of Education* 94 (4) (August 1986): 423.

Kantor's argument recalls the ideas of Antonio Gramsci, who contended that vocational education reinforces class society, by making its graduates privy to the skilled jobs that lead to a rigid hierarchy in society. Antonio Gramsci, "On Education," in *Selections from the Prison Notebooks of Antonio Gramsci*, Quintin Hoare and Geoffrey

Nowell Smith, tr. (New York: International Publishers, 1971), p. 41. Gramsci charged schools with producing intellectual vocations, and persuading people that "studying too is a job, and a very tiring one, with its own particular apprenticeship" (p. 42).

36. Or, as Burton Clark calls it, "educating the expert society". Clark contends that educational institutions do not impart to students "the broader understandings necessary for civilized men in a complicated civilization." See Burton R. Clark, *Educating the Expert Society* (San Francisco, Ca.: Chandler, 1962), p. 283.

I would argue that national service can avoid the problems Clark finds in the schools, but that it still must contend with the issue of technical versus academic education. These two aspects are not necessarily independent of one another. Rather, one can impart specific political skills and people skills (so necessary in our service economy), while at the same time engaging individuals to think critically about important issues which concern their society. This benefits society as it reproduces consciously an ethic of participation, in such a way that the burden of national service withers away.

CHAPTER 6

1. Karl Marx, *Capital: A Critique of Political Economy* 1, tr. Ben Fowkes (New York: Vintage Books, 1977), pp. 299–300.
2. I use the phrase *civic service* here following Charles Moskos, *A Call to Civic Service: National Service for Country and Community* (New York: Free Press, 1988). In using the terms *service, social service*, or *public service* I mean the same things. Often these terms signify social welfare professions or civil service positions. I am not speaking of professionals here, of course, but of NSPs, though I argue below that the two are connected. Civic service subjects the young participants to the norms, rituals, and economy of the service professions. In this way, *civic service* signifies not so much civic duty as it does the professionalization of young servants.
3. Jane C. Kendall, "Combining Service and Learning: An Introduction," in Jane C. Kendall, ed., *Combining Service and Learning: A Resource Book for Community and Public Service* 1 (Raleigh, N.C.: National Society for Internships and Experiential Education, 1990), pp. 22–23. Service learning is a "philosophy of human growth and purpose, a social vision, an approach to community, and a way of knowing" (p. 23).
4. William F. Buckley, *Gratitude: Reflections on What We Owe to Our Country* (New York: Random House, 1990), p. 22.
5. Kendall, "Combining Service," p. 19.
6. For example, Donald Eberly argues that national service must be essentially a service learning experience, where a "person spends his mornings partly in the programmed instruction room and being

taught by a tutor doing his national service, his afternoons on a conservation or construction project at which he is more accomplished
than his morning tutor, and his evenings in bull sessions or seminars on such topics as ecology, politics, sex, sociology, and urbanolo-
gy." Eberly, *National Service*, p. 92. Also see Benjamin Barber, "Service, Citizenship, and Democracy: Civic Duty as an Entailment of
Civil Right," in Evers, *National Service*, pp. 38–43. For the professors of education who argue for a reflective component, see Chapter
10, note 5., in this book.

7. I thank Courtney Walthour, Volunteer Coordinator at the Center for
Service Learning, for informing me about this excellent program.

8. For our purposes VIA and VESEP are the most interesting because
they are nonacademic credit programs, and thus provide a better
model for national service than the for-credit ones. All future reference to the Vermont programs will regard one or the other of these
two.

9. Center for Service Learning, *Vermont Internship Program Supervisors' Planning Manual* (Burlington, Vermont, 1991); Ram Dass and
Paul Gorman, *How Can I Help? Stories and Reflections on Service*
(New York: Knopf, 1985); and Timothy Stanton and Kamil Ali, *The
Experienced Hand: A Student Manual for Making the Most of an
Internship* (Cranston, R.I.: Carroll Press, 1982). The Vermont program has the most fully developed program of service learning I
have seen, and is the one of the few with a relatively sophisticated
understanding of service learning. On the idea of service learning,
see those essays in Kendall, *Combining Service.*

10. Center, *Vermont Internship Program*, pp. 2–3.

11. Ibid., p. 4.

12. Donald J. Eberly, "A Supporting Role for the Federal Government in
National Service," in Evers, *National Service*, pp. 230–31.

13. Kendall, "Combining Service," begins to recognize the contestability
of the concept of service in the section of her essay entitled "The
Importance of the Language Used," pp. 18–26. In fact, she asserts
that "a good service learning program helps participants see their
questions in the larger context of issues of social justice and social
policy—rather than in the context of charity" (p. 20). This is more
practical to do in a politicized learning context, from which many
service learning professionals, and most politicians, might distance
themselves.

Nor does Kendall pursue the implications of her argument, she
simply hopes that a "new public language will emerge that gives
people a way to talk about [service and learning] or that 'service
learning' will gain acceptance in a way that allows it to shed the current baggage of its component words" (pp. 24–25). This is a naive
view of language for it suggests that political connotations of the
concepts can be effaced, and this, I would argue, contributes to a

socialized, and thus weak sense of, citizenship. Nevertheless, Kendall's essay, and many of the essays in the volume, at least recognize the political, economic, and linguistic problems of "service," and thus contribute to its politicization.

14. Roy Lubove, *The Professional Altruist: The Emergence of Social Work as a Career* (Cambridge: Harvard University Press, 1965), pp. 2, 6ff.
15. Ibid., p. 14.
16. Ibid., p. 16.
17. As such it was also taken out of the hands of women and put into those of the more technically skilled professionals (i.e., men).
18. Lubove, *Professional Altruist*, p. 40.
19. Ibid., pp. 55–117, 118–56, 157–82.
20. Ibid., pp. 218, 220–21.
21. Frances Fox Piven and Richard A. Cloward, *Regulating the Poor: The Functions of Public Welfare* (New York: Vintage Books, 1971), p. xiii. For similar effects in France, see Jacques Donzelot, *The Policing of Families*, tr. Robert Hurley (New York: Pantheon Books, 1979). Regarding cycles, maybe national service, as described by Moskos and Nunn-McCurdy, becomes the end of the cycle, in that it liberalizes relief as it reinforces work norms. Clearly, the very concept of national service challenges Piven and Cloward's interpretation.
22. Piven and Cloward, *Regulating the Poor*, pp. 3, 32–36.
23. Ibid., pp. 123–80.
24. Ibid., p. 166.
25. Ibid., p. 324.
26. Alan Ware, *Between Profit and State: Intermediate Organizations in Britain and the United States* (Cambridge: Polity Press, 1989), p. 161.
27. Ibid., pp. 120–21.
28. Ibid., pp. 144–59.
29. Ibid., p. 161.
30. John McKnight, "The Professional Service Business," in Lenore Borzak, ed., *Field Study: A Sourcebook for Experiential Learning* (Beverly Hills: Sage, 1981), pp. 301–14. This essay should be required reading for anybody concerned about national service.
31. One example might be the explosion of therapy groups to employ an otherwise unemployed army of private social workers. Another, of course, is the credit card company that advertises its cards as meeting certain needs: lost wallet insurance, overdraft protection, etc. Whatever service the company may provide it is not a need, *especially* if the customer acts as a rational, prudent consumer.
32. In Marxian terms, capitalist industry and manufacturing require socially necessary, mystified labor in order to produce goods (commodities). Service enterprise, however, requires socially necessary,

mystified "goods" in order to "produce" labor. I have appropriated this comic ditty from Brittain Smith of Loyola University, New Orleans.

33. I am grateful to Professor Stan Makielski of Loyola University, New Orleans, for suggesting this point to me.

34. Ultimately, a national service agency, in engaging in service politics, may grow incrementally as it fights for federal dollars presently allocated elsewhere.

35. McKnight, "Professional Service Business," p. 302.

36. Ibid., p. 303. Ware, *Between Profit and State,* also presents a great deal of evidence that charities and voluntary service organizations are "industries."

37. McKnight, "Professional Service Business," p. 304.

38. Also note the growth in specific environmental concerns (friends of the earth, of the spotted owl, etc.), especially those that are begun by geologists, oceanographers, and biologists who have studied their political concerns with scientific application. See Ware, *Between Profit and State,* for more examples.

39. McKnight makes this same point in "Professional Service Business," p. 311.

40. Ibid., p. 314.

41. Gorham, *National Service,* 222–74.

42. William Graebner, *The Engineering of Consent: Democracy and Authority in Twentieth-Century America* (Madison: University of Wisconsin Press, 1987).

43. T. Zane Reeves, *The Politics of the Peace Corps and VISTA* (Tuscaloosa, Ala.: University of Alabama Press, 1988).

44. Ibid., p. 19. Also, see Gerard T. Rice, *The Bold Experiment: JFK's Peace Corps* (Notre Dame: University of Notre Dame Press, 1985), pp. 256–66; Reeves, *Politics of the Peace Corps,* p. 25. Gerard T. Rice notes that a "radical"—Charles Kamen—was "deselected" by the corps upon completing his training. After this incident, the Congress instituted a loyalty oath to the Peace Corps bill. Rice, *Bold Experiment,* pp. 86–87.

45. Reeves, *Politics of the Peace Corps,* pp. 83–86.

46. Ibid., pp. 91–119.

47. Ibid., p. 160.

48. The functions of certain institutions as agencies of normalization and discipline is well documented. See Michel Foucault, *Discipline and Punish: The Birth of the Prison,* tr. Alan Sheridan (New York: Vintage Books, 1977); Erving Goffman, *Asylums: Essays on the Social Situation of Mental Patients and Other Inmates* (New York: Anchor Books, 1961); William Connolly, *Democracy and Ambiguity* (Madison: University of Wisconsin Press, 1987).

49. Rice, *Bold Experiment,* pp. 117, 118, 127.

50. Ibid., p. 119, from a memorandum dated August 8, 1963.

51. Ibid., pp. 144, 161–63. Between 1961 and 1963, twenty-two percent of trainees were deselected.
52. Ibid., p. 153.
53. Ibid., p. 160. The participants were also subject to an FBI check of their backgrounds and past political affiliations.
54. *National Service Corps: Hearings before the Special Subcommittee on Labor of the Committee on Education and Labor,* HR 5625, United States House of Representatives, 88th Congress, 1st sess., 1963, parts 1 and 2. *National Service Corps: Hearings of the Subcommittee on the National Service Corps of the Committee on Labor and Public Welfare,* SR 1321, United States Senate, 88th Congress, 1st sess., 1963 Willard Wirtz, Stewart Udall, and Robert Kennedy all testified to this at the Senate hearings.
55. Though, as Reeves points out, its advocacy politics soon became quite a thorn on the side of various administrations. *Politics of the Peace Corps,* pp. 120–53. Also, note Donald Eberly's remark: "VISTA has been reform-oriented whereas national service would be service-oriented...[thus] community change [is] wrought through service of sufficient magnitude rather than through confrontation." Donald Eberly, *National Service,* p. 110. There are a number of assumptions underlying this claim: (1) that there is little role for political reform in service programs (this exemplifies the apolitical nature of service I argue above), (2) that reform requires confrontation—a claim that goes unsupported—and (3) that national service should not take VISTA as an example. This last claim indicates that Eberly accepts the Reagan (and presumably Bush) administration's views toward that organization, and thus hides a political statement behind the mask of fact.
56. SR 1321, sections 5(g), 5(k), and 12; HR 5625, sections 5(g), 5(k), and 12.
57. "Information on a Proposed National Service Plan," in SR 1321, pp. 393–94.
58. Ibid., p. 394.
59. Ibid., p. 399.
60. Foucault, *Discipline and Punish,* p. 211.
61. U.S. Department of Labor, *Job Corps: Residential Living Manual* (Washington, D.C.: Manpower Administration, 1972). Note especially the chapter entitled "Corpsmember Discipline," pp. 73–87.
62. Ibid., pp. 3, 7, 15.
63. Ibid., pp. 27–29, 35–36.
64. Ibid., pp. 40–45, 49.
65. For instance, the residence manual does not direct the group or counselor to explore the possibility that the camp organization itself might generate psychosocial pathologies.
66. For example, if a corpsmember misbehaved, counseling only got at the psychological root of the problem; the political and economic

roots remained mysterious. Corpsmembers were generally poor black teenage males—a counselor was not going to suggest to them that the source of their psychological "problems" may rest in an unfair or unjust political system. On those occasions when a counselor might have made that suggestion, there was no mechanism within the service organization itself by which that corpsmembers could have sought help or redress. The service camps attempted to alter the behavior of the individual participant, not provide him with political alternatives.

67. Labor, *Job Corps Manual*, p. 68.
68. Dave M. O'Neill, *The Federal Government and Manpower: A Critical Look at the MDTA-Institutional and Job Corps Programs* (Washington, D.C.: American Enterprise Institute, 1973); Sar A. Levitan, *Antipoverty Work and Training Efforts: Goals and Reality* (Ann Arbor: Institute of Labor and Industrial Relations, 1970); Eli Ginzburg, *The School/Work Nexus: Transition of Youth from School to Work* (Bloomington, Ind.: Phi Delta Kappa Educational Foundation, 1980). See Ginzburg's conclusions on page 78. I note a similar problem for the CCC, in Gorham, *National Service*.
69. Levitan, *Antipoverty Work*, pp. 31–36. Also recall Lubove, *Professional Altruist*, and Piven and Cloward, *Regulating the Poor*, on service as social control: it succeeds because it denies individuals their original communities.
70. See Chapter 6, note 9, for texts in the center's curriculum. I focus on the texts of the center because it presents these texts as essential in learning the ethic of service. I do not engage the arguments for and against service learning emerging from departments of education at universities because I want to look at the implementation of service theory. That is, I want to investigate how service learning theory is actually applied in service programs. Service learning programs have been shown empirically to work quite well, by Newmann, Conrad and Hedin, Shaver, and others. But the goal has always been the inculcation of a service ethic. I have not been arguing that the teaching of a service ethic is impossible or immoral, clearly it is possible and moral, but a developed service ethic often is incompatible with the idea democratic citizenship. Thus, I consider the practice of service learning, and this means also *the theories that are taught to the students* in order to inculcate them with that ethic.
71. Dass and Gorman, *How Can I Help?* pp. ix, 5.
72. Ibid., p. 15.
73. Ibid., p. 32.
74. Ibid., pp. 41, 42, 65.
75. Ibid., pp. 156, 158–59.
76. Ibid., pp. 163–64.
77. Ibid., pp. 163–65, 178.
78. Stanton and Ali, *Experienced Hand*, pp. 7–14.

79. Ibid., pp. 57–65.
80. Ibid., p. 66.
81. Ibid., pp. 71, 72.
82. Ibid., p. 75.
83. Ibid., p. 77.
84. Ibid., p. 84.

CHAPTER 7

1. Charles Price Harper, *The Administration of the Civilian Conservation Corps* (Clarksburg, W.V.: Clarksburg Publishing Co., 1939), p.
12.
2. James J. McEntee, *Now They Are Men: The Study of the CCC*
(Washington, D.C.: National Home Library Foundation, 1940), p. 15.
Charles Price Harper writes, "The War Department broke all American mobilization records in the first three months of the reforesta-
tion program. During that time the Army enrolled, conditioned, and
transplanted to camps more men than it mobilized during the first
three months of America's participation in the World War." Harper,
Administration, p. 27. A sociological study done in 1981 confirms the
effectiveness of the army program. See Michael W. Sherraden, "Military Participation in a Youth Employment Program: The Civilian
Conservation Corps," *Armed Forces and Society* 7 (2) (Winter 1981):
227–45.
3. Ray Hoyt, *We Can Take It: A Short Story of The CCC* (New York:
American Book Company, 1935), p. 114. Also, note Harry Wooding,
Assistant Secretary of War: "The CCC mobilization is to us more
than a great military achievement: it is a dress rehearsal of the
Army's ability to intervene, under constitutional authority, in com-
batting the depression." From "The Militaristic CCC," *The World
Tomorrow* 27 (2) (January 18, 1934): 30. Thus the military was anxious to see the mobilization not only as practice for any future foreign attacks, but also as a means of domestic social control. Some
favored increased military training in order to discipline wayward
youths. Charles Price Harper remarks that more military training is
needed to rid the enrollee "of that slouchiness of bearing characteristic of most of the enrollees." Harper, *Administration*, p. 88. Some
military officers called for the complete militarization of the CCC,
like Major General George Van Horn Moseley, head of the Fourth
Corps Area. But most muted their opinions on this matter. John A.
Salmond, *The Civilian Conservation Corps, 1933–1942: A New Deal
Case Study* (Durham, N.C.: Duke University Press, 1967), p. 86.
4. Hoyt, *We Can Take It*, p. 28.
5. Paul A. Lawrence, *Remembering the CCC* (San Anselmo, Cal.: PAL
Press, 1983), p. 7. Michael Sherraden recounts that some local communities were grateful for army control and discipline, because

some of the boys could become very wild, especially in town. Sherraden, *Military Participation,* p. 240.

6. *Recruiting Regulations,* CCC, 6th Corps Area, Chicago, Ill., 1941, p.
41.

7. Frank Ernest Hill, *The School in the Camps: The Educational Program of the Civilian Conservation Corps* (New York: American Association for Adult Education, 1935), p. 12.

8. *Civilian Conservation Corps Safety Regulations,* Office of the Director, Washington, D.C., 1938, p. 5.

9. Though these uniforms could signify something else to the outside
world: "The CCC uniform told the world that its wearer was unemployed, was usually lacking in higher education and family position,
and was practically a ward of the government due to his poverty and
lack of vocational skill." Jack J. Preiss, *Camp William James* (Norwich, Vt.: Argo Books, 1978), pp. 9–10. Even though the oath represented the influence of the military, its contents could be described
as bureaucratic. What the enrollee swore to were relatively mundane things: (1) that he would remain a member of the CCC until
the end of his term, (2) that he would not make any claims against
the government if he contracted a disease or suffered an injury as a
result of his work in the CCC (in fact, section 16 of the 1937 act con-
tinuing the CCC relieved the government of all responsibility involving property damage or loss, and limited their responsibility for personal injury to $500), (3) that he would not claim any extra
allowances or privileges upon discharge, (4) that he would be
responsible for anything the CCC would lend him during this time,
and (5) that he understood that if he broke a rule or regulation he
might be expelled. See Charles A. Symon, *We Can Do It! A History of
the Civilian Conservation Corps in Michigan, 1933–1942* (Escanaba,
Mich.: Richards Printing, 1983), p. 185.

Therefore the oath functioned like a legal contract. This had a
number of implications: (1) it did not commit the individual to the
country he served, (2) it did not recognize that the CCC was implemented to serve the nation, (3) it bound generally uneducated men
to rules they had not had a chance to read, or maybe could not read
and understand, but most importantly (4) it initiated individuals
into a world of legal and bureaucratic discourse—the enrollees were
not giving an oath of allegiance, they were accepting the hegemony
of a bureaucratic order. Through the oath the enrollees were not
committing themselves to the national community, they were reinscribing themselves in a juridical order which placed them within a
particular bureaucratic regime.

10. Quoted in Salmond, *Civilian Conservation Corps,* p. 48.

11. "The radicals who have been all along charging the Roosevelt
Administration with setting up a militaristic organization in the
name of the Civilian Conservation Corps will find in [Harry Wood-

ing, the Assistant Secretary of War's] words [see note 3] the complete justification for everything that they have said." "The Militaristic CCC," p. 30.

12. James Lasswell, *Shovels and Guns: The CCC in Action,* International Pamphlet no. 45 (New York: International Publishers, 1935), p. 11.

13. Ibid., p. 52. Sherraden, "Military Participation," p. 235.

14. Civilian Conservation Corps Regulations, Sixth Corps Area, Chicago, Ill., January 1, 1936, section 58.

15. War Department, *Civilian Conservation Corps Regulations* (Washington, D.C.: Government Printing Office, 1937), section 13(b).

16. *CCC Regulations,* 1936, section 5(g).

17. "Interference with educational programs, suppression of radical ideas, ambivalence on the question of Negro enrollment—all these charges can validly be laid at the military's door." Salmond, *Civilian Conservation Corps,* p. 85.

18. *CCC Regulations,* 1937, section 6: "The company commander will exercise the normal functions of the company commander in the army, omitting only that of military training, and will temper all his actions to conform to the civilian status of the enrollee."

19. Ibid., section 7.

20. Salmond, *Civilian Conservation Corps,* p. 117.

21. For example, Michael Sherraden remarks that "even though the CCC is now almost forty years behind us, it is not inconceivable that the people of the United States may again call upon the military to play a role in addressing youth employment problems." Sherraden, "Military Participation," p. 228. Of course, the American people did not call upon F.D.R. to bring in the army to mobilize the CCC, a few top bureaucrats including the Chief Forester of the United States did this. Presumably the next call for the army will be like this one. For the comments of other academics in support of the idea of the participation of the army, see Stephen J. Muller, "The Case for Universal National Service," *Educational Record* 52 (1) (Winter 1971): 17–22; Morris Janowitz, "National Service: A Third Alternative?" in *Teacher's College Record* 73 (1) (September 1973): 13–25, and "The Logic of National Service," in Sol Tax, ed., *The Draft: A Handbook of Facts and Alternatives* (Chicago: University of Chicago Press, 1967), pp. 73–90. Also, see the testimony of Congressman Paul McCloskey in *Presidential Commission,* March 13, 1980, p. 11.

Janowitz, in the 1973 article, argues that a national service agency should use agents to recruit for both the military and the national service program. He contends that the Pentagon would have at least partial control over this agency (in conjunction with other departments), and that the army could provide logistical and personnel support for its implementation. Even if only a very small percentage of a national service program is assisted by the army, there is the chance that that aspect will be at least partially regulated under military code. This necessarily constrains the free expression of ideas and activities which could otherwise occur. For example, would homosexuals be allowed to participate in those areas of national service assisted by the military? Would they be allowed to participate in activities in residential camps, like those found in conservation work?

22. Sherraden, "Military Participation," p. 235.
23. Hill, *School in Camps*, pp. 55–56.
24. Federal Security Agency, *Work Experience That Counts* (Washington, D.C.: Government Printing Office, 1941), p. 3.
25. Civilian Conservation Corps, *A Manual for Instructors in Civilian Conservation Corps Camps*, CCC Vocational Series, 15, Washington, D.C.: Government Printing Office, 1935, pp. 22–23. This policy was immediately criticized by the Left. See "Sedition in the CCC," *New Republic*, February 1936, p. 6.
26. John A. Salmond, *Civilian Conservation Corps*, p. 140.
27. Holland and Hill remarked caustically that youths were "attracted by well-illustrated material." Kenneth Holland and Frank Ernest Hill, *Youth in the CCC* (New York: Arno Press, 1974), p. 156.
28. Hill, *School in Camps*, p. 56.
29. Major General George Van Horn Moseley, Commander, Fourth Corps Area, in Alfred C. Oliver Jr. and Harold M. Dudley, eds., *This New America: The Spirit of the Civilian Conservation Corps* (London: Longmans, Green, and Co., 1937), p. 34.
30. See, for instance, General Alva Branstad, in Oliver and Dudley, *New America*, p. 123; Thomas McCarthy, in Thomas Lyons, ed., *1930 Employment 1980: Humanistic Perspectives on the Civilian Conservation Corps in Colorado* (Boulder: Colorado Division of Employment and Training, 1980). Harold Buckles, "This CCC," in *Emergency Conservation Corps*, Washington, D.C.: Government Printing Office, 1935, p. 2.
31. James S. Lanigan, "Education in the CCC: Weapon or Feint," *Education* 61 (2) (October 1940): 93.
32. Dueffort E. Wiedman, "Citizenship through Training in the Civilian Conservation Corps," *Education* 61 (2) (October 1940): 95–96.
33. See, for instance, Nelson C. Brown, "The Civilian Conservation Corps Program in the United States," Paper given at the *Annual Meeting of the Woodlands Section*, Canadian Pulp and Paper Association, January 25, 1933; or Howard W. Oxley, "Analysis of Enrollee Personnel," *School Life* 26 (6) (March 1941): 188.
34. Salmond, *Civilian Conservation Corps*, p. v; Norma Stephenson, "The New Deal and the Civilian Conservation Corps in the Mythology of America," in Thomas Lyons, ed., *1930 Employment 1980*, p. 160.
35. Salmond, *Civilian Conservation Corps*, pp. 6–8; Perry H. Merrill,

Roosevelt's Forest Army: A History of the Civilian Conservation Corps, 1933–1942 (Montpelier, Vt.: Perry H. Merrill, 1981), p. 4.

36. Wesley Cox, in Oliver and Dudley, *New America*, p. 44.
37. Harper, *Administration*, p. 51.
38. Robert Fechner, *Woodsmanship for the Civilian Conservation Corps*, publication no. 1 (Washington, D.C.: Government Printing Office, 1939).
39. Ibid., p. 14.
40. H. R. Kylie, G. H. Hieronymus, and A. G. Hill, *CCC Forestry* (Washington, D.C.: Government Printing Office, 1937), p. 2.
41. Forestry was defined as "the study and application of production and maintenance of the many and varied products of the forest." Ibid., p. 3.
42. Ibid., p. 16.
43. Ibid., p. 9.
44. Ibid., p. 27.
45. They did not train most individuals well because they imparted significant skills to only a very few of the enrollees. Furthermore, the CCC failed to attract many individuals into the profession of forestry.
46. Frank Ernest Hill, *School in Camps*, pp. 3, 82. Hoyt claimed that it was a "new kind of patriotism that springs from the soil." *We Can Take It*, pp. 3, 4.
47. Holland and Hill, *Youth in the CCC*, p. 22.
48. Stephenson, in Lyons, *1930 Employment 1980*, p. 156.
49. Charles H. Judd, "The Induction of Young People into Adulthood" *The School Review* 48 (March 1940): 183; Howard W. Oxley, *Education in the Civilian Conservation Corps*, United States Government Pamphlet, Washington, D.C.: Government Printing Office, May 1936, p. 10.
50. "It was a complete renunciation of every value for which the United States has ever stood. For to be a citizen really means to be able to found your city or your civilization *yourself* if you have to." Eugen Rosenstock-Huessy, in a letter printed in Preiss, , p. 222.
51. Holland and Hill, *Youth in the CCC*, pp. 222–23.
52. Ibid., p. 222.
53. Ibid., p. 229.
54. Ibid.
55. Oxley, *Education in CCC Camps*, p. 6.
56. *Camp Life Arithmetic Workbook 5*, Federal Security Agency, April 1941.
57. *Camp Life Reader and Workbook 1*, Language Usage Series, nos. 1–6, U.S. Department of Interior and Office of Education, 1939, p. 22.
58. Ibid., nos. 1 and 2.
59. This last point was vital to the organization of the CCC, for all agreed that every minute of leisure time had to be constructive for the men-

tal and physical health of the individual. Thus, calisthenics were prescribed, and hobbies were taught. Of course, there is no necessary
connection between these and an informed and active citizenry.

60. Ibid., no. 4, pp. 36–59.
61. Ibid., p. 45.
62. Ibid.
63. Ibid., p. 49.
64. Ibid., pp. 56–57.
65. The practice of atomized individuals associating in this manner is not
surprising, given the nature of American society. Tocqueville noticed
that practice as far back as 1831, and argued that conformity is a fact
of modernity. Alexis de Tocqueville, *Democracy in America*, tr.
George Lawrence (New York: Anchor Books, 1969), p. 615. Tocqueville gives a reason for this: "Men with equal rights, education,
and wealth, that is to say, men who are in just the same condition,
must have very similar needs, habits, and tastes. As they see things
in the same light, their minds naturally incline to similar ideas, and
though any one of them could part company with the rest and work
out his own beliefs, in the end they all concur, unconsciously and
unintentionally, in a certain number of common opinions" (pp.
640–41). The significance of the CCC as a socializing agency, though,
was that it helped "incline" the mind of participants to "similar ideas"
despite their differences. That is, it established an artificial equality
among the poor white males by imposing certain norms of citizenship. The corps helped these individuals "see things in the same
light," but neither the thing nor the light were of their own choosing.
66. See for instance, Sheila Rosenblum, *Youth Corps Case Studies: The
San Francisco Conservation Corps* (Philadelphia: Public/Private
Ventures, Fall 1987). Rosenblum notes that this organization
emphasizes "rules, punctuality, cooperation and productivity," but
that education is a very low priority (pp. 13–14).
67. Donald J. Eberly, "A Universal Youth Service," *Social Policy* 7 (4)
(January/February 1977): 44.
68. For example, see Franklin Thomas, *Youth Unemployment and
National Service* (New York: Ford Foundation, 1983), a speech
before the Economic Club of Detroit, March 7, 1983.
69. The following is taken from United States Department of Labor, *Job
Corps: Residential Living Manual* (Washington, D.C.: Manpower
Administration, 1972), pp. 109–19.
70. *Report on the Conference of Citizenship Education of the Young
Worker*, Arden House, Harrison, N.Y., March 11–13, 1966.
71. Moskos, *Call to Civic Service*, p. 157.
72. Holland and Hill, *Youth in the CCC*, p. 190.
73. Preiss, *Camp William James*, p. 222.
74. *Now They Are Men: The Study of the CCC* (Washington, D.C.:
National Home Library Foundation, 1940), p. 30.

75. Federal Security Agency, *Work Experience that Counts* (Washington, D.C.: Government Printing Office, 1941), p. 3. Self-reliance was another reason the CCC justified sending boys rather far from their homes. Holland and Hill note: "Most CCC officials feel that a distance of 100 to 200 miles is best. The boy then finds it difficult or impossible to go home every week, but he can manage a trip once a month. He does not feel entirely cut off from his home, yet he cannot visit it so often that home contacts prevent him developing a spirit of independence." *Youth in the CCC,* pp. 77–78.

76. Hoyt, *We Can Take It,* p. 82.

77. The leaders of the CCC claimed that sociability was one of the most important aspects to camp life. Indeed, they argued that in learning to get along with 199 other people, one learned "one of the basic lessons of American democracy." This was not the only reason it was good for the boys, though, for "working with other men and learning to pull together as a team is one of the most useful values of CCC experience. Employers want men who have learned this important lesson. That is one reason why they employ so many former CCC enrollees." Hoyt, *We Can Take It,* p. 82. Presumably, though, employers wanted boys who could "pull together" under the direct order of a leader, like the CO. Where they governed themselves, where they organized their own political life in the camps, the "future employees" demonstrated a level of political activism that might have disrupted the conventional industrial workplace. In fact, a protounion organization, the CCC Boys Protective League, formed in many camps to protest conditions, and this was quickly and quietly undermined by the authorities. Lasswell, *Shovels and Guns: the CCC in Action* International Pamphlet no. 45 (New York: International Publishers, 1935).

78. Holland and Hill, *Youth in the CCC,* pp. 126–47. In fact, Holland and Hill, after studying a number of camps, recommended that more enrollee self-governance be tried at the camps as part of a general "program for adjustment." Jonathan Mitchell claimed this as well in "Roosevelt's Tree Army: I," *New Republic,* May 29, 1935, p. 65.

79. Merrill, *Roosevelt's Forest Army.* Also see McEntee, *Now They Are Men,* p. 73.

80. For more details about this camp, see Preiss, *Camp William James,* p. ix. Though this book was published in 1958, Preiss wrote it before 1950.

81. Letter from Alfred Eisenman to Eugen Rosenstock-Huessy, in ibid, p. 27.

82. "The college boys still felt they had an additional responsibility to the others." Ibid., p. 120.

83. See note 11, this chapter.

84. Letter from Eugene Rosenstock-Huessy, in ibid, p. 68.

85. Ibid., p. 72.

86. Ibid., pp. 425–26.

87. Jay G. Hayden, "Vermont Camp Row Seen Threatening CCC Morale," *Boston Globe*, January 30, 1941.

88. Preiss, *Camp William James*, p. 143.

89. This was by no means the only time enrollees tried to take over the functions of the camp in collective action. There had been riots at camps in Pennsylvania, North Carolina, and West Virginia, where the men believed they were being mistreated and decided to take administrative and disciplinary manners into their own hands. But this was the first time an alternative organization had been created.

90. Preiss, *Camp William James*, p. 165.

91. Ibid., p. 223.

92. Algernon D. Black, *The Young Citizens: The Story of the Encampment for Citizenship* (New York: Frederick Ungar, 1962), p. 13.

93. Ibid., p. 51.

94. Herbert Hyman, Charles Wright, Terence Hopkins, *Applications of Methods of Evaluation: Four Studies of the Encampment for Citizenship* (Berkeley: University of California Press, 1962), pp. 94, 96, 109.

95. Ibid., pp. 123–24, 127, 133.

96. Ibid., pp. 138, 157, 143–47, 161.

97. Ibid., pp. 179, 186, 189.

98. Ibid., pp. 209, 212, 219, 215, 216.

99. Ibid., pp. 251–59, 295.

100. Henry W. Riecken, *The Volunteer Work Camp: A Psychological Evaluation*, Cambridge, Mass.: Addison-Wesley Press, 1952, p. 55. Neither Black's book, the Berkeley study, nor Riecken's study are cited in the two most important studies of national service today, Richard Danzig and Peter Szanton's *National Service : What Would it Mean?* and Charles C. Moskos's *A Call to Civic Service*. I have yet to see them referenced in any analysis of national service, yet these projects are no more out of date than the CCC or the Peace Corps.

101. Riecken, *Volunteer Work Camp*, pp. 98, 99, 104.

102. Ibid., pp. 106, 110.

103. Ibid., pp. 114, 116.

104. Ibid., p. 122.

105. Ibid., pp. 125, 136, 146.

106. Ibid., p. 153.

107. Ibid., pp. 168–74.

108. Bernard J. McMullen and Phyllis Snyder, *Youth Corps Area Studies: Katimavik, the Canadian Youth Corps* (Philadelphia: Public/Private Ventures, April 1986), p. 3.

109. Ibid., p. 8. Compared to dropout rates in the CCC this is phenomenal, and it is even favorable when matched against rates for the Peace Corps or Vista. Moreover, it is very low by modern youth corps standards. Moskos, *Call to Civic Service*, p. 165.

110. Michael Sherraden and Donald Eberly, "Canada: Katimavik and Cultural Integration," in Donald Eberly and Michael Sherraden,

eds., *The Moral Equivalent of War? A Study of Non-Military Service in Nine Nations* (New York: Greenwood Press, 1990), p. 15.
111. OPCAN-Katimavik, *Evaluation Report*, Montreal, 1985, p. 14.
112. Moskos, *Call to Civic Service*, p. 185.
113. John Hasek, *The Disarming of Canada*, Toronto: Key Porter Books, 1987, pp. 216–18; McMullen and Snyder, *Youth Corps Area Studies*, p. 9.
114. McMullen and Snyder, *Youth Corps Area Studies*, p. 9.
115. Jacques Hebert, *21 Days* (Montreal: Optimum, 1986).
116. Sherraden and Eberly, "Canada: Katimavik," p. 12.
117. McMullen and Snyder, *Youth Corps Area Studies*, p. 5.
118. Their conclusion that "it is perhaps the lack of emphasis on work that contributed to the program's loss of support after nine years of operation" goes completely unsubstantiated. McMullen and Snyder, *Youth Corps Area Studies*, p. 7. In fact, the most important people opposing it seemed to be military officers—who feared it would attract young people away from military service—and officials of the Mulroney administration, who intended to make large budget cuts anyway. As the publicity of Hebert's hunger strike makes evident, the Canadian people seemed to favor the program.

CHAPTER 8

1. Alan Ware presents a version of this argument in *Citizens, Parties, and The State: A Reappraisal* (Cambridge: Polity Press, 1987), pp. 58–59.
2. David E. Price, *Bringing Back the Parties* (Washington, D.C.: Congressional Quarterly Press, 1984), pp. 111–14. Some even argue that parties define the democratic state. In E. E. Schattschneider's words, "political parties created democracy and modern democracy is unthinkable save in terms of parties." *Party Government* (New York: Holt, Rhinehart, and Winston, 1942), p. 1.
3. To Schattschneider this means "simplifying alternatives." *Party Government*, pp. 50–53.
4. In more mundane terms, they "accept responsibility for the whole conduct of public policy." Ibid., p. 63.
5. Edmund Burke, "Thoughts on the Causes of our Present Discontents," *Works*, vol. 1 (Boston: Little Brown, 1971), p. 151.
6. Leon Epstein, *Political Parties in Western Democracies* (New Brunswick: Transaction Books, 1980), p. 77.
7. Alasdair MacIntyre, "Is a Science of Comparative Politics Possible?" in *Against the Self-Images of the Age: Essays on Ideology and Philosophy* (Notre Dame: University of Notre Dame Press, 1971), p. 266.
8. Austin Ranney, *The Doctrine of Responsible Party Government: Its Origins and Present State* (Urbana: University of Illinois Press, 1962), p. 31.

9. Ibid., p. 74.
10. There were exceptions to this, though. For instance, Ostrogorski argued that democratic participation was "a means to the end of rational, judicious, and unimpassioned popular discussion of public affairs." Ibid, p. 114. Yet he claimed that parties were incapable of permitting this because they were structured essentialy for the benefit of machine politicians. (In this regard, note the pun on the word *end*).
11. Again, by "education" I mean a process of public deliberation and learning, not the transmission of messages or ideology. A party educates in that its members or the voters learn to make political judgments by acting within its structures, and in that its leaders provide reasoned arguments toward a particular principle. Where it transmits messages it informs the public, but this does not guarantee that the public comes to a reasoned understanding of the issue.
12. Martin Wattenberg, *The Decline of American Political Parties, 1952–1984* (Cambridge: Harvard University Press, 1986), pp. 1–2.
13. *Bringing Back the Parties,* pp. 107–16.
14. E. E. Schattschneider, *The Semisovereign People: A Realist's View of Democracy in America* (New York: Holt, Rinehart, Winston, 1960), p. 142; Austin Ranney and Willmoore Kendall, *Democracy and the American Party System* (New York: Harcourt, Brace, 1956), p. 153.
15. Otto Kirchheimer, "The Transformation of the Western European Party System," in Joseph LaPalombara and Myron Weiner, eds., *Political Parties and Political Development* (Princeton: Princeton University Press, 1966), p. 189.
16. Schattschneider argues that this contributes to the inability of American parties to govern effectively (*Semisovereign People,* p. 132), and he suggests that it affects party discipline (p. 133). The discipline that is needed might facilitate common agreement on a political program.
17. Jeane J. Kirkpatrick, *Dismantling the Parties: Reflections on Party Reform and Party Decomposition* (Washington, D.C.: American Enterprise Institute, 1978), pp. 11–12.
18. Ware, *Citizens,* p. 80.
19. Thomas Patterson, *The Mass Media Election* (New York: Praeger, 1980). Here Patterson traces the influence of the media in the 1972 election and its effects on the capacities of the parties to inform and educate people. He concludes that both the press and the parties fail to educate citizens adequately to the basic issues of the campaign. He also argues that parties need to improve their organization in order to retain their effectiveness in educating people politically.

Alan Ware, *Citizens,* p. 83, argues that in America, the effects of television have decentralized political parties enough "so that it is difficult for the citizen to pick out themes and issues which can help to re-form and shape his own political judgments."

20. On the lack of democracy in many parties, see Frank J. Sorauf, *Political Parties in the American System* (Boston: Little Brown, 1964), p. 52; and C. B. MacPherson, *The Life and Times of Liberal Democracy* (Oxford: Oxford University Press, 1977), pp. 64–69. Alan Ware agrees, but argues that they may become democratic in the future. See Ware, *Citizens,* pp. 215–42. Even if they do, though, this is no guarantee that political parties will take their educative functions seriously.

21. Walter Dean Burnham, "American Politics in the 1970s: Beyond Party?" in Louis Maisel and Paul M. Sachs, eds., *The Future of Political Parties* (Beverly Hills: Sage, 1975), p. 265. Here Burnham describes the alienation which occurs due to the lack of moral leadership resulting from exactly this process.

22. Howard Reiter, *Parties and Elections in Corporate America,* New York: St. Martin's Press, 1987, p. 40; Alan Ware, "United States: Disappearing Parties?" in *Political Parties: Electoral Change and Structural Response* (Oxford: Basil Blackwell, 1987), p. 126.

23. "Thus, from being the cornerstone of campaign activity at the end of the nineteenth century, the activist from the party organization has become a resource on which candidates will 'fall back' only when they have to." Ware, *Political Parties,* p. 127.

24. Martin Shefter makes the argument that the relative weakness of political parties today lies not so much in their dealignment or realignment, but in their changing relationship with the bureaucracy. He concludes that "in American politics institutional conflicts are the functional equivalent of party conflicts." "Party, Bureaucracy, and Political Change in the United States," in Louis Maisel and Joseph Cooper, eds., *Political Parties: Development and Decay* (Beverly Hills: Sage, 1978), p. 255. *If* this is so, then new institutions might lead to political conflicts that generate the policy alternatives leading to political change. A "functional equivalent" of the party may be needed, and national service can play this role in terms of civic education.

    This implies a final argument against parties as agents of political education: they are weakening. In Burnham's words, there has been a "critical realignment"—"an astonishingly rapid dissolution between the voter and the objects of his vote at the polls," "American Politics," p. 239. Also see Alan Ware, *Citizens, Party, State,* pp. 132–36, on this point. Shefter and Burnham describe the failure of parties to perform even their most minimal functions of winning elections and managing political campaigns. And where parties cannot run elections successfully, they cannot educate voters towards issues competently or comprehensively. Insofar as parties cannot reform themselves and third parties do not develop, an alternative institution of political education is necessary.

25. Benjamin Barber, *Strong Democracy: Participatory Politics for a*

New Age (Berkeley: University of California Press, 1984). See especially the chapter "The Real Present: Institutionalizing Strong Democracy in the Modern World."

26. Robert Paul Wolff defends TV democracy in *In Defense of Anarchism* (New York: Harper and Row, 1970), pp. 34–37. For another argument on the participatory uses of media technology, see Sidney Kraus and Dennis Davis, *The Effects of Mass Communication on Political Behavior* (University Park: Pennsylvania State University Press, 1976). They argue for a "transactional model" of political communication, in which information is not simply diffused by the media, but is used by the people to influence political decisions.

27. F. Christopher Arterton, *Teledemocracy: Can Technology Protect Democracy?* (Beverly Hills: Sage, 1987).

28. Ibid., p. 193.

29. Kenneth C. Laudon, *Communications Technology and Democratic Participation* (New York: Praeger, 1977), p. 110.

30. Ibid., p. 116. One sees this now in such self-proclaimed interactive TV programming as home shopping networks, "video jukebox," or other television programs asking the viewer to call in—for a price—to purchase their favorite commodity.

31. Amy Gutmann, *Democratic Education* (Princeton: Princeton University Press, 1987), pp. 238, 239.

32. For the argument that technology is not a neutral instrument of social policy I use the term *technology* in a manner similar to Martin Heidegger and George Grant. See Martin Heidegger, "The Question Concerning Technology," in *The Question Concerning Technology and Other Essays,* tr. William Lovitt (New York: Harper and Row, 1977); George Grant, "Thinking about Technology," in *Technology and Justice* (Notre Dame: University of Notre Dame Press, 1986), p. 26; and Edward Andrew, "George Grant on Technological Imperatives," in Richard B. Day, Ronald Beiner, and Joseph Maschiulli, eds., *Democratic Theory and Technological Society* (Armonk, N.Y.: M. E. Sharpe, 1988), pp. 299–315.

33. The evidence for this is overwhelming, on all sides of the political spectrum. On the Right, M. Reed Irvine's group, Accuracy in the Media, watches for "liberal bias." Social scientists like Austin Ranney claim that there is a "structural bias" to the media's reporting, leading them to be antiestablishment. Austin Ranney, *Channels of Power* (New York: Basic Books, 1983). Doris Graber claims that the media serve as a means of social control as they survey, manipulate, interpret, and socialize Americans. Doris Graber, *Mass Media and American Politics* (Washington, D.C.: Congressional Quarterly Press, 1984), on the gatekeeping function of the media and its political effects (pp. 71–96). The gatekeeping function "also yields news that generally supports current political and social institutions in America" (p. 94).

On the Left, the careful analyses of Noam Chomsky and Alexander Cockburn have done much to reveal media bias, especially toward the interests of capital. Noam Chomsky, *The Chomsky Reader,* James M. Peck, ed. (New York: Pantheon Books, 1987), and Alexander Cockburn, *Corruptions of Empire: Life Studies and the Reagan Era* (London: Verso, 1988). For other analyses of media bias and its general influence on discourse in contemporary society, specifically as they support either the most powerful economic interests or the state apparatus itself, see Claus Mueller, *The Politics of Communication* (New York: Oxford University Press, 1973); and W. Lance Bennett, *Public Opinion in American Politics* (New York: Harcourt Brace, 1980), especially the chapter on "Public Opinion and the News Media." In short, regardless of the ideological perspective of the critic, the argument that the media is biased is well documented.

54. Karen Siune and F. Gerald Kline, "Communication, Mass Political Behavior, and Mass Society," in Steven Chaffee, ed., *Political Communications* (Beverly Hills: Sage, 1975). Also see Leon Sigal, *Reporters and Officials* (Lexington: Heath, 1973); Maxwell E. McCombs and Donald L. Shaw, "The Agenda-Setting Function of the Press," in Doris A. Graber, *Media Power in Politics* (Washington, D.C.: Congressional Quarterly Press, 1984), pp. 63–72; and Shaito Iyengar, Mark Peters, and Donald Kinder, "Experimental Demonstrations of the 'Not-So-Minimal' Consequences of Television News Programs," *American Political Science Review* 76 (December 1982): 848–58.

35. Michael J. Robinson, "Public Affairs Television and the Growth of Political Malaise," *American Political Science Review* 65 (June 1976): 409–32. Thus even educational television contributes to the "de-citizening" of the public. For similar conclusions, see Richard E. Dawson, Kenneth Prewitt, and Karen S. Dawson, *Political Socialization: An Analytic Study* (Boston: Little, Brown, 1977); and Steven H. Chaffee, et al., "Mass Communication in Political Socialization," in Stanley A. Renshon, *Handbook of Political Socialization: Theory and Research* (New York: Free Press, 1977).

36. Sheldon Wolin, "Political Theory and Political Commentary," in Melvin Richter, ed., *Political Theory and Political Education* (Princeton: Princeton University Press, 1980), p. 195.

37. Ibid., p. 196.

38. Chomsky, *Chomsky Reader,* Mueller, *Politics of Communication.*

39. For example, I believe that political debate in Britain and Italy is enhanced to some degree by the existence of four or so serious papers, each representing a particular political position, with little pretense to objectivity. Unfortunately, the large media interests are quickly buying these up, and homogenizing them too, so how long these countries can present their political debates in this sort of forum remains to be seen.

40. I am, of course, only talking at the moment of the vast majority of the media. Thoughtful analyses are available to the citizen who looks for them—in the *New York Times,* in the *New York Review of Books,* and in some of the more erudite political journals, like *The Nation* and *Commentary.* But the percentage of people who read these newspapers and magazines is very small (and probably self-contained). The question we must ask ourselves as a society is, why don't more people want to read these sorts of journals?

41. Sigal, *Reporters and Officials;* Graber, *Mass Media,* pp. 37–47.

42. But given what I said above, this would not be a function of the technologies themselves but of how they are used in a democratic format.

43. Richard A. Gabriel, *To Serve with Honor: A Treatise on Military Ethics and the Way of the Soldier* (Westport, Conn.: Greenwood Press, 1982), pp. 150–73. Gabriel claims that by assuming the extra burdens of military life "citizens can truly be ennobled" (p. 174). Also see Eliot A. Cohen, *Citizens and Soldiers: The Dilemmas of Military Service* (Ithaca: Cornell University Press, 1985), pp. 117–33.

44. See, for example, Morris Janowitz, *The Professional Soldier: A Social and Political Portrait* (New York: Free Press, 1971), and the chapters on "Citizenship and the Institutions of Civic Education" and "The American Soldier and the Citizen Soldier Concept" in Moskos, *Call to Civic Service,* pp. 130ff.

45. Moskos, *Call to Civic Service,* p. 128.

46. This ideal contrasts with that of the professional officer corps. See Janowitz, *Professional Soldier,* and Samuel P. Huntington, *The Soldier and the State: The Theory and Politics of Civil-Military Relations* (Cambridge: Belknap Press, 1957), pp. 7–18.

47. Janowitz, *Reconstruction of Patriotism,* pp. 65–72. Moskos agrees, and complains that the all-volunteer force emphasizes "the self–serving aspects of military life." Charles Moskos, "The All-Volunteer Force," in Morris Janowitz and Stephen D. Westbrook, eds., *The Political Education of Soldiers* (Beverly Hills: Sage, 1983), p. 315. Though these sociologists decry the self-serving and unrealistic expectations of the recruits into the military, they seem to forget that this is how the military advertises itself these days. One cannot blame the recruits for thinking they are going to live in exotic places, or to learn how to be a "top gun"; one must blame advertising executives and copywriters who develop these campaigns, military commanders who employ the advertising companies, and politicians and federal regulators who allow this sort of deception to continue.

48. Moskos, "All-Volunteer Force," p. 318. Janowitz makes a similar point when he argues that the soldier "needs to be strongly committed to the basic assumptions of a democratic polity and to the basic 'rules of the game'. Any civic education that takes place in the military establishment must conform to this requirement." Morris

National Service, Citizenship, and Political Education

Janowitz, "Civic Consciousness and Military Performance," in Janowitz and Westbrook, *Political Education*, p. 73. One ought not to learn only "the rules of the game," but how to make those rules just.

49. Many philosophers have demonstrated the fallacy behind the fact/value distinction in political science. See, for example, Charles Taylor, "Neutrality in Political Science," in Alan Ryan, ed., *The Philosophy of Social Explanation* (Oxford: Oxford University Press, 1973); Hanna Fenichel Pitkin, *Wittgenstein and Justice: On the Significance of Ludwig Wittgenstein for Social and Political Thought* (Berkeley: University of California Press, 1972), pp. 177–186; and Leo Strauss, *Natural Right and History* (Chicago: University of Chicago Press, 1953).

50. One empirical study shows that the military does not contribute much to the political socialization of citizens either. John P. Lovell and Judith Hicks Stiehm, "Military Service and Political Socialization," in Roberta S. Sigel, ed., *Political Learning in Adulthood: A Sourcebook of Theory and Research* (Chicago: University of Chicago Press, 1989), pp. 172–202.

51. For an argument to the contrary, see Sebastian De Grazia, "Political Equality and Military Participation," *Armed Forces and Society* 7 (2) (Winter 1981): 181–86. De Grazia argues that "demands for political equality increase when successful military action is believed to require a military technology that utilizes an expanded number of people" (p. 185). But De Grazia, like Barber, presumes that technology is a neutral instrument. Rather, the development of military technology has evolved in such ways that "the people" have been progressively excluded from their use.

The striking fact about today's military technology is that only a few people have the capability of actually understanding it. Thus, contrary to De Grazia's argument, there is no inherent egalitarianism in the military. Thus, the myth of the citizen-soldier perpetuates itself: our technology cannot sustain equality in the military, even among enlisted men, for some have greater knowledge of military technology than others. In an age where not all weapons are equal, this has importance both on the battlefield and on the base.

52. Michel Foucault, *Discipline and Punish: The Birth of the Prison*, tr., Alan Sheridan (New York: Vintage Books, 1977), pp. 135–69.

53. I abstract this argument from Janowitz, *Professional* pp. 215–79.

54. Ibid., p. 224.

55. Gabriel, *To Serve*. See the section on the all-volunteer force.

56. Moskos, "All–Volunteer Force." Also see Charles Moskos, "Making the All-Volunteer Force Work: A National Service Approach," *Foreign Affairs* 1 (60) (Fall 1981): 19–20.

57. Morris Janowitz, *The Reconstruction of Patriotism: Education for Civic Consciousness* (Chicago: University of Chicago Press, 1983), p. 197.

58. In a 1966 conference on the draft at the University of Chicago, Janowitz argued that the present system of military recruitment would create an "all-negro" force. A lottery system was proposed in order to control "this form of disequilibrium." Morris Janowitz, "The Logic of National Service," in Sol Tax, ed., *The Draft: A Handbook of Facts and Alternatives* (Chicago: University of Chicago Press, 1967), p. 88.

    Why these sociologists are so afraid of an all-black or even largely black force remains unclear: (1) they may believe that blacks are un-American, (2) they may believe that blacks are inferior morally—surely the quote from Janowitz in the text suggests this, or (3) they may fear giving blacks the means of state-sponsored violence—that is, military weapons. There is a tragic irony to this last point, because these same sociologists want to take blacks out of the ghetto, and away from weapons. But some of them may balk at the fact that when blacks go into the military they not only receive weapons, but also the legitimacy of the state in using them.

59. This idea was proposed for the Spanish military by Santiago Carrillo in *"Eurocommunism" and the State* (London: Lawrence and Wishart, 1977).

60. Also private schools, but since the vast majority of students go to public schools I am concerned mainly with this school system.

61. Gutmann, *Democratic Education,* p. 63.

62. Democratic education must teach democratic virtue, which, in Gutmann's words, is the "ability to deliberate, and hence to participate in conscious social reproduction." Ibid., p. 46. In this way, too, political education is not political socialization. Political education is the education of free citizens in the practice of making independent political judgments. Political socialization is the training of individuals to accept the civic culture imposed upon them by social institutions and authorities. In this chapter I criticize how dominant American institutions educate citizens politically, not how they socialize them. I am doing the same thing throughout the book for the institution of national service.

63. Gutmann, *Democratic Education,* p. 11.

64. However, there is some empirical evidence that this does not exist in our nation's schools. Stanley W. Moore, et al., in their study of elementary school children in California, maintain that such students are rarely offered a conflictual or dissenting view of the world. "Textbooks, teachers, and perhaps to a lesser extent, parents avoid discussion of the tensions and conflicts that dominate much of our political life. The legitimate interest of the school and the home in promoting order and unity may prompt them, whether consciously or unconsciously, to delay introducing symbols representing divisions in policy-making responsibility and the sources of political tension or conflict. This postponing of *conflictual symbols* is ultimately detrimental to the proper functioning of a vital, participatory democracy." Stanley

W. Moore, James Lane, and Kenneth A. Wagner, *The Child's Political World: A Longitudinal Perspective* (New York: Praeger, 1985), p. 221. They also suggest that presenting conflict actually increases the "diffuse support" for a regime, because it teaches children that their government makes mistakes. Thus, they would be "much less likely to become disillusioned in the future" (p. 229).

Sigel and Hoskin found that high school students were unable to reason about democracy, and offered no more than slogans with which they associated the term. In other words, schools may also present high school students with facile accounts of politics. Roberta S. Sigel and Marilyn B. Hoskin, *The Political Involvement of Adolescents* (New Brunswick, N.J.: Rutgers University Press, 1981), pp. 115–16. Thus, traits acquired in elementary school seem to carry on into high school.

Consequently, school, especially elementary school, may inhibit "nonrepression" in a structural way, because teachers and parents strive for unity. Conflict and dissent may best be presented to individuals later in life. Thus, *another* institution may be necessary to educate individuals in a nonrepressive manner—where they are exposed to a variety of ideas, and are free to choose any means of deliberation. I argue in the next chapter that it ought to be the task of national service to countersocialize (by countereducating) individuals from the ideals and behavior they acquire in schools.

65. The research on civic education in schools is vast, and has been led by educational theorists like Fred Newmann, James Shaver, and R. Freeman Butts. But their analyses are restricted largely to primary and secondary schools, and to schools alone. Gutmann, as a political philosopher, treats education as a lifelong process, thus I focus on her work here.

66. Fred Newmann contends that students need to become competent civically, and calls on schools to introduce programs of service and advocacy learning. Fred Newmann, *Education for Citizen Action* (Berkeley: McCutchan, 1975).

67. Gutmann, *Democratic Education,* pp. 273–81.

68. I am putting aside empirical arguments against the capability of the primary school system to inculcate civic virtue and deliberative skills. These involve such issues as the "hidden curriculum," the technocratic methods used in childhood education which imbue students with "technical reason" rather than "practical reason," the failure of the school system to educate all people equally, the arguments that schools reproduce a capitalist ideology, and the ineffectiveness of many schools in teaching just about anything. I put these aside not because I feel they are not relevant, but because I want to argue that *any* program of primary schooling, no matter how good, may be insufficient to political education. Thus I respond to the *philosophical* grounds for using schools to train the citizen.

CHAPTER 9

1 Mary Jane Turner makes this argument in "Civic Education in the United States," in Derek Heater and Judith A. Gillespie, eds., *Political Education in Flux* (London: Sage, 1981), pp. 59–61.

2. For instance, see Joseph Adelson and Robert P. O'Neil, "Growth of Political Ideas in Adolescence: The Sense of Community," *Journal of Personality and Social Psychology* 4 (3) (1966): 305; Richard M. Merelman, *Political Reasoning in Adolescence: Some Bridging Themes* (Beverly Hills: Sage, 1979); and The William T. Grant Foundation Commission on Work, Family, and Citizenship, *The Forgotten Half: Non-College Youth in America*, Washington, D.C., January 1988, pp. 12–14.

3. Grant Foundation, *Forgotten Half*, p. 13.

4. Judith A. Gillespie, Introduction to Heater and Gillespie, *Political Education*, p. 4.

5. Stephen Esquith justifies this purpose nicely in an unpublished manuscript, "Political Theory and Political Education," Michigan State University, January 1991. He argues that liberal political education involves "a direct confrontation with the consequences of power for those who exercise it, those who endure it, and those who debate, monitor, or just witness its use" (p. 2). These "consequences" occur at many different levels in society, not simply the governmental level.

6. Charles Taylor, "Cross-Purposes: The Liberal-Communitarian Debate," in Nancy L. Rosenblum, ed., *Liberalism and the Moral Life* (Cambridge: Harvard University Press, 1989), pp. 167–68.

7. For a thoughtful defense of this point, see Glenn Tinder, *Tolerance: Toward a New Civility* (Amherst: University of Massachussetts Press, 1976).

8. The studies mentioned in note 2 of this chapter also indicate that by the age of 18 individuals have "full cognitive capacities," and have an "assured grasp of formal thought." Thus, they have the intellectual tools necessary for critical thought. In this sense, national service as a critical education about America challenges the adult mind much more constructively than service programs seeking to socialize individuals to a national ethos. Therefore, service can be a *learning* experience where individuals are asked to question the ways in which they were socialized and the norms to which they were socialized.

9. Shirley H. Engle and Anna S. Ochoa, *Education for Democratic Citizenship: Decision-Making in the Social Studies* (New York: Teacher's College Press, 1988), pp. 12, 28–48.

10. Richard Pratte, "The Civic Purpose of Education: Civic Literacy," in Susan Douglas Franzosa, ed., *Civic Education: Its Limits and Conditions* (Ann Arbor: Prakken, 1988), pp. 22–24. Also, see George H.

Wood, "Civic Education for Participatory Democracy," in the same volume, pp. 68–98, for a similar, if more radical, perspective.

11. Pratte, "Civic Purpose," p. 25.

12. Richard Pratte, *The Civic Imperative: Examining the Need for Civic Education* (New York: Teacher's College Press, 1988), pp. 175–81. These ideas also seem similar to those developed more fully for the public schools by Neil Postman and Charles Weingartner, in *Teaching as a Subversive Activity* (New York: Delacorte Press, 1969). On p. 2 they argue that "schools must serve as the principle medium for developing in youth the attitudes and skills of social, political, and cultural criticism." National service might extend these "attitudes and skills" in adulthood.

13. Michael W. Apple, *Education and Power* (Boston: Routledge and Kegan Paul, 1982); Peter McLaren, *Schooling as a Ritual Performance: Towards a Political Economy of Educational Symbols and Gestures* (London: Routledge and Kegan Paul, 1986); and Pierre Bourdieu and Jean-Claude Passeron, *Reproduction in Education, Society and Culture*, tr. Richard Nice (Beverly Hills: Sage, 1977).

14. The most renowned of these is Paul Willis, *Learning to Labour* (New York: Columbia University Press, 1981).

15. Apple, *Education and Power*, suggests this for schools, pp. 157–59; as does McLaren, *Schooling as Ritual*, pp. 252–55.

16. Philip Wexler suggests that the central problem within schools is not necessarily that of "cultural reproduction" or possibilities of resistance, but that of "suppressed discourse"; and he recommends that social analysts of education rewrite the sociology of education in order to account for this. He also promotes socially transformative readings and community action as ways that all can "re-write" the communities in which they live. See especially his discussion of graffiti artists. Philip Wexler, *Social Analysis of Education: After the New Sociology* (London: Routledge and Kegan Paul, 1987).

17. John E. McPeck, *Critical Thinking and Education* (New York: St. Martin's, 1981), pp. 6, 7.

18. Ibid., p. 11. Here McPeck also criticizes the politically disengaged formulation of "critical thinking" by Robert H. Ennis in his article "A Concept of *Critical Thinking*: A Proposal Basis for Research in the Teaching and Evaluation of Critical Thinking Ability," *Harvard Educational Review* 32 (1) (Winter 1962): 81–111.

19. Ibid., p. 13.

20. Ibid., p. 161. McPeck also argues that reflective skepticism ought to be taught "at some later stage" in the life of the student (p. 160). Thus he too intimates that critical thinking may be an appropriate lesson for older students and adults.

21. Harvey Siegel, *Educating Reason: Rationality, Critical Thinking, and Education* (New York: Routledge and Kegan Paul, 1988), p. 23.

22. Ibid., pp. 55–61.

23. For a similar suggestion, see G. H. Bantock, "The Idea of a Liberal Education," in *The Parochialism of the Present: Contemporary Issues in Education* (London: Routledge and Kegan Paul, 1981), p. 77.
24. Emile Durkheim, *Education and Sociology*, tr. Sherwood Fox (Glencoe, Ill.: Free Press, 1956), pp. 105–06.
25. In John Passmore's terms, national service inculcates a habit, not a mechanical procedure of thinking. John Passmore, "On Teaching to Be Critical," in R. S. Peters, ed., *The Concept of Education* (New York: Routledge and Kegan Paul, 1967), pp. 192–211. In Fred Newmann's terms, it imbues them with "environmental competence"—the ability of individuals to exert influence in public affairs. The goal is "to prevent students from becoming immobilized by the[ir] concerns and to help them work towards resolutions that enhance rather than inhibit their ability to exert influence." Fred Newmann, *Education for Citizen Action* (Berkeley: McCutchan, 1975), p. 93. Newmann argues that "citizen action" must impact the external environment but that this involves reflection as well. He suggests that schools teach environmental competence, but as I have already suggested in the previous chapter, they may be ill equipped to do so in the political sphere.
26. Michael Oakeshott, "Learning and Teaching," in Peters, *Concept of Education*, p. 170.
27. Michael Walzer, "Political Decision-Making and Political Education," in Melvin Richter, ed., *Political Theory and Political Education* (Princeton, N.J.: Princeton University Press, 1980), pp. 159–76.
28. Ibid., p. 160.
29. Charles Taylor, "Rationality," in *Philosophy and the Human Sciences: Philosophical Papers 2* (Cambridge: Cambridge University Press, 1985), p. 142; "Legitimation Crisis?," in the same volume, p. 270.
30. Charles Taylor, "What is Human Agency?" in *Human Agency and Language: Philosophical Papers 1* (Cambridge: Cambridge University Press, 1985), p. 42.
31. Charles Taylor, "Understanding and Ethnocentricity," in *Philosophy and Human Sciences*, pp. 125–26. Also see "Understanding and Explanation in the *Geisteswissenschaften*," in Steven Holtzman and Christoper Leach, *Wittgenstein: To Follow a Rule* (London: Routledge and Kegan Paul, 1981), pp. 205–06. For other versions of this idea see Taylor, "What is Human Agency?" pp. 21, 24, 24n. Taylor himself has suggested that such work exists in social science, for example in Clifford Geertz's *Negara*. Another example might be Octavio Paz's essay, "Thinking Back to the Student Revolt," in *Dissent*, Spring 1975, pp. 148–53.
32. Charles Taylor, "What Is Involved in a Genetic Psychology," in *Human Agency and Language*, pp. 159, 161.
33. Taylor, "Understanding and Ethnocentricity," p. 193.

34. Charles Taylor, "Hegel's *Sittlichkeit* and the Crisis of Representative Institutions," in Yirmiahu Yovel, ed., *Philosophy of History and Action* (Dordrecht, Holland: D. Reidel Publishing, 1978), p. 139.
35. Harold Berlak calls this "raising consciousness". "Human Consciousness, Social Criticism, and Civic Education," in James P. Shaver, *Building Rationales for Citizenship Education* (Arlington, Va.: National Council for Social Studies, 1977), pp. 34–47. In this article Berlak also offers empirical evidence that such consciousness is possible.
36. Wayne A. R. Leys, *Ethics for Policy Decisions: The Art of Asking Deliberative Questions* (New York: Greenwood, 1968), p. 48.
37. Or at least as feasible as any other program for national service. Any program of nationwide service is going to cost a lot of money, taxpayers' money. My program will not pay back in actual deeds done, but rather in intangible benefits—a term service rhetoricians cleverly employ.

CHAPTER 10

1. William F. Buckley, *Gratitude: Reflections on What We Owe Our Country* (New York: Random House, 1990), pp. 3ff.
2. He also learned to reproduce the present health care system by accepting the sorts of econometric analyses produced by business schools.
3. Richard M. Battistoni, *Public Schooling and the Education of Democratic Citizens* (Jackson: University Press of Mississippi, 1985), pp. 175, 181. Also, see Jean-Jacques Rousseau, *Emile*, tr. Barbara Foxley (New York: Dutton, 1974), p. 179.
4. Gilbert Ryle, "Teaching and Training," in R. S. Peters, *The Concept of Education* (New York: Routledge and Kegan Paul, 1967), pp. 105–19.
5. Daniel Conrad and Diane Hedin, "The Impact of Experiential Education on Adolescent Development," in *Youth Participation and Experiential Education* (New York: Haworth Press, 1982), pp. 57–76; Jane Kendall, "A Commentary on 'Facts and Faith: A Status Report on Youth Service'—From Youth Service to Service Learning," in Ann C. Lewis, *Facts and Faith: A Status Report on Youth Service* (Washington, D.C.: William T. Grant Foundation Commission on Work, Family, and Citizenship, 1988), p. 25; Todd Clark, "Youth Community Service," *Social Education* 53 (6) (October 1989): 367; Robert A. Rutter and Fred M. Newmann, "The Potential of Community Service to Enhance Civic Responsibility," *Social Education* (October 1989): 373; James Kielsmeier, "The National Leadership Conference: A Special Niche in the Experiential Spectrum," in Conrad and Hedin, op cit, pp. 151–52; Ernest Boyer, Foreword to Charles H. Harrison, *Student Service* (Princeton, N.J.: Carnegie

Foundation for the Advancement of Learning, 1987), p. xi; and Fred
M. Newmann, "Reflective Civic Participation," *Social Education*
(October 1989): 357.
6. Conrad and Hedin, "Impact of Experiential Education," p. 71.
7. For example the recent national service law, the National and Community Service Act of 1990. The authors of the various parts of this
bill have carefully included reference to "opportunities for reflection"
in all its programs, but they have not specified its meaning.
8. Jane Kendall, whose essay I cite in Chapter 6, note 3, describes community service in political terms. Nonetheless, as I indicate in that
chapter, Kendall does not follow through on the implications of her
suggestion.
9. Roberta S. Sigel and Marilyn B. Hoskin, *The Political Involvement of
Adolescents* (New Brunswick, N.J.: Rutgers University Press, 1981),
pp. 226–29.
10. Abramson and Langton and Jennings find that education and curriculum make little difference in the involvement of youngsters.
These findings, combined with those of Sigel and Hoskin, suggest
that the politicized environment of the young citizen encourages him
or her to participate. Thus, education alone is insufficient, and political work becomes crucial to the nurturing of the active democratic
citizen. Paul R. Abramson, *Political Attitudes in America: Formation
and Change* (San Francisco: W. H. Freeman, 1983), pp. 178–81; and
Kenneth R. Langton and M. Kent Jennings, "Political Socialization
and the High School Civics Curriculum in the United States," in
Jack A. Dennis, *Socialization to Politics: A Reader* (New York: John
Wiley and Sons, 1973), p. 375.
11. Sigel and Hoskin, *Political Involvement*, p. 277.
12. Because form is not the issue when the debate revolves around good
citizenship. The issue becomes what, precisely, is being inculcated.
13. In this regard, read David Thornton Moore, "Experiential Education
as Critical Discourse," in Jane C. Kendall, ed., *Combining Service
and Learning*, vol. 1 (Raleigh, N.C.: National Society for Internships
and Experiential Education, 1990), pp. 273–83.
14. If you doubt this, read Jonathan Kozol's *Illiterate America* (New
York: Anchor Press, 1985).
15. Kozol makes this very suggestion on p. 119.
16. One way to ensure their participation is to levy a tax on property
assessed above a certain value. If property owners above this level
participate in the program, such a tax could be waived. If not, the
proceeds from the tax would go towards hiring competent instructors for these literacy houses.
17. "A political illiterate—regardless of whether he or she knows how to
read and write—is one who has an ingenuous perception of humanity in its relationships with the world. The person has a naive outlook on social reality, which for this one is a given, that is, social

reality is a *fait accompli* rather than something still in the making. One of the political illiterate's tendencies is to escape concrete reality—a way of rejecting it—by losing himself or herself in abstract visions of the world." Paulo Freire, *The Politics of Education: Culture, Power, and Liberation*, tr. Donaldo Macedo (South Hadley, Mass.: Bergin and Garvey, 1985), p. 103.

18. Paulo Freire, *Pedagogy of the Oppressed*, tr. Myra Bergman Ramos (New York: Seabury Press, 1970), p. 69.

19. Barbara Bee, "The Politics of Literacy," in Robert Mackie, ed., *Literacy and Revolution: The Pedagogy of Paulo Freire* (New York: Continuum, 1981), p. 55.

20. Ira Shor, ed., *Freire for the Classroom: A Sourcebook for Liberatory Teaching* (Portsmouth, N.H.: Heinemann, 1987).

21. C. A. Bowers, "Linguistic Roots of Cultural Invasion in Paulo Freire's Pedagogy," *Teacher's College Record* 84 (4) (Summer 1983): 952.

22. For more on the relevance of this type of learning to adults, see Harold Entwistle, "The Political Education of Adults," in Derek Heater and Judith A. Gillespie, eds., *Political Education in Flux* (London: Sage, 1981), pp. 233–55.

23. On "political literacy," see Alex Porter, "Political Literacy," in Heater and Gillespie, *Political Education*, pp. 181–211.

24. Ivan Illich calls this "peer-matching." Ivan Illich, *De-Schooling Society* (New York: Harper and Row, 1971), pp. 19–22.

25. Alternative education of this sort has been found to work successfully within school systems, and at least two researchers argue that such alternative schooling does not put students at a future disadvantage. See Peter Gray and David Chanoff, "Democratic Schooling: What Happens to Young People Who Have Charge of Their Own Education?" *American Journal of Education* 94 (2) (February 1986): 182–213.

26. For an exhaustive survey on the positive effects of "peer teaching," see Lilya Wagner, *Peer Teaching: Historical Perspectives* (Westport, Conn.: Greenwood, 1982), pp. 224–32.

27. See Illich, *De-Schooling*, p. 90, for more on this idea. Also, see Wagner, *Peer Teaching*, pp. 218–24, for a philosophical defense of peer teaching.

28. For more on the idea of action learning centers, see Dan Conrad and Diane Hedin, "Learning and Earning Citizenship through Participation," in James P. Shaver, ed., *Building Rationales for Citizenship Education* (Arlington, Va.: National Council for Social Studies, 1977), p. 71.

29. Ibid., p. 60. Fred Newmann also notes the success of "field research" programs in high schools. See Newmann, *Education for Citizen Action* (Berkeley: McCutchen, 1975), pp. 175–77.

30. "I think what the advocates of national service should do in the

short run is to tell young people that there really is a barrier to a positive vision of the way their lives can be developed—that that barrier is war and militarism. If it can be reduced, then there is a great chance that we can develop social and economic integration, situations of service, situations in which their creative impulses can be genuinely used; and reducing militarism really is the strategy for making all this politically possible." Richard Flacks, in "Discussion on National Service," in Sol Tax, ed., *The Draft: A Handbook of Facts and Alternatives* (Chicago: University of Chicago Press, 1967), p. 421.

31. Charles K. Curtis, "Citizenship Education and the Slow Learner," in Shaver, *Building Rationales,* p. 76.
32. Ibid., pp. 78–79, 83–91.
33. Service for architects, for example, has been suggested by Joe Klein in "The Crisis Corps: A Plan to Start Turning New York Around," *New York,* May 14, 1990, p. 43.
34. Paul Davidoff, "Advocacy and Pluralism in Planning," *Journal of the American Institute of Planners* 31 (November 1965).
35. Which they ought to do out of civic duty to the nation.
36. Joel Wirth, "Servants of Two Masters," *Planning* 46 (11) (November 1980): 14–18.
37. William Rohe, as quoted in Jim Schwab, "Brass Roots," *Planning* 53 (8) (August 1987): 10.
38. Raffaella Nanetti, "Neighborhood Planning in Europe: Vive La Difference," *Planning* (November 1980): 19–21.
39. Note Richard Pratte, who maintains that civic education is not controversial, but the *control* over civic education is controversial. Richard Pratte, *Civic Imperative: Examining the Need for Civic Education* (New York: Teacher's College Press, 1988), p. 15.

SELECTED BIBLIOGRAPHY

For reasons of space, I have included only those books and articles that concern national service directly. For other material, please consult the endnotes. I suggest that those interested in the issue look first at Williamson Evers, ed., *National Service: Pro and Con;* Charles Moskos, *A Call to Civic Service;* Richard Danzig and Peter Szanton, *National Service: What Would it Mean?* and Morris Janowitz, *The Reconstruction of Patriotism.* For a quick introduction, try the Democratic Leadership Council's booklet, *Citizenship and National Service: A Blueprint for Civic Enterprise.*

Barber, Benjamin. *Strong Democracy: Participatory Politics for a New Age.* Berkeley: University of California Press, 1984.

Black, Algernon D. *The Young Citizens: The Story of the Encampment for Citizenship.* New York: Frederick Ungar, 1962.

Black, C. L., Jr. "Constitutional Problems in Compulsory National Service," *Yale Law Reports* 13(19) (Summer 1967):9–21.

Bobbitt, Philip. "National Service: Unwise or Unconstitutional?" in Martin Anderson, ed. *Registration and the Draft.* California: Hoover Institution Press, 1982, pp. 299–330.

Boyte, Harry C. "Democratic Engagement: Bringing Populism and Liberalism Together," *The American Prospect* (6) (Summer 1991):55–63.

Buckley, William, F. *Gratitude: Reflections on What We Owe Our Country.* New York: Random House, 1990.

Coalition for National Service. *National Service: An Action Agenda for the 1990s.* Washington, D.C.: National Service Secretariat, 1988.

Coe, Richard L. *The Kenya National Youth Service: A Governmental Response to Young Political Activists.* Athens, Oh.: Ohio University Center for International Studies, Africa Program, 1973.

Cohen, Eliot A. *Citizens and Soldiers: The Dilemmas of Military Service.* Ithaca: Cornell University Press, 1985.

Committee for the Study of National Service. *Youth and the Needs of the Nation.* Washington, D.C.: Potomac Institute, January, 1979.

Conrad, Dan, and Diane Hedin. "Learning and Earning Citizenship through Participation," in James P. Shaver, ed., *Building Rationales for Citizenship Education.* Arlington, Virginia: National Council for Social Studies, 1977, pp. 48–73.

Conrad, Daniel, and Diane Hedin, eds. *Youth Participation and Experiential Education.* New York: Haworth Press, 1982.

Danzig, Richard and Peter Szanton. *National Service: What Would It Mean?* Lexington, Mass.: Lexington Books, 1986.

Democratic Leadership Council. *Citizenship and National Service: A Blueprint for Civic Enterprise.* Washington, D.C., May 1988.

Eberly, Donald J., ed. *A Profile of National Service.* New York: Overseas Educational Service, 1966.

———. "Guidelines for National Service," in Sol Tax, ed., *The Draft: A Handbook of Facts and Alternatives.* Chicago: University of Chicago Press, 1967, pp. 110–13.

———. ed. *National Service: Report of a Conference.* New York: Russell Sage Foundation, 1968.

———. "A National Service Pilot Project." *Teacher's College Record* 73(1) (September 1973):65–79.

———. "A Universal Youth Service." *Social Policy* 7(4) (January/February, 1977):43–46.

———. "National Service: Alternative Strategies." *Armed Forces and Society* 3(3) (May 1977):445–455.

———. "National Service: Action for Youth." *Synergist* 6(3) (Winter 1978).

———. *National Service: A Promise to Keep.* Rochester: John Alden Books, 1988.

———, and Michael W. Sherraden. *The Moral Equivalent of War? A Study of Non-Military Service in Nine Nations.* New York: Greenwood Press, 1990.

———. ed. *National Youth Service: A Democratic Institution for the 21st. Century.* Washington DC: National Service Secretariat, 1991.

Eddinger, John. "National Service: Uphill All the Way," *Nation's Business,* February 1980, pp. 77–78.

Erikson, Erik. "Memorandum for the Conference on the Draft," in Sol Tax, ed., *The Draft: A Handbook of Facts and Alternatives.* Chicago: University of Chicago Press, 1967, pp. 280–83.

Etzioni, Amitai. "A Remedy for Overeducation—A Year of Required National Service." *Change* 15(4) (May/June 1983):8.

———. "The Case for a New Youth Conservation Corps," *Human Behavior* 5(8) (August 1976):13.

———. *An Immodest Agenda: Rebuilding America before the Twenty-First Century.* New York: McGraw-Hill, 1983.

———. *Towards Higher Education in an Active Society: Three Policy Guidelines.* New York: Center for Policy Research, June 1970.

Evers, Williamson, ed. *National Service: Pro and Con.* California: Hoover Institution Press, 1990.

Fowler, Robert Booth. "Political Obligation and the Draft," in Donald W. Hanson and Robert Booth Fowler, eds., *Obligation and Dissent: An Introduction to Politics.* Boston: Little, Brown, and Company, 1971, pp. 46–62.

Fullinwider, Robert. "Citizenship and Welfare," in Amy Gutmann, ed., *Democracy and the Welfare State.* Princeton: Princeton University Press, 1982, pp. 261–278.

Gorham, Eric. *National Service, Citizenship, and Political Education.* Ph.D. thesis, Madison: University of Wisconsin, 1990.

Greenberger, Ellen, and Laurence Steinberg. *When Teenagers Work: The Psychological and Social Costs of Adolescent Employment.* New York: Basic Books, 1986.

HR 888, United States House of Representatives, 99th Congress, 1st sess. January 31, 1985, section 5(b)(3).

Halperin, Samuel. "What's Wrong with Youth Service." *Streams,* February/March 1989, p. 2.

Harrison, Charles H. *Student Service.* Princeton, N.J.: Carnegie Foundation for the Advancement of Learning, 1987.

Hart, Gary. "The Case for National Service." *USA Today,* November 1985, pp. 11–12.

Huck, Daniel F., and David S. Mundel. *National Service Programs and Their Effects on Military Manpower and Civilian Youth Problems.* Washington, D.C.: Congressional Budget Office, January 1978.

Hyman, Herbert, Charles Wright, and Terence Hopkins. *Applications of Methods of Evaluation: Four Studies of the Encampment for Citizenship.* Berkeley: University of California Press, 1962.

Jacobs, James B. "Compulsory and Voluntary National Service: Analysis of the McCloskey Bill and Other Proposals," in *Socio-Legal Foundations of Civil-Military Relations.* New Brunswick, N.J.: Transaction Books, 1986, pp. 111–47.

————. "The Implications of National Service for Corrections," in *New Perspectives on Prisons and Imprisonment.* Ithaca: Cornell University Press, 1983, pp. 202–12.

James, William. "The Moral Equivalent of War," *International Conciliation,* no. 27. Washington, D.C.: Carnegie Endowment for International Peace, 1910, pp. 8–20.

Janowitz, Morris. "The Logic of National Service," in Sol Tax, ed., *The Draft: A Handbook of Facts and Alternatives*. Chicago: University of Chicago Press, 1967, pp. 73–90.

———. *The Professional Soldier: A Social and Political Portrait*. New York: Free Press, 1971.

———. Introduction, *Teacher's College Record* 73(1) (September 1973):1–6.

———. "National Service: A Third Alternative?" *Teacher's College Record* 73(1) (September 1973):13–25.

———. *The Reconstruction of Patriotism: Education for Civic Consciousness*. Chicago: University of Chicago Press, 1983.

Katz, Michael B. "Missing the Point: National Service and the Needs of Youth." *Social Policy* 10(4) (January/February 1980):36–40.

Kendall, Jane C., ed. *Combining Service and Learning: A Resource Book for Community and Public Service*, vol. 1 and 2. Raleigh, N.C.: National Society for Internships and Experiential Education, 1990.

King, William R. *Achieving America's Goals: National Service and the All-Volunteer Force*. Committee on Armed Services, United States Senate, Washington, D.C., 1977.

Klein, Joe. "The Crisis Corps: A Plan to Start Turning New York Around." *New York*, May 14, 1990.

Kuttner, Robert. "Give the Young a Better Chance to Serve Their Country." *Business Week*, March 21, 1988, p. 15.

Landrum, Roger, Donald J. Eberly, and Michael W. Sherraden. "Calls for National Service," in Michael W. Sherraden and Donald J. Eberly, eds., *National Service: Social, Economic, and Military Impacts*. New York: Pergamon Press, 1982, pp. 21–38.

Lewis, Ann C. *Facts and Faith: A Status Report on Youth Service*. Washington, D.C.: William T. Grant Foundation Commission on Work, Family, and Citizenship, August, 1988.

McCurdy, Dave. "A Quid Pro Quo for Youth." *New York Times,* June 26, 1989.

McGrew, Thomas J. "The Constitutionality of Compulsory National Service." *Public Law Forum* 4(1) (1984):259–267.

McKnight, John. "The Professional Service Business," in Lenore Borzak, ed., *Field Study: A Sourcebook for Experiential Learning.* Beverly Hills: Sage, 1981, pp. 301–314.

McMullen, Bernard J., and Phyllis Snyder. *Youth Corps Area Studies: Katimavik, the Canadian Youth Corps.* Philadelphia: Public/Private Ventures, April 1986.

Mead, Lawrence M. *Beyond Entitlement: The Social Obligations of Citizenship.* New York: Free Press, 1986.

Menzies, Ian. "Why Not a National Service Program for Young Americans?" *Boston Globe,* July 24, 1978.

Moskos, Charles C. "The Enlisted Ranks in the All-Volunteer Army," in John B. Keeley, ed., *The All-Volunteer Force and American Society.* Charlottesville: University of Virginia Press, 1978.

———. "Making the All-Volunteer Force Work: A National Service Approach." *Foreign Affairs* 60(1) (Fall 1981):17–34.

———. "The All-Volunteer Force," in Morris Janowitz and Stephen D. Westbrook, eds., *The Political Education of Soldiers.* Beverly Hills: Sage, 1983, pp. 307–25.

———. *A Call to Civic Service: National Service for Country and Community.* New York: Free Press, 1988.

Muller, Stephen. "The Case for Universal National Service." *Educational Record* 52(1) (Winter 1971):17–22.

New York Times. Editorial, August 28, 1989.

———. Editorial, July 14, 1989.

Noah, Timothy. "We Need You: National Service, an Idea Whose Time Has Come." *The Washington Monthly*, November 1986, pp. 39–41.

Nyhan, Michael J., and Michael Palmer. *National Service in the United States: Problems, Prospects, and Opportunities*. Menlo Park: Institute for the Future, 1979.

Parsons, Cynthia. "National Service for All." *Phi Delta Kappan*, June 1984, pp. 688–89.

Presidential Commission on National Service and National Commission on Volunteerism, Hearings before the Subcommittee on Child and Human Development, Labor and Human Resources Committee, United States Senate, 96th Congress, 2d sess., March 13, 1980.

Proctor, Samuel D. "To the Rescue: A National Youth Academy." *New York Times*, September 16, 1989.

Riecken, Henry W. *The Volunteer Work Camp: A Psychological Evaluation*. Cambridge, Mass.: Addison-Wesley, 1952.

Rosenblum, Sheila. *Youth Corps Case Studies: The San Francisco Conservation Corps*. Philadelphia: Public/Private Ventures, Fall 1987.

Rutter, Robert A., and Fred M. Newmann. "The Potential of Community Service to Enhance Civic Responsibility." *Social Education*, October 1989, pp. 371–74.

SR 3, United States Senate, 101st Congress, 1st sess., January 25, 1989.

SR 1299, United States Senate, 101st Congress, 1st sess., July 12, 1989.

"Sam Nunn Wants You." *New Republic*, June 6, 1980.

Sherraden, Michael W. *The Civilian Conservation Corps: Effectiveness of the Camps*. Ph.D. Thesis, Ann Arbor: University of Michigan, 1979.

————. "Military Participation in a Youth Employment Program: The Civilian Conservation Corps." *Armed Forces and Society* 7(2) (Winter 1981):227–45.

————, and Eberly, Donald J., eds. *National Service: Social, Economic, and Military Impacts.* New York: Pergamon Press, 1982.

————, and Donald J. Eberly. "Individual Rights and Social Responsibilities: Fundamental Issues in National Service." *Public Law Forum* 4(1) (1984):241–57.

"Social Science and the Citizen." *Society* 23(6) (September/October 1986):2.

Tax, Sol, ed. *The Draft: A Handbook of Facts and Alternatives.* Chicago: University of Chicago Press, 1967.

Thomas, Franklin. *Youth Unemployment and National Service.* New York: Ford Foundation, 1983.

Voluntary National Service Youth Service Act and the Select Commission on National Service Opportunities Act of 1985, Hearings before the Subcommittee on Employment Opportunities, Committee on Education and Labor, United States House of Representatives, 99th Congress, 1st sess., September 27, 1985.

Walzer, Michael. *Spheres of Justice: A Defense of Pluralism and Equality.* New York: Basic Books, 1983.

————. "Socializing the Welfare State," in Amy Gutmann, ed., *Democracy and the Welfare State.* Princeton, N.J.: Princeton University Press, 1988, pp. 13–26.

William T. Grant Foundation Commission on Work, Family, and Citizenship. *The Forgotten Half: Non-College Youth in America.* Washington, D.C.: January, 1988.

INDEX

Volunteers in Service to America
(VISTA), 6, 40, 50, 121, 140, 242
Voucher plan, Eberly and Sher-
raden's, 82

Walzer, Michael, 8–9, 12
Ware, Alan, 114, 162, 253, 254
Wertheimer, Alan (on coercion),
32–33, 35
Wexler, Philip, 262
William Grant Foundation, 179

Wolin, Sheldon, 166
Woodsmanship, 135–137
Work camps, 30, 45, 74, 243

YES, *see* Youth Entering Service.
Youth academy, 72, 226
Youth Camps for World Peace, *see*
Katimavik.
Youth Entering Service (YES), 6
Youth Service America, 58